The Revealer

Curt Simmons

The Revealer

The Man,
The Majesty,
The Model

Illumination Publishers International
www.ipibooks.com
ipi

Published by
Illumination Publishers International
1190 Boylston Street
Newton Upper Falls, Massachusetts, MA 02464
www.ipibooks.com

ipi

To my children,
Brad and Brittany:

Thank you for the joy you have brought to my life
ever since the day I discovered you were coming.
If my arms grew an inch every time I thought about you,
I suppose I could reach out and hug the entire universe.

Contents

Introduction
℞ ℟

I'd like to be able to tell you I finished this manuscript in a matter of weeks, thanks to the Spirit of God moving so powerfully within me. And I wish I could say, due to wrapping up this latest effort in record time, I've already begun working on my next literary project. The truth is it has taken me about two-and-a-half years to finish writing this book. If Evelyn Wood offers a class for writers, I obviously haven't heard about it. Though I may be slow to write, this lengthier time of completion has allowed me the opportunity to add a number of things to my "who is Jesus and what does he mean to me?" collection that will hopefully be of help to you.

A lot has happened in my life in the thirty months since beginning this endeavor. I'm sure each choice I have made and each challenge I have endured in that time has contributed to the development of my insights and impressions of Jesus found in this book. In this introduction, allow me to take you on a speedy tour of what has happened in my life the past two-and-a-half years so at least you will be more aware of the backdrop for this book. After that, with very few exceptions, I promise to put it (me) aside and just give you Jesus. After all, he's a whole lot more interesting than I am!

I'm completely convinced that God had always intended for me to write this book during those two-and-a-half-years. No, it's not because I'm so spiritual and somehow I figured out that this was God's will for me way back in the beginning of that time period. On the contrary, I'm just now beginning to understand that this was a major part of God's plan in his perfect oversight of my life during that time. Let me simplify—God is the all-knowing Great Physician and he knew this writing exercise was the medicine I could not do without. God knew for all eternity what would happen to me in those 30 months and how many of those events would supply much of the eye-opening and heart-molding material I needed for this book. I truly hope, in some small way, that this inspiration I received from God in regard to his Son will help to quicken your spiritual step and benefit your life as a disciple of Jesus.

But the way I see it, I'm the biggest beneficiary! As I look back on all that came my way during that time, it has become apparent to me that writing about Jesus played a major role in keeping me spiritually healthy and just strong enough to avoid the need for prolonged hospital stays of the spiritual nature. Regular trips to the doctor's office and a few emergency room visits were necessary, and I felt as though I spent a few days in intensive care. But thank God I'm still alive and kicking and in love with Jesus. I pray that the contents of this book will pass along to you some of the insights I gained about the Lord during those days which served to stabilize and solidify my faith in him. In the process of writing, I have tried my best to describe to you why I still love Jesus and why I have absolutely no plans to change my mind anytime this side of death.

God never tells us exactly what's coming. He just tells us he'll be there when it finally does. I firmly believe God has kept his *"I'll never forsake you"* promise to me ever since I became his disciple, and his continual fulfillment of that vow has not been curtailed at any time (**Hebrews 13:5**). I have had so much of Jesus on my brain and in my heart during this period, and I've tried my best to show him to you in this book. Though I was oblivious to the significance of

> *God never tells us exactly what's coming. He just tells us he'll be there when it finally does.*

writing a book about Jesus at this stage of my life—not two years earlier or ten years later—this has been the best direction I ever could have taken. What I mean is this: While I was busy writing to offer you information about how Jesus trains you to navigate life's dangerous curves, how he warns you of the upcoming potholes of pain and how he empowers you to rise again from the deep ditches of decisions gone wrong, he was doing all of that and more for me.

Why did I need him so desperately? Why did I need to gain more intimate knowledge of his heart and his character that would come as a result of writing this book? I would experience a lot of challenges and difficulties in those two-and-a-half years, and without Jesus being in the middle of my mess, who knows how the losses in my life would have damaged, perhaps even destroyed, what I have been building as a faithful follower of Jesus for twenty-three years. Beginning around November of 2001, here's a sampling of those challenges in my life, just one of nearly seven billion people alive on the planet today who Jesus longs to walk with and work for on a moment-by-moment basis (**I John 2:1-2**).

I moved to St. Louis in March of 1997 to assume leadership of a church, and one of the greatest joys of my life while living there was a member of that congregation, a man by the name of Mike Cruz. Mike typified for me the true friend described in the Scriptures and I leaned heavily upon his friendship a number of times during some challenging situations. But more than that, I just thoroughly enjoyed his company, whether praying or playing, or anything in between. After much prayer and regularly searching their hearts for pure motives, Mike and his wife, Rhonda, decided to move to Indianapolis to be closer to their extended family. A great job opportunity opened up for Mike and the move was one they had been hoping to make for a few years but had humbly postponed a few times to be used by God to help meet the needs of our church in St. Louis. Deep down I was hoping they would change their minds, but God had put it on their hearts to go. In hindsight, I know I sinned and crossed the line of appropriate persuasion in some conversations with he and Rhonda about their need to stay in St. Louis. What I see now in those attempts was much more of a selfishness in my heart arising from a deep need I felt to keep Mike close and our friendship continuing. Eventually I surrendered and, after their move, God really blessed their lives. Their three children continued to do great in all areas, especially spiritually; they were physically closer to family than ever, which made it much easier for them to help those they loved the most to find spiritual guidance; and they've been a great blessing to the church they now attend in Indianapolis. While I truly was happy for them, I really missed Mike's friendship and wished he had stayed in St. Louis.

Just a few weeks later, I was hit with another loss. Jeff Warren, a dear friend of mine for almost 15 years, had come to St. Louis in a serious search for new employment. I absolutely wanted him to come, and he was more than willing to let God work out all the necessary arrangements to relocate his family from Des Moines, Iowa. Jeff needed a change of climate for a number of reasons, and being let go from his job in Des Moines was the perfect opportunity to bring about what we both had desired for a number of years.

Nobody brings me security like Jeff Warren. He is an absolute riot and allows me to unwind and be as goofy as possible without making me feel like a fool or worry that my "private weirdness" will soon be a matter of public record. We had worked together in the same ministries for six years in Colorado, Nebraska, Ohio and Illinois when Jeff was single. He had lost his mother to cancer in the mid 1980s and his dad died in 1991, but God used those tragedies to bond us together like true family. Jeff is a son, a brother, a confidant and, most importantly, a great friend. So for Jeff to move to St. Louis—that would have been about as good as it could possibly get for me. Jeff, his wife Janet, and their three children would have brought much joy to the Simmons' household. They never made it. In short, the job situation in St. Louis that once looked promising fell through and a great employment opportunity presented itself in Colorado Springs, so Jeff accepted the position there. Jeff loves the mountains and the great outdoors and Colorado Springs is a little piece of heaven for him. He has grown tremendously as a Christian since moving there, gaining fresh and valuable insights into his character. It's obvious to me that Jeff needed to be in Colorado Springs, but that didn't do much on a day-to-day basis for me—except make me happy for him. I love Jeff and was looking forward to many wild and crazy times together in the Gateway City and I was greatly disappointed when things didn't work out for him to move there.

Just a few months later, my beloved St. Louis Rams were set to re-capture their Super Bowl winning ways by mowing down the heavy under-dog, New England Patriots. Favored by nearly two touchdowns and considered a shoe-in champion, the Rams were out-hustled and outplayed from the opening kickoff, made a valiant comeback in the waning moments to tie the score at 17-17, only to watch Adam Vinatieri secure the victory for the Patriots with a 45-yard field goal. Now, compared to the losses I've already mentioned and the ones that would follow, that loss was quite trivial. But it still hurt. Who knows what a Rams victory would have done to soothe some pain from my earlier losses? I was depressed for a few days after the loss, the sadness compounded by my son's merciless reminders that his least favorite team, my Rams, had laid the proverbial egg. And oh, how he loved to crack it over my head whenever possible.

That Super Bowl disappointment was just the beginning of what was a series of losses for the city known for its avid sports following. A few months later, the Cardinals made the Major League baseball playoffs but, for the third year in a row, failed to reach the World Series, still in search of their first world championship since 1982. The St. Louis Blues, the city's professional hockey team, made the playoffs for a record 24th consecutive year, but also for the 24th consecutive year failed to hoist the Stanley Cup. And, as if that weren't enough pain, the Rams followed up their Super Bowl loss with a most disappointing 7-9 campaign, completely out of the playoff picture after their 0-5 start to the season. (I must painfully insert here, in this final edit, the 2004 World Series victory gained by the Boston Red Sox over the St. Louis Cardinals in a impressive four-game sweep. Ouch!)

A 20th wedding anniversary getaway to Mexico that summer, scheduled in my day-timer to be a blessing and an absolute blast, proved to be my next major challenge. I'll take you on the trip in a more detailed way in Chapter 28, so I won't say much about it now except this: While my wife and I ordered top sirloin and salivated often as we contemplated its upcoming taste, we were served top-ramen instead and we're still sick from the experience.

In the next few months, a dear friend in the church who our family was very close to decided he no longer wanted to follow God and live as a disciple of Jesus. While we hurt deeply over his departure from the truth and what that meant for him in a spiritual sense, we also just plain missed him and his encouraging presence in our lives. I believe one of the hardest times in a Christian's life is when good friends or family members decide to stop pursuing their relationship with God. And true to form, our family found ourselves in the middle of dealing with all the unpleasant emotions coming as a result of losing a special relationship, and it still stings every time we think about it.

A few months later, I flew in a moment's notice to Portland, Oregon as my father had been taken to the hospital and placed in intensive care. He had not been feeling well for a few months after contracting pneumonia but his illness had not seemed to be heading in a deadly direction. Five days after I arrived, the man who loved me and meant more to me than any other man in my 43 years of living was dead. I cried so many thousands of tears during the next six months as I recalled joyous memories of our life together and as I encountered rough reminders of what was no longer possible. It's now two years later, and I still hurt deeply over the loss of a wonderful father and friend and there are moments when it seems I have to battle just to get the energy I need to smile, serve and give of myself to meet the needs of the people God has called me to lead. Grief is obviously a necessary part of life, but I'm telling you, it's the most ***un-fun*** (I'm sure that's not a word, but nothing seems to fit when you're grieving) part of life, requiring nothing but good, old-fashioned endurance in the race to reach our ultimate goal of heaven.

About the time of my father's death, two of my closest friends were needed in different church leadership situations in Missouri and Oklahoma and, consequently, were no longer part of my immediate life. Chad Reynolds, a dear friend and former minister with the Columbia, Missouri Church of Christ, left to assume leadership of a church in Tulsa. I would no longer be involved in overseeing his life and ministry, and I wouldn't get to enjoy his fellowship at our weekly ministry staff meetings in St. Louis. I would not be able to benefit from his overwhelming support of my leadership or have regular access to his incredible humor which kept all of us laughing, often taking the edge off the burden we felt in discussing our responsibilities in leading and inspiring Christians to stay focused and alert in the spiritual war. And worst of all, I no longer could anticipate with great joy the weekly hang-out time after staff meetings my wife and I would have with him and his wife, Kasey, those treasured times that I think did more to encourage and strengthen me than him. While I'm grateful that others benefited from his convictions and comic relief, what about me?

Vince Hawkins, a fellow St. Louis staff-member and friend-extraordinaire, left a few weeks later to assume leadership of the church in Columbia that had been vacated by Chad. Sure, Columbia was only two hours from St. Louis and I got to see Vince and his wife, Robin, most every week at our staff meetings. But personally, had it been up to me, he would have been about two **minutes** away, and just the thought of him not being in the same city with me bummed me out on a regular basis.

Steve Hiddleson, along with his wife, Keri, and their two young daughters, moved to St. Louis shortly thereafter from Los Angeles to replace the Hawkinses and I really looked forward to building a great friendship with him, one that would help to ease some of the loneliness I was feeling from Chad's and Vince's departure. Due to unforeseen circumstances and a greater need that arose in another church, the Hiddlesons left just one month later in December with their U-Haul fully loaded, headed for Little Rock, Arkansas, to assume leadership of a church there.

After all of that, I was so looking forward to the turning of the calendar year, anticipating that the following year would have to be a series of blessings in order to appropriately counter the pain of the previous year. Surely it would be a year of wins and wonderful moments. But more difficult days lie ahead. The church in St. Louis, and many other congregations in our international fellowship of churches, began experiencing major challenges in maintaining unity, re-examining important beliefs and dealing with stagnant church growth. It was also an important time for me to carefully consider the weaknesses and sins that were present in my life and leadership. Working through those difficult times to repent of my own sins and also keep the Christians in St. Louis positive and focused on God was exhausting. I expended a lot of physical, emotional and spiritual energy helping many people (including myself) resolve relationship conflicts and providing guidance as to the best way to move beyond personal hurts due to sins and mistakes of the past.

About three months later, I made a decision to move our family from St. Louis to Chicago and work with a church there, leaving best friends and a body of believers in St. Louis who we had cherished for more than six years. Though my conscience was clear in regard to the choice I had made, I was afraid that the decision would be judged by some as unwise while others might deem it selfish or the easy way out. Those fears made the final decision process even more challenging, but I had always tried to do my best to make decisions based upon what I believed to be the wisest plans for ensuring that my family and I had the greatest possible chance to stay faithful to God and make it to heaven. And this was my conviction about our move to Chicago. I reminded myself that, regardless if somewhere down the road I realized it was a poor decision, even amid my mistake God would be faithful and *"cause all things to work together for the good"* (**Romans 8: 28**). So we left St. Louis about a month after announcing our decision, ending a six-year stay in an environment that had been a huge blessing to our spiritual lives. It was one of the most difficult decisions I ever had to make and we still miss our wonderful friends and church family there.

The first few months in Chicago went well. My agenda was full of meeting new people, getting reacquainted with those individuals I knew from an earlier stay with the same church from 1993-1995, preaching, teaching and allowing God to use my ministry experience to help steer a big ship with 2,500 disciples of Christ aboard. I still missed St. Louis, but the love of the disciples in Chicago and the excitement of knowing I was being used by God to meet many needs helped to keep me from feeling homesick or entertaining doubts about my decision to move.

Just as things seemed to be moving swiftly in a positive direction on so many fronts for me, I was hit with an illness that has, for the most part, greatly limited my physical activity for the past seven months. I have had several tests administered to determine the cause of my symptoms that include imbalance, muscle weakness, gait disturbance, tremendous fatigue, nausea and poor reflexes. Initially, my doctors believed there was a good chance (I guess it should be ***bad*** chance) that cancer had invaded my body. Moderate atrophy was discovered in my cerebellum, a sign that cancer could be growing somewhere in my body. I dealt with the ensuing emotions of that original diagnosis, everything from "I'm ready to see Jesus" to "I don't want to die so young" to "just let me make it through my son's high school graduation." All the initial tests for cancer came back negative, so the doctors began searching for a neurological problem. I have had three neurologists, five MRIs, an MRA, two CT Scans, a spinal tap, two ultrasounds, an angiogram of the brain (ouch), seven different drawings of blood, two EMG tests for nerve damage (ouch again), a number of different prescriptions to try and combat my symptoms and a visit to the Mayo Clinic. As of today, I am what my doctors are calling "an enigma." While I am grateful that no cancer has been found and that many of the major neurological conditions haven't been visible on any tests to date, I am feeling no better than I was seven months ago and a few of my symptoms have gotten worse. My neurologists believe that I could have a form of Parkinson's Disease, a remote cancer that hasn't been located yet or that I might be in the early stage of some other neurological disorder that will be officially diagnosed in the next few months. The other option, though not very likely, is that I contracted a virus and it is wreaking havoc on my body. If so, it has been completely unwilling to leave my premises, even though I have been very clear about it being an unwanted guest. I have recently begun to take a new medication to combat some of my symptoms and I just finished my 15th week of physical therapy designed to help me gain strength in my legs and learn how to get my balance back in balance.

It's difficult not knowing exactly what it is that is keeping me from enjoying the things I love the most—working for God, hanging out and having a blast with my family and friends and enjoying my physical life to the full. It's also hard to think about what other people are thinking about me and, if I'm that sick, why haven't the doctors been able to diagnose it. It's hard to think about what I might have and that my condition might possibly get worse. It's harder still to think about how I will live my day-to-day life if what I'm experiencing right now never goes away. And it's difficult to think about the possibility of having the beginning stages of something serious, and that I must continue to be patient until it is officially diagnosed. So I will continue to wait, clinging to what I do know—God cares about my situation and could heal or reveal my problem at any time he chose, Jesus experienced every emotion that I am currently facing and can therefore be of great encouragement and comfort to me, I have a Bible by my bed to read and remind me of how men and women of old endured times of challenges in their lives and how Jesus endured pain and suffering all the way to his death on a cross, many people are praying fervently and fasting for my healing, I have access to great medical care and I have family and friends who serve me, write me, call me and visit me—and I will continue to rely upon all of these blessings to make the very best of a not-so-good situation.

Much of my time at home has been spent right here on my computer, working on closing comments for this book. I'm sure some of my last minute changes have come as a result of how I've seen Jesus during this latest seven-month stretch. In that sense, I guess I'm thankful for the illness because it has allowed me to define, redefine and refine my thinking in regard to who Jesus is and what he really means to me.

I guess you might say that losses have been a big part of my life recently. The loss of good health, the loss of being able to work in ministry that I love so much, the loss of physical closeness to dear friends, the loss of a dream vacation, the loss of a good friend to the world, the loss of unity amongst the Christians I am closest to and the loss of a father who I loved so dearly.

If you've ever played sports in a competitive realm, nothing is worse than a loss—especially when you weren't expecting it! I've experienced about eight of the toughest losses in my life, and all of them happened in about 30 months. If you experience enough losses in a short span, it's incredibly easy to begin feeling like a loser. Thank God I was studying and writing about a winner all that time. And thank God, even though all of these losses have occurred, I've been reminded to draw near to the one friend who is still alive, still on call and still the greatest success in the history of the world—Jesus Christ. In doing so, I've been declared a "winner" in the only thing in life that, in the end, really matters.

I pray that God will use my experiences and real-life losses to give you a deeper understanding about whatever has occurred in your life. More importantly, I hope my understanding of Jesus through all these recent trials will strengthen and equip you to endure whatever will happen to you from this day forward. Who knows, maybe I'll need him even more the next 30 months of my life. Maybe the next number of months in your life will be the period of time when your greatest losses to date occur and you'll need him most as well. If so, may you let Jesus do for you what he has done for me—love you, lead you and remind you that, as long as you want him as a friend and as long as you will submit to him as your Lord, he doesn't have any plans other than revealing himself to you in a deeper way than ever before (**Matthew 28:18-20**).

🌿 Chapter One 🌿

May I Have Your Attention, Please?
ꝛꝛ

He was in the world, and though the world was made through him,
the world did not recognize him. He came to that which was his own,
but his own did not receive him.
—John 1:10-11

Grabbing the attention of someone deeply engrossed in the organization and ongoing oversight of their fast-paced and filled-up life is not an easy task. Most people either demand space or space out when their scheduled "busy-ness" is interrupted.

For example, consider the parent who's trying to keep an entire cupboard of plates spinning all at once: Working fulltime and often overtime at an often stressful job with a not-so-often sensitive boss, all the while dealing with the hectic work commute that steals at least two precious hours of their life at least five days a week; trying to restart the part of the brain that hasn't been used in twenty years while valiantly maintaining sanity in helping with their children's homework; making sure the child gets to and from hockey practice, basketball practice or both, and going to the games twice a week, all while being in charge of distributing refreshments to the future All-Americans after each hard-fought contest; taking their ten year-old daughter to piano lessons to bring out the Beethoven they know lies somewhere inside of her; keeping the house visitor-friendly and the yard neighbor-friendly and attending regular sub-division meetings, praying their property isn't on the evening's agenda; scheduling doctor's and dentist's appointments, keeping doctor's and dentist's appointments, scheduling follow-up doctor's and dentist's appointments and attending to any other health concerns in the family; paying the bills, doing their best to avoid a "Tigger-like" checking account (always bouncing) and analyzing the latest Wall Street report, hoping they can still retire before 90; shopping for a two-week supply of groceries which will disappear in one; frequenting numerous stores to buy their children clothes and school supplies that seem to cost ten times what their own did; fixing whatever got broken around the house that day, whether a leg bone or the leaky bathroom faucet; listening to the latest playground crisis or scrambling to help their son finish his 100-point science project due Wednesday morning which he told them about Tuesday afternoon; arranging parties and sleepovers for at least a dozen of their child's classmates and closest friends; remembering relatives' birthdays, anniversaries and other special days, and when blessed with a good memory moment, rushing out to Wal-Mart or Target to purchase a gift; and finally, putting the kids to bed, returning to the room a half dozen times to answer their child's all-important questions and calm their hearts, assuring them after a thorough search that monsters are not under the bed or in the closet, begging God to make this sixth trip the last one for the night, then rapidly inhaling some "children are finally asleep" air before they retire for the night minutes shy of declaring their retirement from parenthood. What are your chances of moving in on that madness for a few minutes and communicating something significant? In regard to most of the parents you will encounter in this position, if it doesn't immediately involve the kids, you're just wasting your time!

Could you possibly convince a teenager to step away from their prime of life for some important adult matter? Good luck even making eye contact with them while their time and attention are focused on homework, homework and more homework; extra-curricular commitments like student government, cheerleading, dance teams, team sports, the school newspaper or yearbook; weekend planning, weekend partying and weekend sleep to make up for the dreaded Monday through Friday 6 a.m. alarms; movie-going and mall madness; satisfying clothing needs that were identified during clothing comparison-conversations with close friends; learning to drive, driving, driving just because they can and driving around those who still can't; video game purchasing and perfecting, television trances and listening to their latest favorite CD; looking for a job, finding a job and working a job; looking for a better job, finding a better job and working a better job; gaining that much-sought-after independence and developing their own identity; dealing with insecurities and worries about weight, acne, popularity, dating, grades and college placement tests; and last but not least on this selection of teenage clock-consumption—mirror time!

If you think that's difficult, try luring a football fanatic into a meaningful conversation while he's watching his favorite team march down the field during a potential game-winning drive in the final minutes of the most important game of the season. You lose!

Or, take a shot at getting a response to your important question from the ***Apprentice*** or ***American Idol*** diehard while they're riveted to a television set watching the season finale. Count on you, not the television, being turned off!

Give a go at getting the attention of the project manager at work facing a deadline, or try convincing a commissions-only salesman near the end of an important month to take a time-out and think about your really important business. Get used to hearing the word "no" and rejoice in the additional "thank you" you might hear occasionally.

Try breaking up the high school sweethearts for a few moments to discuss long-term thinking and building wisely for the future. Good luck making any headway with the ones mesmerized by their new true love, the romance they're convinced will last always and forever. Could something you have to offer produce anything close to the euphoric feeling they've enjoyed since going steady?

How might you go about convincing a recently retired couple that what you have to offer is so much more satisfying than their plans to travel the country in a motor home and just plain relax for the next few months. Does what you have to say stand a chance of topping the quiet hours of fishing on the lake or reading a good book on the front porch they have been looking forward to for so long?

Nobody has dealt more often with this type of dilemma or is more in tune with this sad reality than God himself. Since the beginning of time, God has been hanging gorgeous pictures in front of people, making loud noises or sending soothing sounds in their ears and shining big, bright lights in their eyes in an attempt to draw them in his direction. Granted, some have decided to slow down for a moment in their fast-paced world and have thanked him for his amazing artwork. Some have stopped to acknowledge his warning of danger looming over the horizon and have headed for shelter. Others have heeded the heavenly voice assuring them that their heart's delight could be found in the opposite direction and have gladly made a U-turn. Some have allowed the light from heaven to expose their erring ways, and later welcomed that same light to drive back their darkness. Unfortunately, the vast majority of potentially God-honoring souls just ignore his effort to reach them and continue on the path of independence, oblivious to the One who created them and who currently keeps them breathing. People often ignore God, just like I do with the flight attendant when she explains emergency procedures before take-off—"I've heard it so many times before and, besides, this plane won't be crashing as long as I'm on it!"

It all started with a mind blowing six-day spectacular simply called creation—all of it designed to make it unbelievably easy for all of us to believe in a creator and worship him accordingly (**Romans 1:18-25**). A never-ending sky announces his eternal nature. Deep and vast oceans that surround the earth but rarely engulf its shores speak of the wonderful truth that, though his enormous and unlimited supply of power and wrath could instantly destroy us all, God regularly and willingly restrains himself, having established invisible shorelines called grace to keep us from harm and from going to hell. Majestic mountains rising miles above the earth remind man of God's awesome and immovable nature, strong, sturdy and reliable, and that his ways and his word are firm and steadfast, altered only by an act he initiates. The towering trees that fill the forests and spread their branches to provide shade for man speak of a God who reaches out to his creation and, if they choose to draw near to him, can keep them from collapsing in the sweltering heat called daily living. The bright, blazing sun is a constant reminder that light and direction are available from above— that something so far away and so unreachable can still make its way to earth and touch every inch of its surface—a power that, though it can't always be seen, it can always be felt. The moon and countless stars placed in the expanse above remind us that, even in our dark-

> *The moon and countless stars placed in the expanse above remind us that, even in our darkest hour, light is available from the heavens.*

est hour, light is available from the heavens. The changing of the earth's guard every 24 hours speaks of God's trustworthy nature and provides a continual opportunity for us to realize he loves the idea of a fresh start. The clouds delivering rain to refresh the earth and irrigate the planted fields speak of God's desire to bring freshness to our often-wilting lives and food to our tables. The beasts of the earth, the birds of the air and the biggest creatures of the deep provide for us the privilege and responsibility of reigning and exercising authority, all the while reminding us that someone is reigning over us as well. The lightning makes us run for cover in fear, yet in the same moment helps us to realize power is available in an instant and transferable from heaven to earth. The rainbow allows us the opportunity to marvel at the beauty of God, stand in awe of the colors of creation and better comprehend the creativity and diversity of our Maker. And these are only a small, unscientific sampling of the many messages God has left in his wonderful creation to declare his glory, proclaim the work of his hands and send out his voice to the ends of the world (**Psalm 19:1-6**).

Had we been paying closer attention, God could have been finished with his plan. But we needed more proof so God continued to reveal. He brought a worldwide flood of cataclysmic proportions to warn man for the rest of time that continual evil without a corresponding choice to repent would ultimately bring life to an end (**Genesis 6:5-13**). He confused the one universal language during the Tower of Babel fiasco to teach man how prideful thoughts, pointless pursuits and putting off his original plan to fill the *entire* earth would not be tolerated (**Genesis 11:1-9**). He spoke to man numerous times on a personal level and asked him to pass along his message of truth and grace to a neighbor (**Genesis 12:1-7, Hebrews 1: 1**). He dropped ten devastating plagues upon a top world power to illustrate the absurdity of arrogance and idolatry (**Exodus 7-12**). He raised up Israel, a tiny and inexperienced gathering of sinful people to display to the rest of the world what enormous benefits could come from worshipping and listening to him (**Deuteronomy 9:1-6**). He stopped the regular rotation of the earth and made the sun stand still for an entire day to show he had absolute control over the every day affairs of mankind and would go to any length to bless his people (**Joshua 10:1-14**). He sent prophet after prophet, again and again to tell his chosen people, as well as those on the outside, that though his love was constant and his patience unlimited, his expectations were still to be honored (**Jeremiah 25:1-7**). He later destroyed Israel, his treasured possession, to display to the rest of the world that benefits ended when commitment to him ended (**2 Chronicles 36:15-19**).

These are just a few examples of what God has done to encourage man to seek after him, find him and stay with him as we watch the drama played out in the biblical record. Who knows how many other messages and revelations God sent to earth throughout the centuries to lift eyes and hearts heavenward? God was constantly revealing truth about himself and still, because man's desires were centered elsewhere, man did not fully comprehend him. So God became a human being. For thirty-three years, God lived in a small area in what we know today as the Middle East, spent most of his time with a dozen ordinary and unschooled men who were willing to follow him and proved his deity with startling messages, breathtaking miracles and mighty acts of kindness. He called himself Jesus—the Revealer. In Jesus, God has introduced himself to us personally. He has revealed his love, his power, his kindness, his forgiveness, his patience, his perfection, his teaching, his expectations, his judgments and, most importantly, his directions for obtaining a personal relationship and a permanent home with him.

Even from a limited human perspective, this plan seems to make perfect sense. For example, let me tell you about my wife, Patty. She recently turned 41 but looks much younger, is both bright and beautiful, has an amazingly quick wit and crazy sense of humor, loves her parents and children dearly, is a true servant, has an incredibly competitive nature (especially against me), does the best impression I've ever heard of the wicked witch from **The Wizard of Oz**, whips up the most succulent apple pie I have ever tasted, loves watching **Clean Sweep** and **While You Were Out** on the TLC network and is the only one in our household who still has the compassion to pay attention to our fat and lazy cat since the arrival and subsequent takeover of our home by our dog a few years ago. I know Patty inside and out and love to reveal her to as many as possible, but how would you know if what I just wrote about her was true or not?

After being with Patty for twenty-two years now, I should know a little something about her. And while at times she may disagree, for the most part I've been paying careful attention to her. But in order for you to get to know Patty, you'll need to meet her in person, talk with her, ask her questions, watch her, analyze her and do your best to figure out exactly who she is. In like manner, to get to know God, you'll need to meet him in person, Jesus, and employ the exact same strategy with him.

Now allow me a little space to tell you about my children. My son, Brad, is 19, a freshman in college and he recently moved in to his own place with a few of his friends from church. He's a big man, six feet-three inches tall, broad and strong, yet also displaying enough coordination to juggle and shoot the three with the best of them. He's a disciple of Jesus with a quiet disposition and a soft heart, incredibly easy to be around and hang out with, has never met a movie or a music CD he didn't like or a roller-coaster that he did, has solved the problems of history and science but math remains a mystery to him (his report cards confirmed this), is an all-around good kid and an absolute joy to have as a son.

My daughter, Brittany, is 14 and just began her freshman year in high school. She's tall and thin, is becoming more and more beautiful by the minute, has an abundant supply of the cutest freckles around her nose and eyes, loves to go shopping (surprise, surprise) and has played in a basketball league or on her school's team for the past five years, improving dramatically each year. She is confident, loves all the wild and crazy roller-coasters at Six Flags (she wanted to bungee-jump on our most recent vacation but we felt she wasn't ready for it; the truth is, her parents weren't ready for it), is sharp as a tack and has received one B in her scholastic history that she quickly brought up to an A by the time she got her semester report card.

She loves people, especially little children and, if I were a kid, I'd demand that she be my babysitter at every available opportunity. She's sensitive and has a heart to do what is right in the eyes of God. After studying the Bible, she made her decision to be a follower of Jesus and was baptized into Christ just a few months ago.

But how can you believe all that? Okay, maybe some of it is tainted with prejudice and parental pride, but come see for yourself. You'll see I'm not far off base in my observations. Spend 19 years and 14 years respectively with them and you'll know them intimately—their strengths, their weakness and everything else in between. Do the same with God by spending time with Jesus and you'll know him intimately as well, minus the weaknesses, of course.

If I had more time, I could let you know about my amazing mom, my wonderful sister, my fantastic mother-in-law and father-in-law, the awesome members of the full-time staff of the St. Louis Church of Christ that I enjoyed working with for so many years and my many incredible friends from around the country. But once again, you would just have to take my word for it. Either that, or you would need to spend an extended period of time with each of them and see what you think.

Though he had every right, God didn't wait for us to come and visit him and learn his ways. He heard the rumors had started, knew many of them were wrong and, instead of getting ticked off about the rapidly spreading lies and distancing himself from us, he humbly stepped down from his throne, put on his clothing of flesh, started off in a womb like the rest of us and began his life as Jesus, God in a human body.

No, we weren't there to see him face-to-face. But the written revelation of his activity on earth is just as good. As a matter of fact, it may be even better, because now we get to see so much more of him than those in the first century did, other than the twelve apostles and a few more fortunate individuals who were selected for additional time with him. This book is simply an overall view of what we see in Jesus, the Revealer, contained in the writings of the New Testament. Most of what you will read is purely factual and from the Biblical record, written with a personal twist to try and help you understand Jesus in a clearer and more intimate way. I have, especially in a few places like Chapters 15-16, gone outside the pages of Scripture to speculate on the life of Jesus, especially his early years. These are just my thoughts and opinions and have absolutely nothing to do with the absolute truths found in the Bible. Despite its unproven nature, I hope you'll find this portion to be interesting, thought provoking and enjoyable reading material. I've also taken the liberty throughout the book to insert some verbal comments that those around Jesus may have made in response to what they heard him say or saw him do. (These will be indicated in *italics*) Again, the word **possible** is key here. We know much more was said than what we find in Scripture; just exactly what it was we do not know and never will unless God fills us in once we get to heaven and we're given a full replay of first century history.

The Revealer is written to give you another tool to deepen your understanding, love and appreciation for Jesus Christ. Let's take a trip back in time and witness the one person God was preparing people for even before the time of Adam and Eve and the one he has been pointing people back to for the past 2,000 years. It is to this one man that we must give our utmost attention. Let the journey begin!

🌿 Chapter Two 🌿

Final Statement
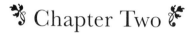

In the past God spoke to our forefathers through the prophets
at many times and in various ways, but in these last days
he has spoken to us by his Son...
— Hebrews 1:1-2

God has delivered many specific statements to human beings throughout the ages since the arrival of Adam and Eve. He left many convincing clues as to his identity and his feelings for mankind in the hundreds of pages we have come to know as the Old Testament. During this time, he also used prophets to relay messages about who he was and what he expected from mankind. He enabled many of these mighty men of old to perform miraculous signs to confirm that the words they were speaking were not of human origin but were sent from the throne of God. God tried on countless occasions, through the written and spoken word, to let his chosen people know he was immediately available for them and wanted what was best for their lives, looking to them to relay those same glorious truths to the general population. Whether it was revealing his law on Mount Sinai through his servant Moses, confirming his love and passion for David and all of mankind throughout the book of Psalms, teaching man his eternal wisdom through King Solomon in the book of Proverbs or encouraging Daniel and the exiled nation of Israel by showing them magnificent scenes of the future, God was getting his message out to man and making sure his truths would be recorded and preserved for generations to come. Unfortunately, many of those who gained access to his word chose not to read it at all, or they read it with an arrogant mindset as though it were optional in nature. So God did what has been a part of his true character for all eternity and what had been a part of his plan for all eternity—he went the second mile and came to deliver the word in person. Truly, the word became flesh.

God, himself, entered a womb and entered time, all the while still upholding the heavens and the earth. He did so in the person of Jesus Christ—the fullness of the deity in bodily form and the exact representation of his being (**Hebrews 1:3**). Jesus did things and said things during one short time span of history to get man's absolute attention. God was shouting loud and long through Jesus because he knew he wasn't going to say it again. Yes, what we have in Jesus Christ is God's *final statement*. Everything written up to that point was pointing to him. Everything written after his arrival looked back to his activity on earth. Jesus, you might say, stopped the heavenly printing presses. Perfection had arrived in the flesh and he was the final headline, story, advertisement and editorial in God's final edition.

The information presented about him in the Scriptures, therefore, is essential for everybody to know and believe. God will not say anything else about the subject that he has not already revealed. He won't send you a personal message or write additional insights in the formation of the clouds. Jesus has spoken and now it's your job to simply listen.

> *Jesus did things and said things during one short span of history to get man's absolute attention.*

What exactly did Jesus say and do that is all-sufficient for all mankind? What truths might someone discover by discovering him that they have been blind to all their lives? Why is there no pressing need for God to send another messenger? What do we see in Jesus that should remind us to no longer look for an answer from heaven? Is Jesus the all-time undisputed champion of spiritual leadership?

Some of my fondest memories growing up are centered around the times my dad and I would sit in the living room with our popcorn and soda watching professional wrestling on Saturday nights, as well as the few times we watched it live in our ringside seats, cheering and jeering as the acrobatic behemoths pounded on each other. But it wasn't until I was about 14 years old that I realized it was much more show than real sports competition.

Everything I was seeing looked so incredibly real. My unsuspicious eyes and overly-trusting heart saw it that way. So many people were telling me otherwise, but surely they were just uninformed or hadn't been watching the action closely enough. Even in person it looked to be the real deal.

Once, while sitting at ringside, one of the wrestlers grabbed the chair next to us and began walloping his opponent repeatedly on the top of his head. Blood was gushing everywhere. And, oh you better believe it—that was real blood! I could tell with my own two eyes that those blows were definitely landing and no doubt causing much permanent bodily damage. That 350-pound champion, descending spread-eagle in mid-air from atop the turn-buckle, most definitely landed with full force right on the mid-section of his dazed enemy lying helpless on the mat. Oh yes, my friend, it was real with-out a doubt. Mad Dog Lonnie Mayne, whose voice and vocabulary actually were closer to canine than human; The Kangaroos, an Australian tag-team of cousins from Down Under who often illegally retrieved a boomerang from down under the ring to turn the tide in matches that had looked like sure defeats; Dutch Savage, who looked old enough and wrinkled enough to be my grandfather, yet was regularly pinning men half his age and twice his size by virtue of his experience in the ring; and my favorite, Jimmy Snuka, the magnificently buffed wild man from Samoa, a good-guy and crowd favorite who resorted to dastardly tactics on occasion just to let the bad guys know he meant business. These were real men: Athletes and fierce competitors in the truest sense. My eyes saw it. My heart felt it. And even if nobody else was smart enough to see it that way, I was always going to believe it and stick up for my heroes who were claiming nothing was staged and that the outcome of each match was left up to the man with the bulk and the best moves on any given night.

It wasn't too long after my 14th birthday that I turned on the televi-sion one Saturday night and noticed that the fierce right forearm to the head of Snuka, sending him flailing to the mat, never actually touched his head at all. My world caught a smackdown and I realized that what I had been defending for the past few years was a mere product of the entertain-ment business looking to make a mint on the naïve minds of professional wrestling believers across the globe. They suckered me into it! With great hesitation and much trembling of the heart, I swallowed massive doses of humble pie and finally admitted what family and friends had been telling me for years.

It's now almost thirty years later and professional wrestling has not changed a bit. Only the names are new—The Rock, Sting, The Under-taker, Triple H, Goldberg and other Goliaths-in-tights excite their fans nightly and entertain millions around the world. I'll occasionally catch a few moments while channel surfing and it's amazingly easy to see through the deception of those finely tuned athletes and entertainers. How come it wasn't so easy to spot back when I could have used the information to avoid being ridiculed by fellow eighth graders? Somewhere along the way my eyes caught a glimpse of the phony grapplers and my heart gained insight into the truth that many in-the-know had been preaching to me all along.

I'm of the firm conviction that professional wrestlers and Jesus Christ have very little in common when it comes to their time on stage. Jesus was the "real deal." Unfortunately, many today don't see it that way and look at Jesus as just another entertainer for those who are into the religious thing. But where do you stand with Jesus at this point in your life? Is he the "real deal" and, if so, are all the glorious accolades we hear attributed to him really deserved? Or, is he simply a product of our religious imagination, cleverly contrived over the centuries so we Christians can shout, "My God is better than your God!" Or, are you willing to admit that, yes, he actually lived, but, no, nobody could actually be *that* awesome. Surely, you say, some of his followers got caught up in the moment and then got carried away with the pen while writing his biography. What do you think?

Regardless of your current belief system concerning Jesus Christ, let this book be your trip back into the video room to watch every match Jesus entered. When the film starts rolling, you'll notice every blow aimed at the enemy actually landed square, and the blood seen running down the entire body of the champion is very real indeed. It will become obvious that every opponent Jesus faced wasn't faking anything or surrendering to him without a fight to the finish. You'll discover that the undefeated and untied record throughout his entire career was truly earned. You'll be especially impressed after reviewing his final match on earth as Jesus looked certain to surrender his championship belt after being knocked out cold and thrown outside the ring onto the stadium floor—only to be revived just short of being pinned by the count of three, coming out of nowhere to score his greatest victory.

My simple prayer is that this look at Jesus in the ring called planet earth, and seeing how he fought and gained a convincing victory against the real forces of evil, will help to open your eyes and your heart to the truth that has always been truth—Jesus is God's eternal champion and the messenger he sent to earth to deliver his *final statement!*

🌿 Chapter Three 🌿

Other Things
❦ ❦

Jesus did many other things as well.
If every one of them were written down, I suppose that even the
whole world would not have room for the books that would be written.
— John 21:25

My main goal in this book is to guide you through the reliable roads of revealed things and to discuss what we know for sure from the Scriptures. We will, however, take some interesting detours onto the paths of perhaps and probably and discuss what might have been in the life of Jesus. It's nearly impossible for me to avoid doing this because, when I begin to contemplate the other things about Jesus mentioned in the above passage, my curiosity levels peak and my imagination runs wild. The possibilities are endless.

God could have left us with hundreds, even thousands of additional gospels recording the most amazing life of his Son. He gave us four: Matthew, Mark, Luke and John, chosen instruments of the Holy Spirit to capture enough moments in the life of Jesus to instruct us, impress us and inspire us. These men have told us the story of the Son of God. Many other things were said and done by him, yet only these were recorded and preserved in the Scriptures. What else might we have known about Jesus if everything about this remarkable man and his remarkable thirty-three years on Planet Earth had been revealed?

Probably many other paralyzed and demon-possessed people crossed his powerful path and were miraculously healed.

Surely more profound parables were presented and eye-opening sermons on the mount were delivered.

Was there more joy than grief at funerals when the Son of God stopped by? How many others went from overwhelming sadness to ongoing smiles when Jesus brought back breath to a loved one?

What comforting words did Jesus use to soothe the pain of parents while at funerals of children he chose not to bring back from the dead?

How many hundreds of ten-minute, life-changing conversations with the previously misguided might be missing from the written word?

How many thousands of ten-second, "you're important to me" moments do you suppose he handed out during his time on earth?

How many lives were changed by his "I'm happy to see you" smile or "I know exactly what you're thinking" glare?

How much more amazed would we be if every one of his early-morning prayer times and late-night rendezvous with God were recorded?

Perhaps an entire city library would be needed to contain all of the books that could have been written to adequately describe what happened the day John the Baptist died and how Jesus dealt with it (**Matthew 14: 1-36**).

What do you suppose the conversations were about at the big bash Jesus attended with newly converted Matthew and all his former partying pals (**Matthew 9:9-13**)? Perhaps each honored guest around the dinner table that night could have contributed a chapter in the book, *I Met the Messiah at Matthew's.*

What about those forty days and forty nights of severe temptation in the desert battling the devil (**Luke 4:1-13**)? Surely we could have been given much more food for thought about the man who refused to succumb to the temptation for food.

What other reading material could we have enjoyed detailing his follow-up visits with all the deaf and blind he healed?

What about a book for each one of Jesus' one-on-one evangelistic efforts and his reaction to their reaction?

What were his innermost thoughts during his nights of sleeping outdoors as he stared at the stars he had made?

What did God in the flesh do to keep his flesh firm? Maybe a book or two could have been written about his time spent in physical training while living in Nazareth.

How about some recorded insight on how Jesus dealt with each of the "all things" he was tempted with during his teenage years (**Hebrews 4:14-15**)?

What did Jesus do on the days when nothing was biting while fishing with his twelve apostles? Did he ever purposely bypass the school of fish he knew were swimming just to the left of the boat to school the fishermen with him on how to be patient?

What were his private conversations with Judas all about?

How many deathbed discussions did he have with people he knew were on the verge of spending eternity in hell? What did Jesus say to them? Did any of them respond and repent? Were there any prototypes of the thief on the cross conversion (**Luke 23:32-43**)?

How about some additional inside information concerning all the undocumented discipleship groups with the apostles? How many other times did Jesus gather the group to dam their flood of selfishness (**Matthew 20:20-28**)?

> *How many other times did Jesus gather the group to dam their flood of selfishness?*

When did he cry when nobody was watching, and what was it that moved him to tears during those moments?

What Scriptures did he cling to during an attempt by those in his hometown to toss him down a cliff (**Luke 4:14-30**)?

How many times do you suppose he told the parable of the sower? What was the setting and synopsis for each one?

What made Jesus laugh? What were the humorous moments of the man from heaven?

What did Jesus do in his spare time? What were his hobbies?

Did he ever have a follow-up talk with the rich, young ruler to offer him one more chance (**Matthew 19:16-26**)?

Did the poor widow who gave all she had get to spend a few minutes with Jesus? Perhaps a few chapters could be written on how he appropriately rewarded someone who wasn't looking for any (**Luke 21:1-4**).

Did he give any dating advice or pre-marital counseling to the woman at the well (**John 4:4-42**)?

What did Jesus think and feel as he wiped the dirt from the feet of Judas (**John 13:1-17**)?

What thoughts and emotions accompanied him concerning your life and the lives of all who have ever lived as he hung on his tree of torture? Ten to twelve billion books, at least, could be written concerning those closing moments.

These questions and others you might be asking at the moment are all very interesting and conversation-provoking. But nobody knows the answers to any of these questions. In his divine wisdom, God chose not to reveal them. Yes, the "other things" are fun to imagine, discuss or even debate, and we will spend a little time doing just that. But none of these "other things" are essential to know. The "revealed things" are! Thank God he has chosen to leave us an abundance of information about the Revealer. And if we commit to learning his heart, his actions and his expectations, and if we make it our number one ambition to become like him in every way, it will keep us occupied and on target for the rest of our lives.

❧ Chapter Four ❦

To Tell The Truth
✄　✄

Dear friends, do not believe every spirit, but test the spirits
to see whether they are from God, because many false
prophets have gone out into the world.
— 1 John 4:1

Will the real Jesus Christ please stand up?

The show was called **To Tell The Truth** and four all-star panelists were given one simple task: Find the fakes! Two of the three contestants they questioned were liars. Only one actually was who he said he was and actually did what he said he did.

The phonies were fully primed. They knew a lot about the truth teller and, without conscience, looked forward to their job of deception. Show regulars Bill Cullen and Kitty Carlisle joined two other panelists on a six-minute exploration for truth, each being allowed 90 seconds to engage in some serious probing of the contestants. Could they catch a pretender off-guard? Was a stuttered answer a dead give away? Was a pause or hesitation a sign of panic from the fake or a decoy from the truth-teller? Were smiles significant? Did one-word answers stem from a lack of deeper knowledge or were they purposefully given to conceal a wealth of information? When the interrogations were complete, the ballots were cast. Who did Kitty select? Did Bill go with his gut or did he just guess? Every night, host Garry Moore would pose the same question to the trios: "Will the real John Brown please stand up?" Down to the very end, the deceivers left the panel and millions of truth-seekers glued to their televisions wondering. Often, an impersonator half stood as if to answer the all-important question, only to sit again while the man with the proper identification rose and acknowledged his honesty.

Those were always an exciting thirty minutes for the Simmons family. Each night I battled with fellow **To Tell The Truth** addicts in the room and had a good time guessing. Like the expert panelists, I won some, lost some.

Today, you're the panelist and it's time to decide. Who is Jesus Christ? What was he like? What did he teach? Do you really know him or are you just guessing? Would you be shocked to see the real Jesus rising from his throne? Would you have selected him?

What would the real Jesus Christ say about the sin present in the world today and, more importantly, the sin present in your life?

What would the real Jesus Christ teach about possessions, tithing, sacrifice and other money matters?

How would the true Son of God deal with an unexpected traffic delay or the slow-moving vehicle in the fast lane?

How would he react to a loose, immoral woman given the opportunity for a "one- on-one, nobody's watching" interaction with her?

Would he be ticked with taxes and how would he fill out his IRS forms?

What would he do in a crisis and how would he get out of a jam?

How would God's eternal Son act as Joseph and Mary's earthly one?

What would be a typical day or a normal schedule for God in the flesh?

Would the real Savior of the world ever bypass a beggar?

Would a leper have a chance for a chat with the Messiah? Could a hug happen for him, too?

How often would the Son of God pray, read his Bible and attend church?

Would the real Messiah ever mess with attending mundane marriage ceremonies?

Would he take naps, ministry time-outs or vacations?

What would the real Lord do with constant interruptions?

How would a true Savior handle humans who are blame-shifting and bellyaching?

Whom would he honor? Who would his heroes be today? For what and for whom would he reserve his greatest applause?

What would he hate? How would he communicate that hatred?

What would be his stance on living together before marriage, a lousy marriage and leaving a marriage?

What would he think about boss-bashing and disrespect for authority?

What would his platform be in regard to negative political campaigns and the not-so-nice way candidates for public office speak about each other?

How would he handle himself if some of his closest friends began to misunderstand and malign him?

How would he deal with physical pain, persistent pressure and praise from others?

What do you think? Do you know the answers to these questions?

The real Jesus Christ is there for all of us to see. Unfortunately, so are the deceivers—Satan's servants looking to tickle your ears, trip you up, take you down, turn your life into unmanageable chaos and tear up your ticket to the heavenly reunion. Thank God you have more than a few minutes to get it right. If you're in your 20s, you've already been given 10 million of them—precious minutes that could have been spent pointing you to the Son of God. Have you capitalized? Have you located the stacks of paper with plentiful insights into the man's personal history? Have you figured out what a true Savior of the world would be like?

> *Without knowing Jesus and making a decision to live for him, you will face some challenging situations in the days ahead that won't make much sense to you.*

Introducing Jesus Christ—a flesh and blood verification of what God had said to mankind for thousands of years prior to his arrival—I love you completely, I want you to know me intimately and I want you to move in with me permanently. Jesus was the God-Man with the eternal, yet simple message: *"I'll go all out for you and give you all you need to go all out for me."*

God desperately wants you to know Jesus Christ. I thank God every day that he has allowed me to know him and that every day for the rest of my life I have the opportunity to get to know him even better. Writing this book is helping me to know him better than ever. Hopefully, reading this book will do the same for you.

Without knowing Jesus and making a decision to live for him, you will face some challenging situations in the days ahead that won't make much sense to you. When they come, and if you're unable to understand them in their proper context, these new situations will greatly complicate matters in your already difficult life. Or, as is the case most of the time, if these life situations are completely misunderstood, they will steal the joy

God has intended for you and, more than likely, steal the salvation God has marked out for you. Neither is worth forfeiting.

For example, consider the man who escaped from the fires of the World Trade Center on 9-11, only to learn a few hours later that his sister and niece had been killed in the terrorist's attack at the Pentagon? What will he do to emotionally survive these terrible losses? How will he go about finding perspective about these horrible events? Why did he live but they didn't? Can he ever make sense of this tragedy without first trying to make sense of Jesus? And how would you have dealt with such tragic news?

What about the children of the heroic firemen and policemen from New York City who were first on the scene after planes flew into the Twin Towers? What will they think about God when they one day come to understand that their fathers died trying to rescue people they most likely knew were already dead? Could knowing the real Jesus help them through this quandary? Could some accurate information about his courageous march to death on a cross (knowing full well that billions would totally ignore his ultimate act of heroism) be used to help keep these kids from the trap of the ultimate terrorist? And if you were the surviving parent, what life lessons would you plan to teach your child?

What can a distraught mother do to ease her painful ordeal after she accidentally kills her two-year old son while backing out of the driveway? Didn't God know he was there? Why didn't he stop this from happening? Could it help her to realize that Jesus' brutal death wasn't even an accident, but that God had actually planned for his Son to die? Could Jesus' acceptance of his Father's plan, stemming from the hope that many would one day be in heaven because of it, inspire this mother to believe that her son's death could possibly bring about some of the same? And what would be your plan for grief-relief and life management if this tragedy were to visit you?

And where can this unfortunate soldier find refuge from his grief? In a moment of elation upon returning from a six-month separation from his family, he embraced his young daughter then raised her into the air after stepping out of a military helicopter, only to watch the still-rotating propeller blade sever her tiny head? Where will he go to now for guidance? Can he ever get on with his life? And where would you turn for help if it were your daughter who had died in a similar way? Would you be able to get on with your life?

Are there answers for these people outside of Jesus Christ, and are there answers for you if a similar tragedy touches down on your doorstep? Is the Son of God able to understand the exasperating emotions of a parent who feels responsible for the death of their child? And can Jesus sympathize and empathize with the daunting challenge of having to move forward and manage life after the death of a loved one?

Will the parents of a 22-year old man ever be able to stop asking "why"? In the summer of 1996, their son was tragically killed, the only person to die in more than fifteen years during the "running of the bulls" through the streets of Pamplona, Spain. Why did it have to be their son? If God really does have control of the cattle on a thousand hills, then why didn't he make the bull miss (**Psalm 50:7-11**)? Why didn't he stop that bull from ruining their lives? Is it possible that knowing Jesus could bring some comfort and understanding into their home and into their hearts?

A father must struggle through his remaining years, looking to make some sense of his pain. It all started with a simple trip to the dentist with the kids on a hot and humid day. After making a stop at the grocery store on his way home, he parked his car in the driveway and left the vehicle, assuming one of the older children would take the sleeping baby out of the back seat. Tired from the heat and groggy from the medication he received at the dentist's office, he decided to take a nap to recover from the difficult day. A few hours later his wife returned home, woke him in a panic and began asking him about the location of their baby. Only moments later they discovered their eight-month old son in his car seat, dead from heat suffocation caused by temperatures that reached 130 degrees inside the vehicle.

Where will all of these people stricken by tragedy turn? Will religion be enough to soothe their sorrow, or is Jesus the only one capable of bearing their burdens and giving them strength to face each new day? Could he possibly know how they really feel?

Could knowing Jesus be the greatest need of all for those nations and individuals who are trying to put their lives back together after the untold death and destruction brought on by the earthquake and ensuing tsunami in the Indian Ocean? Could a simple look into his life, his love and his teachings help them to find some comfort and understanding amid the immense physical and emotional suffering they are now having to endure?

What will you do when your crisis comes? What have you done with the crises that have already arrived? What about the not-so-tragic times that aren't terribly consequential by themselves but, after a few years of steady disappointment and discouragement from enough of them, can leave you bitter for life? Could knowing the real Jesus turn the incoming tide if it's your life that is messed up or mediocre? Could some knowledge of the Son of God bring you the long-awaited perspective on life that may have escaped you to this point? Could an inside look at how he handled his own pressures and how he dealt with people in your shoes two thousand years ago convince you that he's still capable of rescuing you from your perils today? Could Jesus be the vehicle you need while driving in this dangerous world? Is he the Hummer you should purchase before the next crash in your life occurs, or can you be just as confident and secure riding in a Hyundai or a Honda?

Can a look at his life help you to determine how to restore a broken relationship? Can his activity on earth teach you anything about the activity you'll need to be involved in while trying to bring joy and excitement back to your church? Could someone in prison for a crime they didn't commit benefit from a thorough investigation of the life of Jesus? How about someone who's in prison and deserves to be there? Can someone guilty of a crime they haven't been charged with find the courage to come forward and confess it by studying the man who claimed to be all about grace and truth? Or, how about the people who aren't in an actual prison, but still feel all locked up due to being falsely accused by a family member or a former friend? Can a look at the life of Christ be the key to their future happiness? And how about those who are ridden with guilt about some sin they've committed, but a confession won't land them behind bars? Could a husband's look at the life of Jesus bring out his hidden adultery and bring back hope for a decent marriage? Can a closet alcoholic finally admit his weakness and rely upon the strength he sees in Christ to help him say "No" to the sin that is slowly ruining his life? Can bitterness, impurity, deceit and selfishness be more easily eradicated from someone's life if they spend some time searching out the man who claimed to avoid them all?

God is absolutely thrilled to let you and the whole world know about his Son. He works to give each human being a chance to know of his days on earth, his deeds for mankind, his death on a cross, his delivery from the threshold of death and his many days since, sitting at the right hand of God. God delights in Jesus Christ. He longs to show him off. He wants his entire history to be a public spectacle. God is not embarrassed by a single moment or hiding a single flaw. He is righteously proud of the plan and eager to divulge it. Apparently, you've been selected to see him.

As I began writing this book, Americans and many others around the world were plagued with thoughts of past terrorist activities and fears of future attacks. More than 3,500 innocent victims died on 9-11 in New York, Washington D.C. and just outside of Pittsburgh. Since then, some have died as a result of Anthrax poisoning, car bombings, train station explosions, bullet wounds to the back of the head, beheadings, school seizures and other terrorist activities. Others have lost their lives in the fighting in

Afghanistan and the war currently focused in Iraq. Did they know Jesus? Had anybody ever shown these people who he was, what he did and how he could help them? Did their lives end without a true knowledge of the Savior? The people who have been caught in the recent crossfire of hatred and revenge, along with all other human beings who have died since the dawn of creation, are now fully aware. They've been introduced to the real Jesus Christ. Were they surprised? Is that what they thought? Is he similar to what they were taught about him by their parents or their preacher? Is he anything at all like what they had been telling others he was like? Is his real description anything close to what they were teaching their children it was?

Those of us who still live and breathe have been given this additional time to find the true Jesus. We are 21st century panelist on spiritual "To Tell the Truth" looking for the man who has boldly claimed to be the Son of God.

"Will the real Jesus Christ please stand up?"

❧ Chapter Five ❦

The Great Impostor
↩ ↪

Watch out that no one deceives you.
For many will come in my name claiming
"I am the Christ," and will deceive many.
— Matthew 24:4-5

I met Ferdinand Waldo (Fred) Demara when I was nine years old. He was a robust man with a Santa Claus smile and always found time to make me feel special. He was a minister for the one and only church in the small, logging town of Toutle, Washington where I lived from the third grade until my high school graduation. Reverend Demara, as most called him, was well liked and respected and would make appearances at most of the significant community activities. One of the most important of these appearances for me was at my older brother's funeral in 1969, as he was one of the men who spoke during the memorial. I don't remember any of the content of his message that day, but I do remember feeling liked he really cared. And he continued to express his concern for my family's welfare by his many visits to our home following my brother's death.

Reverend Demara moved away from Toutle shortly after my brother's death and, though our family kept in contact with him for a number of years after his departure, my recollection of him ended around age twelve. But his life had a great impact on more than just one child who had lost his big brother. Much of the positive impact from Reverend Demara's life came after a dramatic turnaround of his troubled younger days that ultimately landed him in church work. Demara's hard-to-track trail of deceit became headline news across America beginning in the late 1940s and stretching into the early 1960s, and the story of his life was soon developed into a Hollywood movie with Tony Curtis in the starring role. Fred Demara was better known as "The Great Impostor."

An intense, all-out manhunt led to Demara's arrest and ultimate conviction in 1961, though he spent very little actual time in jail for his crimes. In his more-than-a-decade reign as America's greatest con-artist, Demara was Dr. Joseph C. Cyr, surgeon lieutenant in the Royal Canadian Navy; Ben W. Jones, assistant warden of the Huntsville Prison in Texas; Dr. Robert Lincoln French, head of a college psychology department; and Brother M. Jerome, novitiate in a Trappist monastery, just to name a few. Demara performed admirably at each position, including successful surgeries as a naval doctor, making it even more difficult to detect the hidden truth. He had accumulated very convincing documents for each of the men he impersonated, and, through what he called "the naivety of man," became perhaps the boldest impostor the world has ever known. In the book, *The Great Impostor: The Amazing Careers of the Most Spectacular Impostor of Modern Times*, Demara shared the secrets of his success in weaving his way into even the most challenging of positions. For example, consider his following sentiments on the simple strategies of being a good doctor.

"The seriously sick know they're sick and so do you. Those you send to a hospital. The rest are all going to get better sooner or later, and anything you do for them will seem right, and because they think you're a doctor, they'll automatically feel better."

Demara's successful reign as the Great Impostor was a clear indication that those in charge of the hiring process weren't looking closely enough into important matters. He lived out his many lies with forged, stolen or non-existent qualifications. Exhaustive background checks with corresponding photographs and eyewitness confirmations of identity were deemed unimportant by those in a position to employ him. The many worlds he ventured into needed immediate help and Demara was always there to oblige.

The world you and I live in is the arena Satan has been allowed to temporarily occupy (**Revelation 12:7-12**). It's a world with millions crying loud and often for help. And the echoes of "Fix me God," "Heal me God" and "Save me God" have Satan and his cleverly disguised demons rushing to the doorsteps of these desperate souls, ready to offer them a delightful array of quick-fix Messiahs. "You're fixed," "You're healed" and "You're saved" are the promises they make to many naïve individuals who are looking for the simplest and most satisfying salvation scenarios.

But our world also has millions of people who would be interested in following Jesus, but they can't get around their thoughts of "I can't change," "I've never really succeeded at anything in my life" and "I'm no good anyway." Satan is eager to agree with them. "You're beyond fixing,"

"You'll never make it" and "You aren't worth saving" are a few of the thoughts he loves to plant in the minds of those who remain trapped in the basement of the skyscraper called self-esteem.

The biggest problem with both of these presentations is that little or no biblical backing is included. But the naïve seekers don't really seem to care about seeing any hard and fast evidence or biblical proof about the new position with God they're being promised. Too much information might just take away the warm and fuzzy feelings they need in order to continue wading through their shallow lives.

Too much information might just take away the warm and fuzzy feelings they need in order to continue wading through their shallow lives.

"*That Jesus sounds so good to me, why, who could ever turn him down?*"

Sadly, those searching for identity, self-worth and a place to belong tend to believe the hellish lies just as quickly upon receiving confirmation of their total unworthiness. They quickly retreat with their heads hanging low to dark, yet familiar dungeons of "I told you I couldn't do it," "Who was I fooling anyway?" and "Why did I get my hopes up again?"

"*That Jesus sounds so intense, why, who would ever be able to follow him?*"

Unfortunately, too many people are either following the wrong Messiah or their interest in following the right one has plummeted to an all-time low.

Let's take some time now and see if we can spot some of the defective "Messiah merchandise" up for sale. You've probably encountered some of it while watching the "Jesus Goes to Hollywood" blockbusters casting the frail and effeminate man with a British accent in the starring role. Others you may have been introduced to while tuning in to Sunday morning church services on television from the comfort of your bed, or maybe you remember meeting the one in Sunday school who spent most of his time smiling for no apparent reason, or the one talking quietly to the 5,000 people on the mountainside who are supposedly hearing and hanging on his every word, or the one petting the precious lamb lying on his lap. Or, perhaps the one you can identify with the most is the one wearing the permanent scowl, or the Jesus who is looking as if he is dazed and confused, his head completely in the clouds and acting as though this trip-to-earth strategy was a big mistake and an even bigger bummer. Maybe none of these situations apply to you but, instead, you've developed your impressions of Jesus from books, best friends or out-of-context Bible passages. Here are some frequently spotted impostors of Jesus that have been set free from the gates of hell. Consider this book an all-points bulletin from heaven that will help you to identify these criminals of chaos while they remain at large. Once you've locked up these bad guys, don't relax! Other demons have been ordered by Satan to remain at home and work feverishly on new inventions of Jesus designed just for you.

In regard to the first seven impostors we'll discuss, most of us would find them very attractive and very appealing. The last five you'll be introduced to, however, are unbelievably ugly. All are false.

First let's look at the product for sale. Then we'll listen to the Satanic sales-pitch that follows.

Impostor #1: The Believe What You Want About Me Just as Long as You Believe Jesus.

"After all, it wouldn't be like a loving Savior to shove truth down your throat. If you want him to be Lord, he'll surely oblige. If not, take the good you see in him and do what you can to imitate it."

"So, you think he is *the* Son of God? Great! He'd actually settle for *a* Son of God. Is Confucius your cup of tea? Go ahead and drink, just sip on Jesus every now and then. Is Mohammed more of what you're looking for in a Messiah? Is the Koran more comfortable reading material? Enjoy your reading and, if you have the time and when you get the chance, grab a gospel or two from the Good Book and learn a little something about his fellow prophet."

Impostor #2: The Everyone Is Going to Heaven Anyway Jesus.

"Wasn't the main purpose for his arrival to get you to heaven and not necessarily to teach you good morals or a better way of life on earth? Sure, you'd probably improve your quality of life eventually if you did things his way while on this planet, but right now you look like you need some freedom, and those "deny yourself" statements are going to have to be denied. Thank God the Cross says we're all going to make it to heaven anyway."

Impostor #3: The Do Your Best to Work Me Into Your Schedule Jesus.

Certainly Jesus must be pleased with your once-in-a-while prayer, Bible study and church attendance. Why, billions of people never engage in those kind of spiritual activities, so he must be ecstatic that you at least take the time to occasionally be with him and his people. After all, with the stress of living in today's fast-paced society and keeping your job intact, your family happy and your bank account positive, the opportunities for those extra exercises of spirituality just aren't there like they were when you were younger. Aren't you glad Jesus understands the rigorous demands of life and doesn't expect all that much from you?

Impostor #4: The Hey, No Big Deal, Mellow Out a Minute Jesus.

"You saw the movie, didn't you? Wasn't Jesus cool! Absolutely nothing bugged him. He even told those guys who nailed him to the cross that they were going to be forgiven. Now, I know you haven't been that bad! My guess is, had Jesus been living in the 60s, he would have owned a Volkswagen van, shown up at Woodstock and hung out with the hippies. You saw it: He didn't even take the time to get his haircut or shave. He was always real low-key, wore the same clothes, went to the biggest parties, made tubs of wine at dragging wedding receptions and even took naps in the middle of the day. Now isn't that your kind of Messiah?"

Impostor #5: The Follow Me and Your Financial Future is Secure Jesus.

"Haven't you heard that if you commit your life to Jesus you'll better your business prospects? Give him just a little of your time and you might be holding the winning lottery ticket real soon. Tithe your janitor's paycheck and the CEO position you've dreamed of is right around the corner. You've heard his promises—ask for anything and it will be given to you! There is absolutely no way that God would want you to be poor or even middle class. Think about it—if you were to make a million, what could God do with that kind of money?"

Impostor #6: The Won't You Be My Neighbor Jesus.

"Did you know that Jesus was a lot like Mr. Rogers? He was sensitive at all times, donning the cardigan sweater for a softer touch and ready to appeal to our childlike hearts on a regular basis. Jesus was as popular with the adults as Fred was with the kids. No kidding, you can mess up big-time all the time and still be his neighbor any time."

Impostor #7: The All Your Problems Will Go Away If You Follow Me Jesus.

"Could this be the reason why your marriage has been a bit rocky lately? No wonder your kids haven't been listening or obeying you. Now you can understand why you didn't get that promotion. Just a little more commitment to Jesus and you should be problem free before long. Wow, isn't this incredible? Even your in-law problems are history!"

These first seven impostors (I've only named a few) are all quite attractive. Most of us would have few, if any, problems devoting our lives to any of these so-called saviors. We'd be frantically searching for a pen, willing and eager to sign on the contract's dotted line because they all have a seductive appeal to our selfish and sinful natures.

Now that we've considered the more enticing Messiah types, let's discuss some models of Jesus on display that won't have many people standing in line to take a peek. None of these will win any popularity contest, nor will they do well on a public approval poll. Nevertheless, they are equally devastating. While the first seven impostors lead people to a false sense of security with God and their salvation, these last five can cause people to greatly dislike the coach and decide against trying out for the team or finishing the season.

Impostor #8: The Don't Bother Trying, You Won't Be Able to Make it Anyway Jesus.

"Who could really do all that disciple stuff anyway? According to Jesus, you're committing adultery daily and murdering your fellow man on the freeway. I think that's somewhere in the Sermon on Mount Everest! Even if you did decide to stop sinning, how long could you last? Who's going to help you? The only people you know are the spiritually blind, and didn't Jesus tell a parable about that? And look at Peter and Judas. They spent three years with Jesus, day in and day out, and look what happened to them—Judas hangs up his Christianity by hanging himself and Peter can't even get the guts to witness to a young girl. And you think you can do it? You just need to go your own way, do your best and roll the dice in regard to judgment day."

Impostor #9: The I Can Walk on Water But Can't Keep Your Life From Sinking Jesus.

"Weren't the miracles simply to show you convincing proof that Jesus was from God? And isn't the power of God more of a show to keep you in line rather than proof that when you're in trouble he'll throw you a line? If the loaves and fishes are intended to mean something beyond a simple banquet on the hillside hosted by a local magician, then explain Ethiopia, Somalia and the multi-millions living today with little or no food. And what about your history of horrible relationships? If Jesus is so powerful, then why do you only attend weddings and never star in one? And why did your divorce happen? Jesus can't really help you with your marriage issues because he was never married. And sure, Jesus did okay with other people's kids, but he never had any of his own."

Impostor #10: The I Never Have Time to Have a Good Time Jesus.

"Self-denial. Cross bearing. Coming in last. Giving up your seat. Praying in closets. Renouncing recognition. Turning the other cheek. No place to lay your head. Have you heard enough yet? No wonder Jesus always looked so unhappy! Couldn't you tell from watching that Easter special that he was always serious, rarely smiled and often appeared stern and business-like? Did all work and no play make Jesus a dull boy? I thought you said you were looking for a schedule full of fun, excitement and adventure? Looking at Jesus, that definitely won't be happening if you follow him!"

Impostor #11: The Leave Me Alone, I'm Talking to God Jesus.

"Wasn't Jesus too lofty to bother with us low-life's? He was probably carrying an attitude from having to leave heaven in the first place. From what I can tell, either he was in prayer, in church, leading a Bible study, having an extended spiritual conversation or meditating on a mountain? What in the world would he want with you anyway? And besides, you can't possibly relate to all of that. You need a little (okay a lot of) "r-and-r" in your life."

Impostor #12: The Let Me Get These 33 Years Over and Get Back to Heaven Jesus.

"Jesus didn't really want to be here. Wasn't he doing this become-a-human-thing out of duty? Didn't he die because he had to? Don't you think he would have gathered a much larger gallery if he were sincerely in love with the human race? And if he didn't really care deeply for the people on earth that he could see and touch, chances are slim that, two thousand years later, you and I have much hope of getting his attention now that he's back in heaven."

Perhaps you're walking hand-in-hand right now with one of those first seven impostors. Never mind how secure it feels, read the rest of the book and see if you should announce a break-up.

Maybe you met your Prince Uncharming (impostors 8-12) at an early age and up until now you've had no interest in jumping on his white horse and being rescued from your oppressors. Read the rest of the story and then decide if the one in the saddle is different than you thought. Maybe he knows where "life more abundantly" is located after all.

In the case of the Great Impostor, had the victims spent just a little more time looking into the applicant's background and adequately investigating his credentials, all fooling would have failed. It's absolutely no different in the spiritual realm. Have you possibly employed Satan and don't even know it? Has the true Great Impostor perhaps been successful in claiming another victim (**2 Corinthians 11:13-15**)?

Let's take a quick trip through the Gospels, watch the real Jesus in action and hear what he has to say. Perhaps you'll once and for all be able to say "No" to any and all Satanic sales-pitches, contact the Better Bible Bureau and help put these impostors behind bars where they belong. In some later chapters, we'll search more thoroughly for the correct picture of Christ and, once we find it, we should never again be so gullible. The prosecution (me) would now like to present its opening statement (a few verses) and commence the trial of these hoaxes from hell.

Consider these words from the Special One about Impostor #1, The Believe What You Want About Me Just as Long as You Believe Jesus.

I am the way and the truth and the life. No one comes to the Father except through me (**John 14:6**).

Moreover, the Father judges no one, but has entrusted all judgment to the Son, that all may honor the Son just as they honor the Father. He who does not honor the Son does not honor the Father, who sent him (**John 5:22-23**).

Let's hear what heaven's one and only census taker has to say about Impostor #2, The Everyone's Going to Heaven Anway Jesus.

Not everyone who says to me, "Lord, Lord," will enter the kingdom of heaven, but only he who does the will of my Father who is in heaven. Many will say to me on that day, "Lord, Lord did we not prophesy in your name, and in your name drive out demons and perform many miracles?" Then I will tell them plainly, "I never knew you. Away from me you evildoers" (**Matthew 7:21-23**).

Make every effort to enter through the narrow door, because many, I tell you, will try to enter and will not be able to. Once the owner of the house gets up and closes the door, you will stand outside knocking and pleading, "Sir, open the door for us."

But he will answer, "I don't know you or where you come from."

Then you will say, "We ate and drank with you, and you taught in our streets."

But he will reply, "I don't know you or where you come from. Away from me, all you evildoers" (**Luke 13:24-27**).

The Lord made sure he worked into his schedule a few moments to warn us about Impostor #3, The Do Your Best to Work Me Into Your Schedule Jesus.

He said to another man, "Follow me."

But the man replied, "Lord, first let me go and bury my father."

Jesus said to him, "Let the dead bury their own dead, but you go and proclaim the kingdom of God" (**Luke 9:59-60**).

A certain man was preparing a great banquet and invited many guests. At the time of the banquet he sent his servants to tell those who had been invited, "Come, for everything is now ready." But they all alike began to make excuses. The first said, "I have just bought a field, and I must go and see it. Please excuse me." Another said, "I have just bought five yoke of oxen, and I'm on my way to try them out. Please excuse me." Still another said, "I just got married, so I can't come." The servant came back and reported this to his master. Then the owner of the house became angry and ordered his servant, "Go out quickly into the streets and alleys of the town and bring in the poor, the crippled, the blind and the lame."

"Sir," the servant said, "what you ordered has been done, but there is still room." Then the master told his servant, "Go out to the roads and country lanes and make them come in, so that my house will be full. I tell you, not one of those men who were invited will get a taste of my banquet" (**Luke 14:16-24**).

Here are a few "big deal" statements concerning Impostor #4, The Hey, No Big Deal, Mellow Out a Minute Jesus.

And if anyone causes one of these little ones who believe in me to sin, it would be better for him to be thrown into the sea with a large millstone tied around his neck. If your hand causes you to sin, cut it off. It is better for you to enter life maimed than with two hands to go into hell where the fire never goes out (**Mark 9:42-44**).

Anyone who breaks one of the least of these commandments and teaches others to do the same will be called least in the kingdom of heaven, but whoever practices and teaches these commands will be called great in the kingdom of heaven. For I tell you that unless your righteousness surpasses that of the Pharisees and the teachers of the Law you will certainly not enter the kingdom of heaven (**Matthew 5:19-20**).

Let's cash in on a golden opportunity to expose Impostor #5, The Follow Me and Your Financial Future is Secure Jesus.

Do not store up for yourselves treasures on earth, where moth and rust destroy and where thieves break in and steal. But store up for yourselves treasures in heaven, where moth and rust do not destroy, and where thieves do not break in and steal. For where your treasure is, there your heart will be also (**Matthew 6:19-21**).

No servant can serve two masters. Either he will hate the one and love the other, or he will be devoted to the one and despise the other. You cannot serve both God and money (**Luke 16:13**).

Let's watch the biblical Jesus as he drops by for a few visits with Impostor #6, The Won't You Be My Neighbor Jesus.

From this time many of his disciples turned back and no longer followed him. "You do not want to leave too, do you?" Jesus asked the twelve (**John 6:66-67**).

Jesus said to them, "If God were your father, you would love me, for I came from God and now am here. I have not come on my own; but he sent me. Why is my language not clear to you? Because you are unable to hear what I say. You belong to your father, the devil, and you want to carry out your father's desire. He was a murderer from the beginning, not holding to the truth, for there is no truth in him. When he lies he speaks his native language, for he is a liar and the father of lies. Yet because I tell you the truth, you do not believe me! Can any of you prove me guilty of sin? If I am telling the truth, why don't you believe me? He who belongs to God hears what God says. The reason you do not hear is that you do not belong to God" (**John 8:42-47**).

The real Jesus made sure we wouldn't have a problem discovering the deceit in Impostor #7, The All Your Problems Will Go Away If You Follow Me Jesus.

I have told you these things, so that in me you may have peace. In this world you will have trouble. But take heart! I have overcome the world (**John 16:33**).

Remember the words I spoke to you: "No servant is greater than his master. If they persecuted me, they will persecute you also. If they obeyed my teaching, they will obey yours also" (**John 15:22**).

Your efforts will be rewarded if you ignore Impostor #8, The Don't Bother Trying,You Won't Make It Anyway Jesus. The following verses will attest to that.

Come to me, all you who are weary and burdened, and I will give you rest. Take my yoke upon you and learn from me, for I am gentle and humble in heart, and you will find rest for your souls. For my yoke is easy and my burden is light (**Matthew 11:28-30**).

The disciples were even more amazed, and said to each other, "Who then can be saved?" Jesus looked at them and said, "With man this is impossible, but not with God; all things are possible with God" (**Mark 10:26-27**).

How about drying off from the effects of Impostor #9, The I Can Walk On Water But Can't Keep Your Life From Sinking Jesus. Here are a few fluffy towels.

Believe me when I say that I am in the Father and the Father is in me; or at least believe on the evidence of the miracles themselves. I tell you the truth, anyone who has faith in me will do greater things than these, because I am going to the Father. And I will do whatever you ask in my name, so that the Son may bring glory to the Father. You may ask me for anything in my name, and I will do it (**John 14:11-14**).

Jesus replied, "I tell you the truth, if you have faith and do not doubt, not only can you do what was done to the fig tree, but also you can say to this mountain, 'Go throw yourself into the sea,' and it will be done. If you believe, you will receive whatever you ask for in prayer" (**Matthew 21:21-22**).

We'll have a blast as we examine the evidence against Impostor #10, The I Never Have Time to Have a Good Time Jesus.

Then because so many people were coming and going that they did not even have a chance to eat, he said to them, "Come with me by yourselves to a quiet place and get some rest." So they went away by themselves in a boat to a solitary place (**Mark 6: 31-32**).

While Jesus was having dinner at Matthew's house, many tax collectors and sinners came and ate with his disciples (**Matthew 9:10**).

On the third day a wedding took place at Cana in Galilee. Jesus' mother was there, and Jesus and his disciples had also been invited to the wedding (**John 2:1-2**).

I have come that they may have life, and have it to the full (**John 10:10**).

I definitely think it's time to interrupt Impostor #11, The Leave Me Alone, I'm Talking to God Jesus.

Jesus entered Jericho and was passing through. A man was there by the name of Zaccaheus; he was a chief tax collector and was wealthy. He wanted to see who Jesus was, but being a short man he could not, because of the crowd. So he ran ahead and climbed a sycamore-fig tree to see him, since Jesus was coming that way. When Jesus reached the spot, he looked up and said to him, "Zacchaeus, come down immediately. I must stay at your house today." So he came down at once and welcomed him gladly (**Luke 19:1-6**).

People were bringing little children to Jesus to have him touch them but the disciples rebuked them. When Jesus saw this, he was indignant. He said to them, "Let the little children come to me, and do not hinder them, for the kingdom of God belongs to such as these. I tell you the truth, anyone who will not receive the kingdom of God like a little child will never enter it." And he took the children in his arms, put his hands on them and blessed them (**Mark 10:13-16**).

Let's get to the evidence as fast as we can and expose Impostor #12, The Let Me Get These 33 Years Over and Get Back to Heaven Jesus.

I am the good shepherd; I know my sheep and my sheep know me—just as the Father knows me and I know the Father—and I lay down my life for the sheep. I have other sheep that are not of this sheep pen. I must bring them also. They too will listen to my voice, and there shall be one flock and one shepherd. The reason my Father loves me is that I lay down my life—only to take it up again. No one takes it from me, but I lay it down of my own accord (**John 10:14-18**).

O Jerusalem, Jerusalem, you who kill the prophets and stone those sent to you, how often I have longed to gather your children together, as a hen gathers her chicks under her wings, but you were not willing (**Matthew 23:37**).

The prosecution will rest its case for the time being. I'll have an abundance of additional evidence in later chapters about the real Son of God.

Sadly, most people's perception of Jesus is based on a single snapshot and few have bothered to methodically turn through the pages of his entire photo album. Most, at best, have seen a few pictures of the baby and perhaps a few additional photos of his last days on earth, but what about the 33 years in-between?

I'm sure glad I don't have to be judged by a single snapshot—one that was taken by a good friend of mine in 1992. Eight of us from Cincinnati were on a four-day trip in a rented Winnebago, off to Miami, Florida to watch Nebraska play Florida State in the Orange Bowl. We had stopped for gas early one morning and I had just awoken from a brief rest during a night when sweet sleep was in short supply. I had on black sweats, a red-and-white striped, long-sleeved shirt that was tucked in on one side but not on the other, and my hair (more plentiful then) was severely matted in some places and pointing straight up or out in others. Knowing the picture was about to be taken, I decided to add a little humor to the pose (gross humor for sure) by pretending to pick my nose as I pumped the gas. To make matters worse, the picture was a close-up and, much like most of our worst photos, came out perfectly developed. There I was, Curt Simmons in living color, looking about as bad as I had ever looked, supposedly searching for nose remnants. Now, if that was the only photo of me in your possession and you had never personally met me, your perception of me might be a tad tainted.

Instead, come on over to my house. Let me show you my baby book and some pictures of me from elementary school. Check out my wedding photos and look at me in moments of better dress. See me wearing a coat and tie and notice the combed hair. Take a look at hundreds of other pictures—there's not one where you will find a finger in the wrong place and my shirt is tucked in every time. Granted, the shirt is from the 80s, but so is the picture!

You have one, too. The picture you wish was never taken. The picture you wish your mom had never kept. The picture that doesn't accurately depict the real you. Could it be that you've done the same thing with Jesus? Have you gotten a picture that's out of focus or out of context?

Did somebody you know take a picture of him then give it to you? How did you know that was really Jesus? Could Satan have momentarily disguised himself and now you own a picture of the devil but somehow think it's the Lord? My prayer is for you to be able to collect key photos of the real Jesus Christ and to gather the necessary information to expose any impostors. God has cleared a path for you to spot the Savior. But to do so, you must collect all the available pictures of Jesus. Then, and only then, will you get *the* picture!

Fred Demara died of a heart attack in 1982 at the age of 60. He fooled a lot of people in his era as the Great Impostor and made efforts later in his life to bring truth to others. From pretender to preacher, Demara appeared to have taken a significant step in the right direction. But the only question that really mattered upon his death was this: Did the real Great Impostor, Satan, persuade him to follow a phony Jesus and did he accept the offer? And it's the only question that will matter for you and me as well when we depart from this world.

❧ Chapter Six ❧

Saturday at the Synagogue
〜 〜

All spoke well of him and were amazed
at the gracious words that came from his lips.
"Isn't this Joseph's son?" they asked.
— Luke 4:22

Most of the synagogue-goers were familiar with the man who was scheduled to be one of the speakers that Saturday morning. He had lived there as a boy, and many adults had seen him interact with their children on the streets, in the schools and at the synagogue. Some had watched as he and his father worked tirelessly under the Nazareth sun to build or repair houses. Or, they had seen him in their own homes giving an estimate of what it would cost to repair a leaky roof. Business owners knew of him from the times he would come to their stores and buy the family's food for the evening meal or take his father's tools to be sharpened by the town smith.

"He was a good boy," they said.

They all agreed he never got into trouble like most of the other youngsters, honored his parents to the point of making the other children jealous and seemed to be a fair, honest and hard working carpenter-in-training looking to one day take over the family business. He was a positive in the city known mostly for negatives. People had marveled at his regular synagogue attendance, his propensity for memorizing Scripture and his zeal to arouse a lukewarm heart. His baptism in the nearby Jordan River had been deemed a bit unusual with rumors of doves and deep voices but, hey, those were only rumors. A forty-day desert disappearance seemed slightly strange, but everything seemed back to normal for him upon his return. Actually, many Israelites were holding out hope that he might indeed be the one they had been reading about in Scriptures around the dinner table and talking about almost every Saturday at worship for as long as they could remember.

John the Baptist said he was the one. And John was a well-respected prophet, even considering his lack of clothing savvy and the highly unusual diet of locust and honey he followed.

"Was this the son of David?" they cautiously asked one another.

"Was this the Messiah? Was he the fulfillment of Old Testament prophecy? Was this the time for God to rally Israel once again? And could all this "good" happen here in Nazareth?"

That Saturday morning many would be making up their minds. They were ninety percent convinced already. But how would he preach? Would he communicate with as much heart as David did in the Psalms? Would his wisdom be as obvious to them as Solomon's was to those he taught? What angle would he come from? How many points would there be in his lesson? Would the first letter from each point spell something? Would his main points rhyme? They were all eagerly anticipating the greatest Saturday their synagogue had ever witnessed. This lesson would be sure to stir even the lukewarm and cold-hearted members to action. Everybody would be signing up after service, bound and determined to be on the team. It was just a matter of what position they would be playing. When convinced he was truly on a mission from God, they would be the first to enthusiastically jump on the "Jesus is the Messiah" bandwagon. The stage was set. This was going to be just the beginning of big things in Israel. Everybody could anticipate the Sunday paper's front-page headline.

"NAZARETH MAN HERALDED AS SAVIOR OF ISRAEL"

See inside—*Mayor declares his allegiance and urges all residents to rise to the occasion, risk it all for the obvious "God-send" and never rest until everyone knows about Jesus, Nazareth's hometown hero.*

Attendance at the synagogue was about double the norm that day. People who hadn't been spotted in weeks managed to drag their "leave me alone, this is the Sabbath" bones out of bed and into the crammed auditorium. Everybody wanted to say they saw him first—the Messiah—making his inaugural speech as President of Promise Land Recovery. Late-arrivers pushed and shoved their way closer to the front, frantically fighting for position and a closer glimpse of the great one.

And there he was, looking very stoic, sitting attentively, listening to the synagogue leader's opening comments and waiting for his opportunity to read, then remark on a few Old Testament passages.

Finally, it was his turn. As he began to read, each soul in the synagogue felt as if the words he read were actually a part of him. He was so poised and polished. But in a strange way, it was nothing fancy, almost as though he was trying desperately to draw attention away from himself, unlike others of high rank who regularly appeared on the program in the Nazareth synagogue.

When he finished reading and rolled up the sacred Isaiah scroll, nobody said a word for about a minute. They had never heard or seen anything quite like him before and they were speechless. Soon the silence turned to quiet whispers as compliments started to emerge.

"Best, by far, that I have ever heard."

"Did you hear that voice?"

"He can't stay in the carpentry shop!"

"I sure hope he's speaking next week, too."

"My daughter really needs to meet that man."

Others looked at each other but said nothing. They didn't need to. They knew what each other were thinking. Thoughts of, "This is him, yes, this is really him," engulfed their minds. Then they spoke.

"We knew he was going to be something someday."

"I can't wait to shake his hand on the way out, let him know how much I appreciated it, and that I'm definitely coming back."

"I wonder what he'll want me to do in his kingdom."

"I can't wait to hear his specific strategy for getting our nation back on top again."

"This is going to be better than the days of David and the stories we've heard about Solomon's success."

Everybody had something to say. None of it was critical. Yet only minutes later, fury bore its way through the thick synagogue walls and into the hearts of those present that morning. With unprecedented heights of hate in their hearts replacing the outpourings of praise from only moments earlier, those listening to Jesus rose from their seats, drove the man out of their synagogue then out of their town and had plans in motion to kill him by throwing him down a cliff.

Something in his additional comments threw them down a cliff. It was that "something" about the Gentiles and they just couldn't stomach it. Surely, they thought, a true Jewish king eager to overthrow the reigning Gentiles and bring Jehovah back to the top wouldn't dare mention **them**, let alone highlight individuals.

*"**Naaman**? No way!"*

*"A widow from **Zarephath**? Wrong!"*

"How dare he try to challenge us during his first sermon."

"Surely if he were the Son of God he would have allowed us to warm up to his style before he tried to go after our hearts."

"And what about all the good we've done? I didn't hear anything about that."

"What happened to a good Moses analogy and how he can't wait to lead us to the Promise Land?"

"How about some applause for each of us just being here and not abandoning our faith in the midst of this unfair Gentile domination?"

"How about cutting us some slack instead of cutting us to the heart?"

"I knew his upbringing was questionable."

"I thought he looked a little glassy-eyed at times."

"I always thought it was a bit strange how much time he spent reading the Scriptures and talking to the rabbis."

"My gut about him was right. I should have gone with my first instinct."

"We've got to stop him now before Nazareth slides further down the ladder of most unlivable cities."

> Jesus wasn't what they expected that Saturday morning at the synagogue. His message wasn't even close to what they had in mind.

"We should have known a carpenter could never be groomed for such an important political role."

"Hey, Jesus. Go back to your hammer and nails and leave us alone."

Jesus wasn't what they expected that Saturday morning at the synagogue. His message wasn't even close to what they had in mind. To them, his takeover strategy was stupid, suspect at best. So they missed him. They missed the Messiah. The God who had made the heavens and the earth was sitting in their synagogue that Saturday and somehow they believed, for heaven's sake, it was best to rid the earth of him.

❧ Chapter Seven ❧

My Kind of Messiah
❧ ❧

Jesus said to them, "If God were your Father, you would love me, for I came from God and now am here. I have not come on my own; but he sent me. Why is my language not clear to you? Because you are unable to hear what I say."
—John 8:42-43

Chalk it up to preconception. Personal bias. Private interpretation. Pride. Prejudice. Whatever it was, it was pathetic. Can you believe it? They were about to murder the Messiah—and this after just one message! And the sermon wasn't even that long! And, if not for a heroic Houdini act by Jesus, managing to slip away from the angry mob, they would have succeeded (**Luke 4:14-30**). But before we get too judgmental and pat ourselves on the back because "we would never do such a thing," perhaps why so many of us love the Lord is because we haven't heard enough of his sermons and become aware of his standards. Maybe we haven't heard any of his sermons. Maybe if we did, we'd have a problem, too. Maybe our problem is that we've created a better 21ˢᵗ century Jesus. Better for our lifestyle. Better for our kids. Better for our schedule. Maybe we've glanced over any Scripture that might tempt us to get mad at him or question his mental capacity, so tossing him down an imaginary cliff has never been an option for us.

Jesus has always been a big problem for anybody looking for their own kind of Messiah. He's a huge problem for those searching for the most popular path or the latest line but not seeking to submit to a Lord. Billions have missed Jesus over the years because he didn't fit. He didn't make sense initially. He didn't look like, talk like, walk like, dine like or live like a Son of God was supposed to. And, as a result, many people, religious and pagan, didn't like him. For most of the religious Jews, Jesus became labeled as a false prophet, a pain in the neck and a possible disruption to the compromised peace they were able to enjoy under Roman rule. To the Gentile pagan, he was just another Jew who was claiming to have the inside scoop on matters pertaining to their Law. No doubt, they felt, he was a hypocrite like all the others had been, possessing selfish motives. He, too, they believed, would disappear in due time, never to be heard from again.

Initially, however, Jesus fit for many of the Jews, and his amazing display of miracles seemed to nearly close the deal, arousing "Could the Christ be here?" questions from those who were witnesses to the unexplainable.

"So, you think Moses had the touch, do you? He only parted the water—Jesus walks on water! Sure, Moses gathered manna—Jesus produces manna!"

In the first century, Jews longing for the Messiah's arrival were in the ready position and anxiously awaiting the crowning of a new and improved King David. They firmly believed he would confidently lead their nation in conquest of Rome, the stated and hated enemy of Israel who were currently occupying their God-given Promise Land. So, at first, upon encountering Jesus, many of the Israelites seemed ready and willing to follow him. The "I'll march to war with you" contract was all but signed, sealed and delivered. Jesus was destined for greatness in their minds, and it appeared to be only a matter of time until the reigning Caesar in Rome would fall and be replaced by the Christ who would rule the world.

"Move over Rome, here comes Jerusalem!" they were saying to themselves.

It looked to be a sure victory for Israel—a permanent food supply, a control of the weather to aide them in developing major battle strategies, power to raise the dead and maintain a never-ending supply of soldiers and plenty of wine for the victory celebration.

Then, one by one, they heard him speak—on a hillside, in a neighbor's home, at the synagogue or by the lake. They discovered his unconventional battle plan. Then Jesus discovered their motives. Little about loving their fellow man could he locate in their hearts. Turning the other cheek to these Israelites was nothing more than tongue-in-cheek. Going the second mile for someone was at least a mile off base. Treasures in heaven were nice, but quickly overshadowed by the here-and-now hopes for treasure on earth. Throughout his three-year public ministry, Jesus constantly searched to find the heart of a trusting and faithful follower but, upon closer scrutiny, he discovered that most of the Israelites who crossed his path were selfish, still searching for their kind of Messiah.

At one time, all spoke well of him when they heard him teach. Soon, very few had anything good to say about him. At one point in his ministry, the masses were willing to escort him to a conference with the Jewish higher-ups to discuss attack strategy (**John 6:14-15**), but then he started talking like a fool and saying something strange and masochistic about how his greatest victory would be achieved when he was lifted up on a cross. The problem was obvious—they wanted him as their commander in chief while Jesus talked about being their crucified chief.

Somewhere in our sinful natures, we all want our own particular type of Messiah and Lord. That's why God chooses. We can easily become self-righteous when we analyze the rejection of Jesus by the first-century Jews, but Jesus would have been met with opposition had he come to any group of people at any time in the history of mankind. Consider some of the following possibilities of Jesus coming to America as the Messiah in the past 65 years. Do you think Americans would have had a problem following any of them?

1940 to 1950—Half American, half Japanese; last seen preaching at a peace rally promoting the destruction of all atomic weapons.

1950 to 1960—African-American; factory worker; last seen eating at an all-white restaurant and preaching social reform.

1960 to 1970—Long hair, hippie type; wearing tie-dye T-shirt with humungous peace sign; last seen talking to pot smokers at a rock concert.

1970 to 1980—Vietnam veteran; unemployed and paralyzed from the waist down; last seen in Washington D.C. preaching about equal opportunity for the handicapped.

1980 to 2005—Middle Eastern descent; mother from Iran, father from Iraq; distant relative of Ayatollah Khomeini and Saddam Hussein; raised in Libya and Afghanistan; last seen speaking with Al Qaida radicals in a mountain cave.

> *Somewhere in our sinful natures, we all want our own particular type of Messiah and Lord.*

Perhaps now you can better understand the Jews and their struggle with Jesus. What exactly was their issue? For most, it was worldliness—their physical, emotional and national desires had taken precedence over their desire to engage in an invisible spiritual war. They were more interested in greed than God; more interested in real comfort than a real Christ; more interested in demanding their rights than doing what was right; more interested in politics than people; more interested in heroics than heaven and more interested in dealing with Rome than dealing with their sin. And there stood Jesus, right in the midst of a nation that was in desperate need of spiritual revival.

He had already been introduced by angels and had been announced by a highly respected prophet as the Son of God. But, alas, he was a ***carpenter*** from ***Nazareth*** with a ***questionable conception***.

Strike 1: A questionable conception.

"Is he really Jewish? How can we be sure Joseph was actually his father? Perhaps he really is a half-breed—a Samaritan! The real Messiah would never leave those important questions unanswered."

Strike 2: A carpenter.

"But he's working class. Blue-collar. Uneducated. How could he possibly develop successful plans to overtake Rome and, even if he did, how could someone from that background lead our nation to long-term peace, security and financial prosperity?"

Strike 3: Nazareth.

"A Messiah from Nazareth? Not in a million years! They're the city of low-lifes. It's last place on the list of cities most likely to settle in. No past leader of any magnitude came from within twenty miles of there."

There were many more strikes to add to the list, but for most first-century Messiah-seekers, these were enough to declare Jesus **OUT!** Those who were willing to look beyond those three issues might likely get hung up on some of the following.

"He hangs out a lot with losers like tax collectors, drunks and prostitutes" (**Matthew 9:11**).

"He really has nothing that attractive or alluring about him physically. Who's going to be drawn to him anyway?" (**Isaiah 53:2**).

"Doesn't his own family even think he needs professional help?" (**Mark 3: 20-21**).

It really didn't matter what he did or how he did it. Most of his own countrymen weren't going to accept Jesus as the Son of God. If he preached the most incredible, "I've never-heard-anything-like-it-before" sermon, they found a loophole (**John 6:32-66**). If he miraculously healed a lifetime invalid, it was done on the wrong day (**John 5:1-12**). If he claimed to have given sight to the blind, that miracle had to have been performed by someone else only he decided to take the credit, or he really did perform it but only through the power of Satan (**John 9:13-34**). Even when he raised Lazarus from the dead, his popularity was becoming so widespread that many nervous and jealous Jewish leaders believed it to be in the best interest of their nation to end his life (**John 11:45-53**). At the end of his days, the surrendered, never-complaining Savior lay down his life on a cross. But to most people, that, too, was a sure sign that he wasn't God's Son. Certainly, in their minds, if he were the actual Son of God, a heavenly rescue operation would have started long before he found himself in that awful predicament (**Matthew 27:41-43**). And when Jesus walked out of the tomb breathing after three days dead, many Jews quickly discarded the resurrection option and accepted the fabricated story of the stolen body (**Matthew 28:11-15**). For most people, there was absolutely no way. The odds of Jesus being the Messiah were about as good as a last place Pop Warner team beating the New England Patriots. Nothing seemed to fit. *"Jesus,"* they conferred, *"is not our kind of Messiah."*

What kind of Jesus have you created? What does he have to be or have to say? What does he have to look like? What does he have to believe? What is the picture of Jesus you have hanging on your wall and in your heart? Does his message of discipleship threaten your religious peace? Is he too religious and narrow-minded for your "all roads lead to the same place" philosophy?

The Bible and its revelation of Jesus will, without a doubt, address your pride and preconceptions. It will do with Jesus in written form what Jesus did to the Jews in word and deed in the first century—tell the truth and refuse to change a single thing. You may like what you see. You may not. You may enjoy some of him, most of him or all of him. But until you are willing to completely accept him and his message, you, too, will miss the most amazing man who ever lived.

❧ Chapter Eight ❦

The Survey Says
ॐ ॐ

When Jesus came to the region
of Caesarea Philippi, he asked his disciples,
"Who do people say the Son of Man is?"
— Matthew 16:13

Everybody in Israel seemed to have an opinion about Jesus, ranging from "Watch out, he's a demon" to "Oh my, he's a deity" and everything else in between. Almost everybody in Jerusalem and throughout all Judea had at least heard about him. During his three-year public ministry, thousands had seen him or heard him preach. Some had talked with him on a casual level, while others were given the opportunity to have a more lengthy conversation with the controversial man from Nazareth. Everyone who was privileged to have been in his presence had seen and heard exactly the same things. There were miracles to convince even the greatest skeptics, speeches to amaze even the most polished and educated listeners, acts of kindness to soften even the hardest hearts of those who witnessed them and astounding claims to arouse even the totally disinterested bystanders.

To the general observer, Jesus appeared to be consistent. His messages were always crisp and to the point. His kindness was viewed as a constant and without prejudice, and he had nothing on his previous record to indicate that he might be a potential problem. But what would the surveys and public opinion polls have revealed about people's feelings toward this man from Nazareth—Jesus, the son of Joseph and Mary?

Let's take a quick trip through the Gospels and learn what some of the three million residents of Israel were saying about Jesus. Whether these opinions were being shared because people relied on incomplete information, quickly believed the latest rumor, succumbed to peer pressure, owned a bad heart or had a believing faith, one thing was for sure—Jesus was the talk of the town. If God had decided to send his Son to earth to begin his ministry in 2005, a story about him and his most recent exploits would likely appear in nearly every edition of **USA Today** and your local newspaper (pictures included), his latest activities would be a regular topic on **Nightline**, **48 Hours** and **60 Minutes**, and he might even make an occasional appearance on those shows. Oprah would seek to secure him as a guest on her program, and Leno and Letterman would find a way to weave him into their nightly monologues. He would be kept under constant surveillance by the local and national authorities, and high-ranking government officials would go undercover to gather valuable information from him and his disciples, just to make sure the potential troublemaker didn't get out of hand.

While carrying out his ministerial duties on earth, information about Jesus was streaming in to the religious authorities, likely kept in a "Top Priority" file. Many interviews with childhood friends, teachers, neighbors, those who did business with he and his father Joseph at the carpentry shop, fellow synagogue members, relatives, close friends and even with Jesus himself were no doubt being conducted. With the onslaught of information being circulated around Israel—some of it right, some of it wrong and some of it way out of context—the public had become incredibly divided on what their proper response to Jesus should be. Should they ignore him or hang on his every word? Should they arrest him or follow him? Should they bury him or believe in him?

Here is a sampling of opinions about Jesus that were offered up by those who heard about him and those who came in contact with him.

"What kind of man is this?" (**Matthew 8:27**).

The twelve apostles selected by Jesus were able to see him in rare form a lot more often than most people. On this occasion, the twelve had witnessed Jesus calming a storm through a simple command with his voice. It was one thing, they reasoned, to be able to accurately predict the weather. In those days, even being correct fifty percent of the time would have been respectable and the makings of a meteorologist. But nobody who they could recollect had ever been able to figure out how to change the weather. So the bewildered boys who sailed with him in the boat that day began to alter their stance on his human-only status.

"This fellow is blaspheming" (**Matthew 9:3**).

These remarks, made by a few teachers of the Law, came in response to the promise Jesus had just made to a paralytic of a cured step and a clean slate. These observer of the miracles that day ignored the wonderful truth that the once-crippled man's severed spinal column had been miraculously sewn back together without a surgeon's knife. Never mind the opportunity they had before them to celebrate the fact that he was now set free to walk and wander. Instead, they chose to focus on what they felt was a preposterous claim being made by Jesus, livid that he would have the audacity to announce that he, a human, had the authority to forgive sins.

"Who does he think he is, God?" they asked sarcastically.

Well, now that you mention it . . .

"Here is a glutton and a drunkard, a friend of tax collectors and sinners" (**Matthew 11:19**).

"Certainly, nobody could spend that much time with the dregs of society unless he was one himself," critics assumed.

"Sign him up for Overeaters and Alcoholics Anonymous."

"I'm almost positive Jesus is doing drugs, too. My guess is, he's probably teaching those tax collectors a new money-making trick to help support their addictions."

Jesus knew that in order to be with the people who needed him most, he would open himself up to slanderous speculations and ridiculous rumors like these. Consequently, he would often be classified with the "losers." But, in line with his mission and purpose for coming to earth, Jesus would rather save an alcoholic from emptiness and an eternal hell than simply hang out with the proper people who chose to stay sober. And he absolutely loved to offer grace to a prostitute. He must have been thrilled to take these former "hookers" and hook them up with some men who wanted to talk to them and treat them with respect instead of taking them to bed. That was a whole lot more important to Jesus than to only associate with the pure and respectable crowd who spent more time ridiculing these women's choices and making fun of their vices than they did in offering them a helping hand.

"Could this be the Son of David?" (**Matthew 12:23**).

You can almost hear it in these individual's voices. They wanted to believe it. They really did. They needed a Messiah, they were ready for a Messiah, they had been looking for a Messiah and they had been hoping and praying for the Messiah to arrive in their lifetime. And there he was—Jesus, the Messiah, in their lifetime and the answer to their nightly prayers. But most of those hoping for the "Hope of Israel" to appear simply kept on praying for a second option because his political agenda seemed drastically different than that of David, the greatest of Israel's former kings.

"But wouldn't the Son of David think like David and employ military strategy like him?" they asked one another.

So they kept waiting and wondering. They didn't close the door completely to the idea that Jesus was the head of God's house, but they left it open only ever so slightly. Most Israelites agreed, however, that if any more strange wind of doctrine came blowing from the direction of Jesus, the breeze would be enough to slam it shut forever.

"We're open to your ideas Jesus, but we need more time and more information before we'll get too excited. It took a while, you know, before David proved his worth and actually ascended to the throne."

So for three solid years, Jesus proved his obvious right to the eternal throne. He waited patiently for his people to notice the royal robe of righteousness he wore daily and the royal crown of humility he would wear at his death.

"Isn't this the carpenter's son?" (**Matthew 13:55**).

Blue-collar, plus middle class, plus carpenter skills, equals the Messiah. It didn't compute for these Israelites who were expecting a much more sophisticated pedigree for the new King of Israel. Their calculations about who he would be, where he would be from, how he would look and what he would do once he arrived had always worked out quite nice whenever they sat down to figure out how God would lead his chosen people. Now Jesus was calling himself Israel's teacher, but this new math he was introducing on the Messiah made absolutely no sense to them.

"God would never train the Messiah with a hammer and nails, would he?"

"Wouldn't he be off at military school or in private training with the top rabbis?"

"He's thirty years old, for goodness sake, and his only experience is as a carpenter. He's already missed the best years for leadership training."

"How can building houses help you to prepare to destroy an empire?"

"John the Baptist, Elijah, Jeremiah or one of the prophets" (**Matthew 16:13-14**).

According to the twelve apostles, it's what many of the people were saying. This popular view of Jesus, that he was just another prophet in a long line of God's prophets, was a safe place for many Israelites to take up residence in the beginning stages of Jesus' ministry. After all, similar to Israel's Hall of Fame prophets and the one who would soon be inducted, the messages Jesus preached were powerful and packed with excitement. And the miracles, much like those from the days of Elijah and Elisha, were even better.

"He must be from God," they agreed, *"like all the other great prophets, he's just not the Messiah."*

There was still way too much about Jesus' message and his means to an end that they didn't agree with, and it kept many of them from surrendering to all of the truths he was proclaiming.

"Perhaps," they said, *"When the time is right, he'll let us in on the whole truth and tell us more about the man God has **really** chosen to lead his people to victory."*

"You are the Christ, the Son of the Living God" (Matthew 16:15-16).

The Teacher had just asked a simple "Who am I?" question, and the impulsive pupil who usually had his hand up first but often answered incorrectly finally got one right! Simon Peter added everything up in his mind concerning Jesus—the miracles he saw, the incredible insight into spiritual truth he had access to, the late-night discipleship lessons he had received to refine his character, the love he had felt and seen on a daily basis, the powerful preaching he had heard and so much more. The answer to his simple addition problem couldn't be wrong, he determined. Despite what all the educated Israelites were concluding, this was the only answer that made complete sense to him.

Unfortunately, shortly after proving his mathematical prowess, this confident student would begin to incorrectly subtract and ultimately disagree with his Teacher, claiming that the answer to the question about how God would save the world was certainly not found in a crucified Messiah.

"Hosanna to the Son of David" (Matthew 21:9).

The shouts of "glory-glory" from the exuberant crowd that day stemmed from a hope that Jesus actually was their long-awaited king. Those lining the streets proudly heralded Jesus as their leader of destiny while they watched him make his way into Jerusalem, the city of kings, riding on a donkey.

"Our new and improved David has arrived to kick some tail," they thought.

"Get ready Rome, your days are numbered!"

But when Jesus refused to rally his troops, fought off every temptation to remove the cross from the battle plan and kept all miraculous escape possibilities in his back pocket, he was soon arrested and discarded as a Messiah-wannabe by the residents of Jerusalem and by the thousands of visitors in the sacred town, there to enjoy another Passover celebration. It was only a few days later when louder shouts of "Crucify him, Crucify him" were heard from a similar crowd as Jesus stood before Pilate waiting to hear the announcement concerning his ultimate fate.

"This is Jesus, the prophet from Nazareth in Galilee" (**Matthew 21:11**).

Jesus—such a common name.
Nazareth—such a sorry town.
Even as they said it, doubts about his possible greatness entered their minds.

"Now this is a huge stretch for Nazareth!" they muttered. *"Okay, maybe he's a prophet, but the Messiah? We're certainly not ready to go that far!"*

"He is worthy of death" (**Matthew 26:66**).

To the religious hierarchy in Jerusalem, criminals and blasphemers headed the "worthy of death" list. Many of the Jewish leaders viewed Jesus as both and, therefore, he had to be eliminated. Once Jesus had been taken into custody and the public's opinion of him was rapidly turning negative, the time was ripe for the decision about his punishment to be swift. In their minds, there was no need for a stay of execution or another last hour appeal to free Jesus from the death he so justly deserved.

"Listen!" they shouted to any possible sympathizers. *"He's on death row, so he must be guilty. What are we waiting for? Get it over with! Kill him and kill him quick!"*

"Surely he was the Son of God" (**Matthew 27:54**).

Something out of the ordinary had happened during those six hours that the Gentile centurion had been with Jesus. The Roman leader of soldiers had been responsible for hundreds of crucifixions in his time on the job, but he had never witnessed anything quite like what he was seeing in Jesus. None of the lawbreakers that he could remember had ever offered themselves to be nailed to simplify the crucifixion ordeal. On the contrary, he had suffered numerous bumps and bruises from the kicks and out of control swings of the previously condemned. Even the two thieves crucified earlier that day had landed a few blows. And all the others he had observed being nailed to their crosses had violently cursed at him and spat on him. Jesus said nothing.

"Why is he so surrendered?" he kept thinking to himself.

After being lifted up from the ground and left to die on a cross in a most hideous way, the typical man who was being crucified looked for any opportunity to curse God and ridicule any others who he had felt wronged him during his life. But Jesus prayed for his accusers, asked a friend nearby to take care of his mother and quietly surrendered to death, as if to say the battle was over and that he had already won.

"And," the centurion thought to himself, *"when has there ever been an earthquake and a total eclipse of the sun during a previous crucifixion? Are all of these strange occurrences merely coincidence or is this a clear sign from God?"*

Surely this centurion had never experienced the uneasiness he felt in his heart on that day. Thoughts of "Maybe we really shouldn't kill this man," and "Maybe this job just isn't suited for me anymore" worked their way through his heavy heart. Little by little he became convicted of his wrongdoing in this latest brutality, and it wasn't long before he realized the true identity of the man he had nailed to a cross only hours earlier. Finally, this tough, unrefined and unbelieving Gentile soldier confirmed the work God had been doing in softening his heart. He withstood all temptations to chalk everything up to coincidence and publicly verbalized his newfound belief in Jesus, that surely this man was the Son of God.

"That deceiver" (Matthew 27:63).

What could possibly lead any individual to hurl this accusation at a man who had never lied? Here are some possibilities.

When someone has little or no desire to deal with the sin in their heart, they call him a liar.

When someone doesn't like being challenged about certain decisions they've made, they call him a liar.

When someone doesn't think the Messiah would be average age, average size and average looking, they call him a liar.

When someone gets caught red-handed in a sin and they don't want to admit their guilt, they call him a liar.

When someone thinks it's totally ludicrous that God himself would ever consider becoming a man and living with his creation, they call him a liar.

When the plan Jesus announces calls for cross bearing instead of arms bearing and someone doesn't agree with the strategy, they call him a liar.

When admitting the truth and following Jesus would be a costly, relationship-ending decision for someone, they call him a liar.

And that's exactly what thousands of people did to sear their consciences and dismiss Jesus. They allowed themselves to become convinced that Jesus was just another idiot who needed to be institutionalized before he could hook others with his ever-enlarging fish story.

"We have never seen anything like this" (**Mark 2:12**).

Wilt Chamberlain, Bill Russell, Kareem Abdul Jabbar or Shaquille O'Neal? Who's the most dominant center in the history of the NBA?

Hank Aaron, Babe Ruth, Willie Mays, Mark McGwire or Barry Bonds? Who is the greatest home-run hitter of all time?

George Washington, Thomas Jefferson, Abraham Lincoln, Franklin Delano Roosevelt or JFK? Who did more good for the United States of America during their time serving as President?

Raiders of the Lost Ark, **Temple of Doom** or **Last Crusade**? Which is the greatest of the Indiana Jones' thrillers?

At most barbershops and bus stops today, the debate continues and the final answer to these questions will never be settled. Just imagine the talk at the local barbershops and marketplaces in the first century when Jesus was being matched up with the greatest in Israel from the past.

"Yes, Moses parted the Red Sea and then walked through on dry ground, yet we know from Scriptures he was a man who often seemed to be on the edge of frustration. Jesus walks on top of the water without the benefit of a staff and emotionally he always seems to be under control. All in favor of Jesus say "aye." It's unanimous!

"Okay, David did write some pretty inspiring stuff in the Psalms, but he seemed to have a problem at times with the ladies. When Jesus speaks, he inspires me to want to change and give my life to God, but he doesn't seem very interested in getting time alone with the women he meets. Anybody want to go with David?" Silence.

"Sure, Elijah ignited a watery sacrifice and defeated 850 prophets of Baal, but after that he got all wimpy and got intimidated by Queen Jezebel. Jesus raises the dead and he doesn't seem to be afraid of anything or anybody. So, what are we thinking here?"

These legendary leaders were Israel's "Three Musketeers"—Moses, the giver of the Law, David, their greatest king and Elijah, their number one prophet of all-time. But Jesus was rewriting the record books. He was shattering the long-held high-marks of any and all predecessors, the same records that most Israelites said could never be broken.

"You are the Son of God" (**Mark 3:11**).

While earthlings struggled to grasp this amazing truth, evil residents from hell had no problem coming to conviction about Jesus when he ordered them to "come out" of the humans they were tormenting. The demons knew, in Jesus, they were facing their fiercest competition to date, and they wanted nothing to do with setting up any future matches. As they considered the power and one-time glory of their leader, Satan, they realized that their current boss had impressive credentials, but only according to their lowered selfish standards. But never had they encountered such a powerful and imposing being like Jesus, and they quickly recognized his rightful role of deity.

"He is out of his mind" (**Mark 3:20-21**).

Ouch! Now that one had to hurt. Usually mom and dad are the first ones you think about contacting if you need a good character reference. Not in this case! Those who had been with Jesus the longest finally concluded that their son and sibling had crossed the line of bad choice and had entered the space called borderline crazy. They had had enough! It was time to pull Jesus back down to earth, have a crisis intervention with him, take a few weeks off and go on a long-overdue family vacation, get him back living in their house so he could enjoy some much-needed home cooking, settle him down and, hopefully, in doing all this, get him off the Messiah kick once and for all.

"He is possessed by Beelzebub" (**Mark 3:22**).

It was the final place for bad-hearted people to go when nothing else was working. It was blasphemy in its purest form. It was end of the rope, bottom of the barrel, last-shot-language spoken by many Israelites in an attempt to shut down the Savior and deter other observers who might have been thinking about following him from taking another step in his direction.

"John the Baptist has been raised from the dead" (**Mark 6:14**).

Few Jews in the first century had ever seen a man as radical as John the Baptist. They would have needed to search long and hard in the Old Testament scrolls to find anybody who was comparable to John with his head like flint and heart like flesh. And few could imagine anyone being as powerful as John in the days to come. So the conclusion for some was obvious—this Jesus must be John the Baptist raised from the dead, only now he's gone undercover. *"And this time,"* they said, *"he's back with miraculous powers."*

The Israelites were reminded of John whenever they heard Jesus preaching. Like John, Jesus wasn't afraid to bring out the "brood of vipers" accusation to his listeners, and he refused to move toward the waters of forgiveness unless real repentance was seen in a hearer's heart (**Luke 3:1-14**). He was hard line, to the point and always calling people to a decision. Jesus was also known to mix it up and go toe-to-toe with both his disciples and his detractors. He always seemed ready to be ridiculed, but he never retaliated or over-reacted. And it never seemed to be about popularity or percentage growth for his movement. Jesus was willing to watch everyone turn away from being or becoming his follower, and he would still refuse to compromise his message. Ultimately, like John the Baptist, Jesus was prepared to die to keep the truths of God alive.

"He is a prophet, like one of the prophets long ago" (**Mark 6:15**).

Initially, most everybody in Israel conceded this prophet-point about Jesus as evidence mounted with each passing day.

*"Yes, Jesus is a man **sent** from God, but he isn't the **Son** of God."*
*"Yes, Jesus is a man **with** the word of God, but he isn't **the** word of God."*
*"Yes, Jesus is a lot **like** Moses, but he isn't **greater** than Moses."*
*"Yes, Jesus is making **waves**, but he didn't make the **world**."*
*"Yes, Jesus is worthy of **respect**, but he isn't worthy of **worship**."*

Comfortable thoughts. Cautious observations. Clearly wrong!

"Good Teacher" (**Mark 10:17**).

Nobody could argue this point about Jesus—people always seemed to learn a lot whenever he would teach. Their notes actually made sense when they came home to review them. Those who heard him preach and teach were growing in their knowledge of God, understanding things from the Scriptures they had never been able to discern. Many loved what they were hearing from Jesus, but they were also hoping that he would tone it down and tame his tongue just a bit.

"If he would just bag the Messiah part," they said, *"I bet he could even start his own school of theology before too long and make quite a name for himself."*

"If he would just stay away from using the term Lord so often to describe himself, I'm sure that all of these people wouldn't be leaving his camp."

"That Nazarene, Jesus" (**Mark 14:67**).

Even the best of the breed in Nazareth carried the awful stigma wherever they went. Some had probably lost a good job opportunity along the way just because of this piece of information. If ever there was data that a Nazarene would like to delete from their re`sume`, this was it. If ever there was something they would pray to never be asked about in an interview, it was, "So, where were you raised?" Nobody of note had come from there. No great prophet came to anyone's mind. None of the highly respected scribes and Pharisees lived there. None of Israel's top executives or Sanhedrin members had graduated from any of her schools. We're talking about Nazareth here, not Jerusalem or Jericho. It was, people said, a town to avoid, not vacation in; a town to move out of, not into; a town mostly for losers and boozers; a town that had been booed and bad-mouthed by many for years. Unfortunately, most of the residents there had done little or nothing to try and shed the nasty label. If anything were true, many Nazarenes had come to tolerate, even accept the negative publicity, and few who lived there expected much of themselves, or anybody else in town for that matter.

*"Jesus is from **where?**"* people asked.

*"And he claims to be **what?**"*

"Doesn't he understand how absurd and ridiculous that sounds?"

It was so far-fetched and virtually impossible for most Israelites to believe. This man, Jesus, from Nazareth, just couldn't be the Messiah. Believing that about Jesus, for them, was like someone in the early twentieth century believing that man would one day walk on the moon—sheer lunacy!

"Lord" (**Luke 5:8**).

Hallelujah! Peter got one right!

And it all started with a bad day of fishing. What Peter couldn't locate all night, Jesus pointed out to him with no prior net experience in a matter of seconds. With a prideful, "Okay, if you say so," Peter promptly dropped his nets into the suggested area and brought in the biggest catch of his life. Peter knew that either Jesus had created those fish right there on the spot, or he had direct lines of communication with the underwater world. Either way, "Lord" was the only thing that came to his mind.

"By Beelzebub, the prince of demons, he is driving out demons" (**Luke 11:15**).

The miracles of Jesus were perfect and provable. Those who had been raised from the dead by Jesus told tales of Paradise and Hades that could never have been derived from a drug high or an over-stimulated imagination.

Upon request, those who could now perfectly hear would proudly display their diplomas from the deaf institutions they had attended.

Five thousand men could be interviewed separately and each would gladly testify that nobody from a nearby bakery had brought the extra bread to quiet their grumbling stomachs.

So after a while, the critics stopped claiming that the unexplained events Jesus was displaying were merely the work of a master magician and turned to making much more vicious claims, similar to this Satanic one.

"Who gave you this authority?" (**Luke 20:2**).

This radical and unannounced act of Jesus was perhaps the final straw in the minds of many Jews. The camel's back had been broken and most of the Jewish leaders felt Jesus needed to be broken before he got further out of control.

Merchants and shoppers, enjoying a typical day at the temple, were suddenly frozen by Jesus, postponed for the moment in their "let's make a deal frenzy" by his not-so-typical display of righteous indignation. The turtledoves were out of their cages and flying away to freedom. The cattle were stampeding down the busy streets of Jerusalem and upset owners frantically raced to find their own. Unclaimed sheep hurried off to find the nearest pasture. Shepherds, seething from losing their greatest sale in months, couldn't decide whether to locate their lost sheep or locate the one who had just lost his mind and give him a piece of theirs. Worst of all for the buyers and sellers there that day—money was scattered everywhere and merchants and beggars both were scurrying to grab what was theirs and what wasn't.

Nobody had ever remembered a full-blooded, true-blue Jew coming to the temple and turning things upside down. A few Gentiles, yes; but never one of their own!

"How dare he," they said.

"Why, the nerve of this guy!"

Early on in his ministry, people were praising Jesus for speaking with such authority (**Matthew 7:28-29**). Now they were demanding proof of his authority. Prior to this unprecedented "temple tantrum," Jesus had simply preached against the evils of hypocrisy and using God and religion as a means of making money. Now these temple retailers were feeling the disappointment and wrath of God in their pocketbooks. In their opinion, Jesus had most definitely crossed the line with this outburst.

"This," they vowed, *"will never happen again!"*

"We and our temple should never be treated with this kind of disrespect."

"Look, the Lamb of God who takes away the sin of the world" (**John 1:29**).

After hearing so many people get it wrong, Jesus must have appreciated the few times when someone finally proclaimed his true identity. John the Baptist was the proud deliverer of this profound truth, although, at a later point in his life, even he doubted if Jesus really was the ultimate deliverer the Israelites had all been waiting for (**Matthew 11:1-6**). But the Lamb of God said it all. According to John's theology, Jesus was the fall guy, the one who would gladly take a hit for a friend. He was the innocent one who would willingly be led naked to the slaughter, just so others could be fully clothed. He was the righteous one who willingly would be taken away long before he would have the chance to live out his days on earth, just so the sins of others could be taken away, allowing them the chance to live with him for all eternity.

"Rabbi" (**John 1:38**).

The life-changing, "fresh-bread" word of God had turned stale in many of the synagogues, thanks in large part to the lack of conviction shown by the local Jewish rabbis who had been serving it to the people. But now the word was becoming fit for consumption once again, full of spiritual nutrition. God's message for man was coming back to life in every lesson given by Jesus. His rabbinical reputation was growing and gaining popularity. People were leaving his lessons with looks on their faces that simply said, "Wow!" Student after student headed out from their time with Jesus excited to discuss what they had just learned with fellow listeners, friends and family back home.

"This man must have studied with the other top rabbis for a long time."

"Boy, is he ever good at dissecting the Torah."

"Interesting. I've never heard the Scriptures explained quite like that before."

"Sure, I'd be willing to take a course or two from him."

"I sure wish he were teaching in my synagogue."

"The Pentateuch, the Psalms and the Prophets—I can't find a weakness in his teaching yet."

"You are the King of Israel" (John 1:49).

In Nathanael's initial encounter with Jesus, the apostle-in-the-making was thoroughly impressed with what he considered to be other-world eyesight in the one who was claiming to be the Messiah. Perhaps the fig tree Jesus spoke of knowing about in Nathanael's world was his favorite private getaway and spiritual hiding place. No one, including Jesus, could have known it was the place where he often went to find God and find peace, and he had never been willing to share his divine secret with a single soul. But somehow, Jesus already knew about his favorite fig, and Nathanael knew that if somebody knew about it, they must possess omnipresent qualities.

"Anybody who can see me without seeing me must be a king sent from heaven," he thought. *"Move over David. Stand down Solomon. Jump back Josiah. A new and improved king has finally arrived and I'm ready to go to war for him."*

"The Savior of the World" (John 4:42).

First came the startling testimony from the woman at the well. It had been extremely helpful to her fellow-Samaritans, but could they really trust a troubled woman who couldn't keep a spouse with the statement that she had found the Savior?

"Could it really be?" they wondered. *"We're curious and open to you being right, but we really need to meet this man for ourselves."*

Then came the personal visit. The "Jesus Train" made an extended whistle-stop in their town, and after a couple of days, all wondering had ceased.

"He told the woman at the well everything she ever did without knowing what she did and now he's doing the same thing with me. I'm a believer!"

Maybe each man and woman in attendance during those two days had a private, award-winning **This is Your Life** presentation by the star of the show, Jesus. Whatever it was, these Samaritans became convinced that Jesus wasn't just there for the Jews, but he was the Savior of the **entire** world. And whether you were a half-breed Samaritan, such as they were, a purebred Jew or a no-bred Gentile, everybody in the world had equal access to his saving power.

"Is this not Jesus, the son of Joseph, whose father and mother we know?" (John 6:42).

Ordinary, sinful people: It's what Joseph and Mary were being called by those who knew them. When those in Israel considered Joseph and Mary's checkered past and their normal current status, they concluded that the blue-collar couple just didn't have the spiritual wherewithal to raise the king of the Jews. Due to an abundance of worldly thinking in regard to whom God chooses for important roles in his kingdom, statements began to surface about what people said were the sinful similarities between Jesus and his parents.

"You know what they say! The fruit never falls too far from the tree."

"Well, I know one thing. If he's anything like his mom or dad . . ."

"You know, it's been a while. Could you remind me again what happened when they got engaged?"

"They can't be very good parents. We babysat his brothers a few times and, boy, were they a pain!"

So Jesus' family tree became the root of the problem for many people who were still not convinced of his right to occupy such a high position in the nation of Israel.

"He is a good man" (John 7:12).

People who came in contact with Jesus certainly couldn't dismiss this truth. Too many old ladies had been seen taking his arm and crossing a busy street of Jerusalem during the Jewish feasts. Too many children had been seen playfully wrestling with him in their back yards. Too many people had seen Jesus drop off groceries at the orphanage on a regular basis. Too many people remembered how often he gave up his VIP seat at the over-crowded meeting hall and stood in the back instead. Too many people had been recipients of a friendly smile from him, a pleasant "good morning" or a sincere "hope to see you soon" farewell. Too many people had seen too many good deeds performed by Jesus to buy into any demon-possessed or insanity accusations. Yet most weren't willing to take it to the next level and say, "He is a perfect man!"

"How did this man get such learning without having studied?" (John 7:15).

It was a fair question posed by these people, and one designed to lead each interrogator to a final answer—God! Unfortunately, most of them assumed a more earthly response.

"How could anyone have so much insight into the Scriptures without some expert training along the way?"

"He must have secretly been taking some correspondence courses."

"Funny, I don't remember seeing him for a few years in his teens. Maybe his parents sent him off to some rabbi prep school."

"I know. It's that photographic memory a small percentage of the population have been blessed with that enables him to quote all those passages on demand."

Nobody doubted his understanding of the Scriptures. But few were open to the idea that he had actually lived through the history recorded within its pages.

"But we know where this man is from; when the Christ comes, no one will know where he is from" (John 7:27).

Wrong again! Like so many other times before, chalk this one up to a blatant lack of Bible knowledge.

"No one ever spoke the way this man does" (John 7:46).

Spellbound. Gripped. Astounded. People were actually staying awake through his sermons.

"He says things that convict me and make me mad, but somehow I can't dis-count what he's saying."

*"That was **two hours**? No way! It seemed like about twenty minutes."*

"So, when is he scheduled to come through town again? I think I'll be back."

"That was **AWESOME***!"*

Even those who listened to Jesus speak and hated what he said usually agreed that the way he said it was quite impressive. Even his staunchest critics couldn't counter his wisdom and debating skills.

In similar fashion, millions of Major League Baseball purists today find little problem in communicating their hatred for the New York Yankees. With claims of "They're the best team money can buy" and "The Yanks own the banks," many baseball fans opt to cheer for those organizations with shallower pockets. Ridicule them and rip into their financial advantages if you choose, but you certainly can't argue the fact that the Yankees are quite impressive in playing the American pastime, winning more World Series titles than any other professional baseball franchise in recent history, four in the past ten years.

But unlike today's Yankees-haters, opponents of Jesus couldn't justify their hatred toward him. They couldn't make claims that he was wealthy and had an unfair advantage over other messengers of God's word because he was privileged to attend the most prestigious universities and receive the finest education. Nor could they dismiss his amazing ability to communicate the truths of God by pointing to an obvious genetic link, one to prove that Jesus had been born into a family of talented and trained speakers.

"Now that's strange. We've never seen Joseph preach or teach. We've seen him pound a lot of nails, but we've never seen him pound on the pulpit."

"I'm guessing he's been taking some public speaking courses from the top orators of Rome."

"Who do you think you are?" (John 8:53).

Many people considered Jesus to be arrogant, brash and cocky.

"Say what? You're telling us that you were around before Abraham?"

"You actually have the audacity to say our father is the devil?"

"Now, let me get this straight. You and God are one?"

So they hurried off to gather rocks for an impromptu stoning of Jesus because his claims of deity didn't register with their present theology.

"This man is not from God, for he does not keep the Sabbath" (John 9:16).

Because Jesus didn't comply with the Pharisee's carefully thought out additions to the biblical Sabbath, these religious leaders concluded he couldn't be from God.

"Doesn't he have a calendar?" they quipped.

"For God's sake, has he forgotten this is Saturday?"

*"Any **real** Jew would be very familiar with our weekend regulations."*

Like these misguided religious zealots, anybody who is more into tradition than truth will miss the real Jesus. They'll create a Savior to better fit their traditions and teachings, or they'll dismiss him altogether. Both are equally damning.

"He is demon-possessed and raving mad" (John 10:19).

Out of control. Hysterical. Insane.

"No wonder he hangs out with those zombies in the cemeteries."

"This guy needs to be put away for a long time."

"I know a good psychiatrist who might be able to help this guy."

"Counseling won't be enough. He'll need some serious medication."

"I know a great anger management course I could recommend to him."

Though not one moment of his life was out of control, hysterical or insane, these labels were securely sewn on Jesus' character. Though not one time did the term "raving mad" describe his true behavior, many loosely shared this opinion of him with their family, friends and fellow truth-haters.

"You, a mere man, claim to be God" (John 10:33).

Mere. Regular. Run of the mill.

"But I've seen you take naps and my Scriptures say God never sleeps."

"I saw you drink that glass of wine. Why, God would never . . ."

"Isn't that sweat I see on your brow? And what's that about God never tiring?"

"You're a bit short, Jesus, and you surely don't stand out a great deal. Even if God did become a man, he surely wouldn't look like you."

"Okay, so if you really are God, who is controlling the universe at the moment?"

Was it hard for the Israelites, or anyone for that matter, to comprehend Jesus being God in the flesh? Absolutely! Was it impossible? Absolutely not! There are many things I don't fully understand in life, but I surely don't discount them or write them off as wrong. I'm not quite sure how a big ball of fire 93 million miles away warms the earth, but it does so without my help and I plan on reaping the benefits of the yellow sphere for as long as I'm alive. I'm not totally aware of the intricate details that allow my car to take me from my home to my intended destination, but I'm smart enough to know that it needs gas and four workable tires, and I'm still planning on driving most everywhere I go. I'm not exactly sure how the brain in my body works—the blood vessels, the tissue, the unique compartments that control my various bodily functions and all the other human computer parts you can find within it, but I do know it works (most of the time) and I plan on using it to help me for as long as it will let me.

Understanding how God became flesh in Jesus, yet all the while maintaining the order of the entire universe, is beyond my ability to totally grasp, and I can't offer you a mathematical equation to help you better understand it. But the concept to me makes complete sense, much like you and I getting on our hands and knees and engaging in baby talk to better communicate with a one-year-old. Or going to the inner city with no job, no money, no car, no friends and no place to stay, and doing it in the dead of winter just to better understand the daily struggles facing a homeless person. That God would do it seems completely consistent with his loving nature. And though it boggles my mind to try and understand how he did it, it doesn't take away from the fact that he did. Evidently, these religious people had minimized God's ability to do the impossible and refused to accept some of the simplest and most basic truths that comprise true religion and a belief in an Almighty being—that God is beyond our means of understanding completely and his abilities and choices are often beyond our means of reason and common sense. Jesus was proving both to be true.

"My Lord and my God" (John 20:28).

Thank you, Thomas! Though it took you a little while, you arrived. Thomas kept climbing and eventually arrived at the high place God wants every human being to reach—the conviction about Jesus' true identity of *our Lord and our God*. He wanted this glorious truth to be understood by first-century face-to-face observers and he wants it to be grasped by those of us reading about Jesus in the 21st century.

And what about you? Who do you say he is?

❦ Chapter Nine ❦

A Letter From a Friend
∽ ∾

(The following is a letter that could have been written in the 21st century had Jesus been introduced to the world at this time. It's written by someone familiar with Jesus, near what would have been the end of his three-year ministry, and is addressed to a friend who is seriously considering becoming a follower of Jesus.)

Dear Friend,

I felt it was a matter of extreme importance and urgency to pass along some information I've received about this man called Jesus. I understand you have been entertaining the possibility of following him and, I must admit, this greatly concerns me. Having spent personal time with him on occasion, and knowing many people on both sides of the issue, I'd ask you to please hear me out. I would hate to see you do anything rash and get caught up in something so destructive. This new religious movement has already ruined the lives of way too many good-hearted people for me to remain silent at this time, especially to someone who is so close to me. We've always been the best of friends, so I am asking you to trust me as I share these things.

Because I've talked with Jesus a few times myself, most of what I am telling you is from first-hand knowledge. Some of it is from information I've received from others who both of us know and a few of the items are from those who neither of us know, but who are very respected in the community. Either way, the information is from those you can totally trust. I've known you for many years now and have always seen your zest for life, but also your ability to judge things fairly and accurately. If you can continue walking on that path, you will not regret it. However, if you continue on the path to follow Jesus, you will be giving up the chance to see most of your dreams realized. You will end up losing most, if not all, of your closest friends. Of course, I won't stop being your friend. But after talking with a few people who used to be a part of his group, you'll be discouraged from associating with me since I'm not a member there. And your new friends, from what I've both seen and heard, are extremely needy, socially awkward and desperate for love, to say the least. That doesn't describe you in any way and I'm surprised that you haven't been able to pick up on those weaknesses in his group yet.

But let's get down to the real issue: The leader of this group. If the leader is someone with a questionable character or a shady reputation, then his followers will likely be cast from the same mold. I'm sure you're not aware of most of the information I'm going to tell you about him, but here is what I've come to learn. This Jesus is a very hard guy to pin down and he seems to be eluding his critics and their questions. He hasn't even given a full interview to any of the networks yet and that seems a bit strange to me. I would think that to go on television and clear up these disturbing accusations would be very helpful to his cause; that is, if he really has nothing to hide. Or, at least he could grant a story to the local paper, or perhaps he could even write an autobiography.

And doesn't it seem strange to you that he never stays in one place for very long? He doesn't have a permanent address (not even a post office box) and his own family gets frustrated just trying to determine his whereabouts. How could you trust someone that intangible? In addition to that, a number of people have been searching for months and still can't find any certifiable information about his life from age 12 to 30. Where was he anyway? What was he doing during that time? Eighteen years is a long time to just disappear. Did he even go to high school or is he a drop-out? Did he pursue a college education and get a degree? Has he ever held down a real job for any length of time? Does he have any references and, if so, are they reputable? How can you trust a man to lead you who has no formal education and no credible work history? Now, if he went to college somewhere like Harvard, Pepperdine or Stanford, or even to one of the state universities, I wouldn't be this concerned. Or, if he could produce a résumé and we could get some evidence of his employment with, say, a broker on Wall Street or perhaps a Fortune 500 company, then I'd feel a whole lot better about the decision you're making.

As far as I can tell, he hasn't worked anywhere of note, and now he's using women (even widows I hear) to financially support his ministry efforts. He doesn't own a home, which seems pretty ignorant in today's financial climate. But what's even more disturbing is that he doesn't even have a rental history. Still somehow he always seems to have a home to stay in, and he spends most of his nights in some of the nicer ones in the suburbs. Many of us have seen him sailing in some of the bigger boats out on the lake. We're wondering if those are actually his boats or, if not, how does he weasel his way into the wealthier social circles? Does he just find clever ways to mooch off of others and live the high-life and, if so, what kind of scam-artist is he anyway? I'm sure you haven't heard about this, but one time he approved of a widow giving her entire Social Security check to his church, leaving her with nothing left to live on. Sure, the money helped him, but did he even bother to find out how she planned on surviving until her next check?

I hear as well that he may not be paying his taxes. He avoids answering the straightforward questions he's being asked about his responsibility toward the government and their role in his life. And if you stop and think about it, it looks like he might possibly be a predator of sorts, preying on the weak? Look at the kind of people who are following him. Even most of his associate ministers aren't from a real respectable background. Check and see for yourself. I think a few of them worked for a while as offshore fishermen before going into the full-time ministry and working at his church. Most of them don't even have a high school diploma, let alone a degree from a respected seminary. And one of his closest followers is an anti-government radical with an arrest record. These things I'm sharing with you should cause you to take more time, ask more questions and look into these matters more thoroughly. It seems obvious to me that if you can't feel good about those at the top of the organization, you shouldn't get involved with it at all.

I've also heard that the local police are trying to arrest Jesus and they think they might have a pretty good case. Even the other church leaders in the area, who you would think should come to his defense, are in full support of bringing him in for questioning. Two ministers from a couple of the largest churches in the city are heading up a campaign to petition for his arrest. Why would they be so upset with him if he really were promoting God and the Bible? Isn't that what they want, too?

Obviously, something seems a bit strange here. But what's even worse in my opinion is that Jesus has the audacity to claim that those same ministers aren't even preaching the truth. I've heard he says they're all going to hell. And these men are the leaders of churches that have been around for more than one hundred years and are heading up some of the most respected religious organizations in the city. Sure, Jesus claims to be religious, but why isn't there even one church in the city that will support him and why don't any of them agree with what he's teaching. Even the most conservative churches who have strict interpretations of the Bible say he's way off base and dangerous, especially to those who are desperately looking for a fresh outlook and a more exciting religious experience. He promises some new type of worship experience and sucks people in before they have time to realize how ridiculous his methods really are. I just don't want to see you, of all people, end up being hurt, or even worse, brainwashed. I'm sure you would realize after a while what you had done, but perhaps it wouldn't be until you really had done some damage to your life. You might even end up putting a wedge between you and your family. And, worst of all, you will miss out for a few years on the good life that God really wants you to enjoy.

Let's look at the facts. Jesus says you can have this "full life" if you follow him, but then he teaches stuff about relationships with the opposite sex that seem more like the Amish way of doing things. I've also heard that he encourages most of the single people he meets to never get married, period. Add to that the high likelihood you'll have to give up your chance of maintaining a good career if you go to his church. And will you have any time to do the recreational activities you so enjoy, or will you be able to use the vacation time you've built up at work over the past ten years? Probably not! Instead, I'm predicting you'll be spending most of your nights doing everything you're required to do as a member of his church, and I've heard that's a ton. You have such a great job right now and I'd hate to see you run the risk of losing out on the incredible career path you're on. Besides, how many others in your company are following him? And will your boss feel good about your decision, because I'm sure he'll find out about it soon enough?

Also, this no sex policy seems so hypocritical in my opinion. Think about it for a minute. What do you suppose Jesus does with all his time? There have been many occasions when people haven't been able to find him anywhere for a few days. Where does he go? There have also been a few times when people finally figured out where he was, and he was alone with a woman. In a few of those cases, the women he was with were those with questionable lifestyles, and one was even a known prostitute. Another was with a woman who has been married five times and is currently living together with her boyfriend. Sounds like the type you would see on The Jerry Springer Show. And I don't believe for a minute that nothing sexual happened between the two of them? Besides all of that, there are two other women who live in the suburbs (I think Mary and Martha are their names) who are pretty involved with him. I've heard he stays with them in their home a lot when nobody else is there.

But what's even more frightening than that is the question that many have about his sexual orientation. Most people I know are convinced he's bisexual. It's pretty apparent he has some homosexual tendencies, isn't it? Why else would he spend so much time with those twelve men? Where do they go when nobody else is allowed to go along? What do they do on their getaways? Why are they out on the lake in the middle of the night? Why is Jesus off climbing mountains at three in the morning? Is he really alone like he claims to be? And consider this: The only evidence we can find of Jesus at a younger age was when he was twelve. And where was he found then? He was at a church building with some ministers, supposedly asking them Bible questions. With all the news lately about the sexual abuse by the priests, could it be that Jesus was a part of that as well? He definitely displays a lot of physical affection to the men he's with, and he even hugs strangers at times. Apparently, some people spotted him massaging his disciple's feet and taking a bath with them. There are even more rumors from reliable sources that he struggles with an attraction toward young boys, maybe even babies. Why do you think he spends so much time with children? Someone said they heard a ten-year-old boy is about to come forward and talk about the time Jesus inappropriately touched him.

I know I'm writing a lot here, but I want to make sure I don't miss anything because I really care about you and want you to know everything I know. Once again, I have to say it seems like Jesus is very hypocritical. He talks a lot about not getting drunk, but then he goes and brings in a bunch of wine at a wedding reception where most of the people had already had too much to drink anyway. There are numerous reports that he's spending a lot of time with those who have drinking problems. Nobody has caught him drunk yet, but that doesn't mean he hasn't been. Maybe he's an alcoholic, too, but he knows how to hide it better than most. That truth will come out eventually, I'm sure.

Now, obviously, I'm not saying that everything I'm writing to you is one hundred percent accurate. But it sure seems like most of the evidence is pretty solid. And with all these questions and accusations about Jesus, shouldn't you take a break from this, clear your head, get away for a few days and then make your decision? Of course, you're free to do what you want, but as a friend who cares for you deeply, I just don't want to see you throw away a good life. Hey, maybe I could clear my schedule for a few days and we could go on a little getaway together. That would give us more time to go over some of these things in greater detail. I could also let you know more about the church I've been attending recently. I think you'd like it a lot and it would be a good alternative to what Jesus is trying to persuade you to join. Listen, you're going to heaven anyway, and you've always been very confident about that. Why would you want to go and do this now if it really has absolutely nothing to do with your eternal status?

There are just a few more things I need to tell you. I'm sure Jesus has some good qualities, but a lot of what I'm hearing is very troubling. Were you aware that even members of his own family have a difficult time figuring him out? I know how much your parents mean to you and also how proud they are of you, so how could you agree to follow that kind of example? Did you know he once told a crowd that they had to hate their own father and mother if they wanted to follow him? One time his whole family came to see him, but he said he was too busy and basically blew them off. Now, I know you've never done that to your family. That was incredibly disrespectful and downright rude. But then he turns right around and preaches in his next sermon that you're supposed to honor your father and mother. Doesn't that sound a little psychotic to you?

Have you heard about the vandalism charges that may be filed against Jesus? I guess he walked into a church building, of all places, and right before the service he started turning over all the pews in the sanctuary and the book and tape table in the foyer. We also heard he went to the city park on the south side of town and poisoned some of the trees there. It appears to me, and many others, that he cares very little about other people's property. He even encouraged a woman to pour out an entire bottle of perfume on his feet that was worth more than $1,000. What a waste! You, on the other hand, have always been so sensitive and thoughtful when it comes to other people's property and space. Why would you want to get involved with someone like Jesus then?

Another thing I want to point out to you is his approach to people and their existing beliefs. You've always been very understanding and respectful when people have disagreed with you on the Bible or spiritual matters. But Jesus isn't that way at all. It's either his way or no way. And he's becoming known as the biggest hell-fire and brimstone preacher in the city. He's even started talking about his followers needing to cut off their body parts to help them stop sinning. Talk about extremes! I know you're not an extremist. You've always been so careful and cautious when it comes to spiritual matters. Boy, it's a good thing most people aren't giving in to his all-or-nothing-nonsense. They can read between the lines and see he's on a power trip. And can you really feel good about following someone who says, "I'm the only way?" Have you forgotten about what Jim Jones did in the early 80s? Don't you remember David Koresh and what happened to him and most of his followers a decade later? Jesus seems to have many similarities to those two men, as well as some of the other religious crazies who have been able to get a few desperate people to follow them. Unfortunately, most of those misguided souls ended up dead at an early age. Don't you see that if you follow Jesus you could possibly end up dead, too? Is that what you really want to do with your life? My prediction is that Jesus will be dead within a year, maybe even sooner. Do you really want to follow someone who won't even be around for much of your life?

I'm almost certain that Jesus isn't for real. He claims to do miracles, but when the coalition of church leaders came to meet with him and asked him to prove his radical claims by simply showing them a miracle, he couldn't do it. Wouldn't that have been the ideal time to convince the world? These men have thousands of members in their churches. If they had seen proof of Jesus' power, surely they would have encouraged their members to get excited about him, too. But none of that happened. Why? It's because he doesn't really have the power. He isn't really who he says he is. I believe he's a fake. But I'm sure he won't be able to fool you.

Thanks for letting me share my concerns. We've always been close and I know you trust my opinions. I look forward to meeting with you face-to-face. Perhaps we could grab some coffee at Starbucks next week and talk about this some more. I love you a lot and will do anything I can to help you see the truth.

Sincerely,

Satan

❧ Chapter Ten ❦

The Savior Says
≫ ❧

Jesus answered, "Even if I testify on my own behalf, my testimony is valid, for I know where I came from and where I am going. But you have no idea where I came from or where I am going."
— John 8:14

While it is rather interesting to consider the many opinions that were formulating about Jesus, only one opinion really matters. What did Jesus say about himself? Who did he claim to be? Was he vague and confusing about his identity or was he very clear?

Upon reading through the four Gospels, it becomes apparent that most people were not confused with Jesus' claims, but instead they were outraged! His messages about his exact identity weren't cryptic and did not need to be deciphered by linguistic scholars to discover the real meaning. There was no hidden agenda. There was no secret code that only computer geeks could uncover two thousand years later. He never wore Clark Kent glasses. He claimed to be Superman, acted like Superman and was Superman. He boldly spoke of his God-liness, God-likeness and God-ness. He made no apologies for being the Scripture-fulfiller, the Savior and the Son of God. He humbly spoke of an eternal position that came with eternal privileges and that every individual's eternal placement was dependent upon his final decision.

So let's get right to the source and examine some of the ways Jesus referred to himself during his time on earth.

"The Son of Man" (**Matthew 8:20**).

Though Jesus often heralded his rightful claim to deity, he never steered away from talking about his humanity as well. The title, Son of Man, was the one Jesus used most often when referring to himself. Though he was the fullness of God in bodily form, he was also called to serve as God's human representative to act on behalf of other human beings. It was a title borrowed from references to Daniel and Ezekiel in the Old Testament, and one that many in Israel had attached to the coming Messiah. Now, Jesus was claiming to actually be this Messiah figure, the one Daniel saw in his vision of a coming deliverer to Israel (**Daniel 7:9-14**). This was a fairly safe title for Jesus to use in the early days of his ministry, as it emphasized his complete union with mankind. This strategy would also allow additional time for the nation of Israel to warm up to the more radical truth of Jesus being the Son of God.

"No one knows the Father except the Son" (**Matthew 11:27**).

With a right focus and a concentrated effort, we humans can acquire a lot of knowledge about God in our average lifespan of 70 to 80 years. But even then, how thorough can that knowledge be? We could live a million lifetimes, study out his nature every single day and still never totally comprehend God (**Romans 11:33-36**).

The angels know even more about their Master than we do. They've been bowing before him, singing to him and praising him for thousands of years. They've watched him work, delivered many soul-saving messages to man on his behalf and bailed out his people from spiritual jail on numerous occasions (**Hebrews 1:14, 13:2**). Still, the Bible says, their information as to the exact nature of God and his specific plans for creation are incomplete (**1 Peter 1:10-12**).

Jesus, however, knew God completely. He claimed an intimacy and an absolute oneness with him, and all this from a man who was only in his 30s. Only an eternal being who is equal with God could claim this lofty oneness—someone who had been around for as long as God had, was with God the entire time and was now living as God on earth, his glory veiled only by human flesh.

"The Son of Man will send out his angels" (**Matthew 13:41**).

The Scriptures teach here, and in other passages, that Jesus is the master of the heavenly beings. He is the coordinator, conductor and song-selector of the heavenly angelic choir, those who minute by minute sing to promote his praise. He's Charley to billions and billions of angels. When he calls, they answer. When he speaks, they listen. When he commands, they obey. When he stands, they bow. When he sits, they worship.

This was an important piece of theology to those who thought Jesus might just be a powerful angel on an extended visit to earth, in the same elite class as a Michael or a Gabriel, but nothing more. This, clearly, was not how Jesus saw himself. Sadly, there are still many today in fast growing religions that lower him to this position of "just another angel" or "just another important messenger of God."

"I will build my church" (**Matthew 16:18**).

Jesus never said that he was the minister of the church. He most certainly wasn't a mere member of the church and he never claimed to be one of the founding fathers of the church. He was the architect, builder and one and only owner of the one and only church.

Starting this church was decided upon only by his will and timing. Doctrine in this church was determined only by his binding words. Past and present members of this church were added to the roster only by his approval. And the welcome sign on the door to this church will be forever removed upon his return.

"The Christ" (**Matthew 16:20**).

Jesus boldly claimed to be the holy and anointed one of God. He was the one who had volunteered to come to earth and engage in a radical and risky rescue mission. He was God's knight in shining armor, racing with sword in hand to the front of earth's most intense conflicts to save mankind from eternal damnation and show them the way to an eternal Camelot. Jesus was the only one with sufficient (eternal) credentials making him worthy enough to be selected for the most important job in the history of world civilization, that of bringing sinful and lost souls into a saved relationship with God.

"The King of the Jews" (**Matthew 27:11**).

Notice Jesus said that he was ***the*** king and not ***a*** king. He was the perfect composite of the men from Israel's past whom they respected the most. Jesus possessed king David's heart, only much softer (**1 Samuel 13: 14**); he had king Solomon's wisdom, only in far greater amounts (**1 Kings 3:1-28**); he displayed king Asa's conviction, only much more thorough (**1 Kings 15:9-24**); he walked with king Jehu's zeal, only more refined (**2 Kings 9:14-10:17**); he showed king Joash's concern, only more urgent (**2**

Kings 11:1-12:21); he had king Hezekiah's resolve, only for an entire lifetime (2 **Kings 18:1-20:11, 2 Chronicles 32:24-33**); he led with king Josiah's firmness, yet with far greater approachability (2 **Kings 22:1-23:30**).

If you took all the top spiritual qualities of Israel's greatest kings and wove them together into one amazing king, Jesus would dwarf that king in greatness as a great white shark would a guppy.

"All authority in heaven and on earth" (**Matthew 28:18**).

If angels were given a help-a-human assignment to come and visit earth, marching orders went through his office. If the street of gold was in need of polishing, he approved the budget. If Satan wanted a temporary visitor's pass, he would need an interview with him. If any angels succumbed to Satan tactics, he was there to pronounce expulsion. If any human sought entrance through the pearly gates, he was the one and only security guard posted at the gate demanding proper identification.

It was, and still is, no different on earth. Nobody's heart is softened or opened without a prior search by Jesus for pure motives. Nobody could then, or now, change or improve upon a single word he spoke during his time on earth. Nobody can receive the blood he spilled on the cross unless they follow his specific instructions for a transfusion. And nobody can remain in his church while on this earth without receiving satisfactory remarks on his regular reviews (**Revelation 2-3**).

Jesus seeks permission from no one and answers to no one. No heavenly or earthly congress can veto any law he writes. He is truly the Branch—the executive branch, legislative branch and judicial branch (**Zechariah 6:9-15**). He is President, Speaker of the House and Chief Justice of the Supreme Court. He makes laws, passes laws and enforces laws. Yet, unlike so many of the authority figures today, his motives are one hundred percent pure, and his purpose in using this authority is to build us up in this life and bring us up to heaven in the next.

"The Lord" (**Mark 11:3**).

Though he never forced his will or way on any follower or potential follower, not once did he demand a retraction from someone who bowed before him and uttered these words. And never did he stutter or stall when using this description about himself. He was the Lord, not merely a messenger of the Lord. He was the Lord, not merely one of the higher-ups in his organization.

"The Son of God" (**Luke 22:70**).

This is where much of the trouble began for Jesus with the Jews. Most Israelites were perfectly fine with Jesus being *a* Son of God. After all, in a sense, that's what they were, too—children of God and part of his spiritual family. They also had little or no problem with Jesus being one of the many *sons of God*, an offspring of a righteous man, or an angel, as the term had been used in the Old Testament (**Job 38:6-7**). But *the* Son of God! Now that was pushing it!

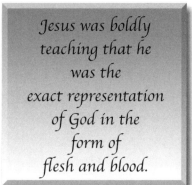

Jesus was boldly teaching that he was the exact representation of God in the form of flesh and blood.

The Jews had trouble with the title because they knew exactly what it meant. In making this claim, Jesus was stating that he was equal with God. He was unashamedly announcing that the Holy Spirit himself had been planted in a young woman's womb and had arrived in physical form nine months later (**Luke 1: 35-37**). Jesus was boldly teaching that he was the exact representation of God in the form of flesh and blood (**Hebrews 1:3**).

"We've never heard of anything like that before," critics argued.

"Hey, Jesus, God is bigger than the universe and you're not even that big for a human."

"How can a mere man and a mighty God ever be equal?"

"Besides, if God ever did visit our planet, he'd be a lot more impressive than you."

"The Son gives life to whom he is pleased to give it" (**John 5:21**).

Giving life to whatever and whomever he desired had never been a big problem for Jesus. He was an active agent in the creation of the universe (**Colossians 1:16**). He had been knitting babies in their mothers' wombs for centuries and no life came to be without his planning and performing. The same was true in regard to spiritual life. If he spotted a caring heart, he was pleased to grant it eternal privileges and didn't pass his decision by anybody else. When a lifetime criminal asked for an eternal home in his last few hours on earth, Jesus promised him Paradise without a committee's inquiry concerning whether or not the request was sincere.

"The Scriptures testify about me" (**John 5:39**).

All of the Israelites had been trained to be somewhat skeptical about anyone who made boasts of being the promised Messiah. They had undoubtedly encountered a few of these liars through the years who had made the radical claim of being the Christ, long before Jesus came on the scene. But every one of these phonies had come without power, without proof and without a passport stamped by God.

"We don't see it in your life and we don't see you in the Scriptures," they would argue.

Many would come after Jesus and claim to be the one. They would muster up a small, but fanatical following and they, too, were shown to be false (**Acts 5:34-37**). With no spiritual backing, no scriptural roots and no previous prediction about their arrival, they failed to impress the majority of people they sought to recruit.

Jesus wanted the skeptics to get their Bibles out. He wanted them to go back to Genesis and check out the final king coming from the tribe of Judah (**Genesis 49:8-12**). He wanted them peering into Micah and discovering the born in Bethlehem connection (**Micah 5:2**). There was so much they could find out about him in the Scriptures and Jesus longed to make them aware of it. He wanted them to check out the Messianic Psalms and see if he didn't fit (**Psalm 22**). He hoped they'd spend a little time in Isaiah and notice that an average looking Messiah was par for the course (**Isaiah 53:2**). And he hoped they'd stay tuned for more detailed information about his upcoming crucifixion between two thieves (**Isaiah 53:12**), his burial in a rich man's tomb (**Isaiah 53:9**) and his miraculous escape three days later (**Isaiah 53:11, Psalm 16:8-11**).

"I am the Bread of Life" (**John 6:35**).

In the desert it was manna—the only God-given source of physical sustenance that kept the Israelites alive on their journey to the Promise Land. It was sent from heaven, satisfying to the taste, sufficient for life and supplied daily by God himself.

Now it was Jesus claiming to be the new and eternal manna—the only source of spiritual sustenance to keep humans spiritually alive and able to reach their heavenly home. He, too, came from heaven, was more than satisfying to those who hungered for righteousness, was completely sufficient for spiritual life and, as God in the flesh, made himself available on a daily basis to all who sought him out.

"I am the Light of the World" (John 8:12).

The first-century world was full of philosophers, religious zealots and wisdom-seekers, all doing their best to shed a little light into a world arena that was full of confusion and darkness. They promoted their latest thoughts and ideas on how to acquire a better life and a deeper understanding of deity. They promised a clearer picture of God and a clearer path to God. But none of their light lessons had the capacity to keep people from their dark, sinful ways. Their fine-sounding arguments (**Colossians 2:4**) couldn't release any of their listeners from spiritual bondage, and they certainly couldn't get them into heaven. In a light sense, it was wisdom with no wattage, ideas with no illumination and religion with no rays of sunshine.

But Jesus was different. The one who had made the sun, the moon and the stars came to earth with an even brighter message—*"I am the Light of the world; whoever follows me will never walk in darkness but will have the light of life"* (**John 8:12**).

If you listened to the teachings of Jesus, the sun had risen. If you obeyed his teaching, it never set.

If you saw his example, the light in the tunnel appeared. If you imitated his example, you were all the way out.

If you heard about his death on a cross, the stars became brighter. If you embraced it and believed it to be the only means for you to be acceptable to God, they fell into the earth's atmosphere.

Many people throughout the centuries prior to Jesus' arrival had brought some light. Jesus brought himself. Spiritual patriarchs, such as Noah and Abraham, built campfires. Jesus built a bonfire. Good kings of Israel, such as David and Josiah, shined flashlights. Jesus shined floodlights. Powerful prophets, such as Elijah and Jeremiah, flashed lasers. Jesus flashed lightning.

"Before Abraham was born, I am" (John 8:58).

Jesus was the one within the burning bush proclaiming his name to Moses approximately 1,500 years before his arrival on earth—*I AM* (**Exodus 3:1-14**). Jesus was, Jesus is and Jesus always will be an eternal being with no beginning and no end. He was not an angel created by God, but the creator of the angels. He was not a prophet sent to deliver a message from God, but the actual Word of God. Jesus was not just a good man in the flesh. He was God in the flesh!

He would feel much sorrow for people's sinful condition, but never need to apologize for his own: *I AM caring and I AM complete*.

He would weep over lost souls and cities, but never find a better way to reach them: *I AM passionate and I AM perfect*.

He would face every temptation known to man, but never succumb: *I AM sympathetic and I AM sinless*.

He would bend over backwards to assist people, but never dodge the truth about their sin: *I AM helpful and I AM hard-line*.

He would suffer physical torture, bleed, die and be buried, but never have a moment of decay: *I AM real and I AM risen*.

"I am the Gate" (John 10:7-9).

In the Gospels, Jesus never uttered the words, "Let me show you to the gate." He **was** the gate and only he had the power to swing himself open for eternal rewards. Only Jesus had the power to allow people access to him. Only Jesus had the power to open up a listener's heart to follow him. And only Jesus had the power to change lives once someone finally decided to surrender to him. With this amazing power of Jesus now being made available to man, many gates began to be opened by the Gate.

The gate of forgiveness: *"Then neither do I condemn you"* (**John 8:11**).

The gate of peace: *"I have told you these things, so that in me you may have peace"* (**John 16:33**).

The gate of freedom: *"If you hold to my teaching, you are really my disciples. Then you will know the truth, and the truth will set you free"* (**John 8:31-32**).

The gate of fruit: *"If a man remains in me and I in him, he will bear much fruit"* (**John 15:5**).

The gate of confidence: *"I tell you the truth, anyone who has faith in me will do what I have been doing. He will do even greater things than these, because I am going to the Father"* (**John 14:12**).

The gate of access to God: *"I am the Way, the Truth and the Life. No one comes to the Father except through me"* (**John 14:6**).

The gate of heaven: *"I tell you the truth, today you will be with me in Paradise"* (**Luke 23:43**).

"I am the Good Shepherd" (John 10:11).

Israel had experienced their share of bad shepherds throughout Old Testament history. Ezekiel had pinpointed Israel's major problem to be exactly that in his day, but then reminded his fellow Israelites that God had something better in mind for them in the days to come (**Ezekiel 34: 1-31**). It was Jesus he had in mind. In Jesus, God had come to the sheep pen himself to show the world just how sheep were to be treated.

Jesus knew every sheep. He loved every sheep. Baby sheep frequently found their way into his arms. Sheep without a full complement of wool were always on his daily rounds. Crippled sheep were made to feel an important part of the flock and seemed to get greater attention than the rest. Retired sheep were paraded as heroes in the barnyard, not has-beens. Black sheep were considered special and unique, not strange and unworthy. Regular, healthy, wool-giving sheep were not just one of the flock, but a coat for a cold day. Every sheep had a name that was remembered. Every sheep had protection from the elements and the enemy. Every sheep had food to eat, pasture to roam and fence to contain. This was the day-in, day-out description of Jesus and his involvement with people. No human being had ever loved one of their best friends anywhere near the way Jesus loved his enemies. Every person he met, whether friend or foe, received the royal treatment when they appeared before the shepherd king.

Nobody had ever treated every individual they encountered with absolute respect. Then Jesus came.

Nobody who was in a hurry had ever made every single person they crossed paths with during those busy moments feel like they were of great importance. Then Jesus came.

Nobody had ever made every outcast they touched feel like an insider. Then Jesus came.

Nobody had ever considered every single person they had ever met to be better than they were. Then Jesus came.

Nobody had ever made the sheep feel more important than the shepherd. Then Jesus died.

"I am the Resurrection and the Life" (**John 11:25**).

It's one thing for a person to die and then, without their prior knowledge, have a power outside of themselves to bring them back to life. We see this occurring at times in both the Old and New Testaments (**2 Kings 4:8-37, Acts 9:36-42**). It's another thing altogether to predict you will die and how you will die, declare you'll be resurrected soon after your death and confidently reveal that you're the one with the power to make it all happen. Jesus did all three.

Never in the history of mankind has there been a recognized religious leader, claiming to be sent from God, who predicted he would resurrect from the dead. There has never been a religious leader of note whose followers claimed their designated leader had indeed been resurrected. There has never been a spiritual leader who actually rose from the dead, hung out with others for forty days afterwards, then commanded his followers to make spreading the knowledge of this truth their mission in life. Again, Jesus did all three.

"I am the Way, and the Truth, and the Life" (John 14:6).

Jesus is the Way: He is the **right** way, the **best** way, the **complete** way and the **only** way. Jesus is the way of **peace**, the way of **hope** and the way of **God**.

Jesus is the Truth: He is the **amazing** truth, the **sobering** truth and the **entire** truth. Jesus is the truth that **reveals**, the truth that **convicts** and the truth that **sets people free.**

Jesus is the Life: He is the **good** life, the **true** life, the **abundant** life and the **full** life. Jesus is the life of **service**, the life of **sacrifice**, the life of **love** and the life of **perfection**.

"My Lord and my God" (John 20:24-29).

Thomas spoke it. Jesus didn't argue. That settles it!

These are some of the astounding claims Jesus made about himself. Who else in history had ever made such claims? Who else after him would dare to even try? These claims were nothing short of outlandish. But what is even more bizarre is that Jesus believed them, backed them up and made acceptance of them the basis for being his follower.

Who else in the history of mankind has ever come close to being as amazing as Jesus Christ? Putting any past, present or future life on trial would bring about a quick acquittal: Not guilty of being the Savior! Jesus was put on trial for thirty-three years. Just one prophecy about him remaining unfulfilled would have made him just another man. One sinful and selfish outburst of anger would have made him just another failed attempt at saving mankind. One look of lust at a beautiful woman would have rendered his blood useless. One ounce of deceit would have meant every other word from his mouth could not be trusted. One angry stare or retaliatory remark while he was being nailed to a cross would have left us looking for another Lamb of God. One bone found from his grave would have meant we all would have to settle for only what this life has to offer. But none of that happened. Jesus was everything he was cracked up to be, and more!

The preview of the "Jesus" movie made most people eager to purchase a ticket to the show. The actual movie didn't disappoint true fans and was even better than expected. The raving reviews of the movie, written and spoken by believers both past and present, haven't changed for the past two thousand years. And just in case you haven't seen the movie, it's still playing in Bibles everywhere.

❧ Chapter Eleven ❧

Tales From the Tax Man
❧ ❧

As Jesus went from there, he saw a man
named Matthew sitting at the tax collector's booth.
"Follow me," he told him, and Matthew got up and followed him.
— Matthew 9:9

Imagine for a moment that you had never heard of Jesus before today and you opened up your Bible to the book of Matthew and started reading. Upon completing your reading of the first Gospel to appear in the New Testament, you then proceeded to read the next three Gospel accounts of Mark, Luke and John. Do you think the picture of Jesus you would develop would be the same one you have indelibly etched in your mind at the moment?

Much of the problem leading to the tragedy of missing the real Jesus is that so many people already claim to have a good idea about him before they ever get to the Gospels. Consequently, when they begin reading the Biblical account of Jesus, most of these people will tend to rationalize certain passages, skip by some passages altogether, read over a few important passages without considering their implication or make the clear and simple passages cloudy by the bad weather they are bringing in.

When you think you're right about something, isn't it hard to see it any other way? When you think you have the correct answer to an important question, especially a spiritual one, isn't it hard to admit you got it wrong? When you think you know Jesus, isn't it incredibly challenging to humble up and confess you had the wrong man? Of course, the answer to all these questions is a resounding *yes!* It's hard! It's really hard!

If possible, it would be advantageous to begin your pursuit of discovering Jesus without any pre-conceived ideas of who he was or what he was like. Your chances of finding the same Jesus that the apostles knew would dramatically improve if you had just arrived in the modern world after being rescued from a remote island where you had lived your entire life without the possibility of being brainwashed by any of the older generation's traditions and religious biases of the Bible. But since this better way of being in the know probably isn't feasible, you will need to do your best to forget the Jesus you've been introduced to so far, just in case he's not similar to the one you can read about in the Bible.

Quickly now, erase the tapes of *Jesus of Nazareth, The Greatest Story Ever Told, The Historic Jesus, The Last Temptation of Christ* and any other big screen portrayal of Christ you may have viewed in your life and record the four Gospels over them. (The recent presentation of *The Passion* would be an exception, but it only covers the last few hours in the life of Jesus) Forget the Sunday school lessons you were taught about Jesus for just a while and listen to the people who were actually there to hear his lessons first-hand. Or, at least gather your "Jesus" information from those who knew someone close to him. Allow them, and only them, to tell you the story. Deny and dismiss the Jesus you would personally like to create for your perfect world and let God show you the one who emerged from Mary's womb.

Since it appears first in your New Testament, let's start our search for Jesus with the Gospel of Matthew. What you will discover (among many things) as you read his account are three crucial elements concerning the life and times of Jesus Christ—the prophecies about him, the parables he told and the power he displayed.

The Prophecies

As a full-blooded Jew, it was Matthew whom God selected to convince his chosen people that Jesus was indeed the one who prophets of the Old Testament had pointed toward as the Messiah. As a tax collector, Matthew was trained to be meticulous with details. Now he would use that training to detail the crucial information that the Israelites would need to accept Jesus as the promised Messiah. As a greedy and often deceitful collector of revenue, no doubt he was highly efficient in taking full advantage of every opportunity made available to him to squeeze some extra cash out of a fellow-Israelite. Now, as an author, he would squeeze as much information as possible into his biography of Jesus.

Matthew's work was primarily concerned with proving to the Jews that they owed Jesus the honor of being called Messiah and Lord, and his writings were the means to confirm it. From the prophet Isaiah's specific predictions about a coming king for Israel (**Isaiah 9:6-7**) and the arrival to earth of *Immanuel, God with us* (**Isaiah 7:14**), to David's recorded despair of,

"My God, my God, why have you forsaken me?" in the book of Psalms that would later be repeated by a crucified Savior (**Psalm 22:1-2**), Matthew wove a masterpiece of undeniable truth giving every Jew the best possible chance to accept Jesus as the promised Messiah.

Was it a mere coincidence that Jesus was born in Bethlehem? Or, did Joseph and Mary go there unknowingly to register for a census at the exact time Jesus was to be delivered in order for the first of God's many flawless predictions about his Son to come true (**Micah 5:2**)?

What about those crazy first few months for Jesus and his parents, moving from Nazareth to Bethlehem, from Bethlehem to Egypt, from Egypt to Galilee, and finally from Galilee back to Nazareth? Did *"Out of Egypt I shall call my Son"* happen due to luck and chance? Was it all due to an even more worldly explanation—simply because Joseph just couldn't keep a job? Or, had God led the Israelites out of bondage in Egypt and into the Promise Land to foreshadow what he knew would be Jesus' return from Egypt to Israel 1500 years later?

What could adequately explain the directions and warnings Jesus gave to disciples and demons, telling them they were not to reveal his divine identity to anyone in the early stages of his ministry? Was this silent strategy a fear of the stage, or was it a setting of the stage for Isaiah's prophecy about the original outreach plans of Jesus to be fulfilled (**Isaiah 42:1-4**)?

When Jesus rode into Jerusalem on a donkey, announcing his right to the throne of Israel, was it just a desperate effort to arouse those on Messiah-watch to action? Or, was it an actual event that God had revealed to Zechariah nearly 400 years prior to the time of Jesus, revealing another specific occasion in the life of the king who would arrive to lead Israel (**Zechariah 9:9**)?

Was the overturning of the tables in the temple a last-ditch effort by Jesus to stir some of the Jewish zealots to action and follow him? Or, was it a sign that someone even greater than Jeremiah had arrived? Seven hundred years prior to Jesus' arrival, Jeremiah had stated that God was carefully watching his children's behavior. Could this "upsetting" event mean that God was actually there at the temple in person, not merely watching his people from a distance, but finally doing something in person to challenge their ongoing hypocrisy (**Jeremiah 7:1-13**)?

Were the thirty silver coins the Jewish ruling council paid to Judas for his betrayal of Jesus a mere coincidence? Or, was it another indication that Zechariah, though unaware at the time, was being led by God to help those in the future pinpoint the Messiah (**Zechariah 11:4-13**)? Could Jesus have cleverly manipulated this situation to make himself more believable?

And if the Jewish leaders wanted to prove once and for all that Jesus was a joke and not the Messiah he was claiming to be, why didn't they just make the betrayal price twenty-nine pieces of silver?

If Jesus only fulfilled a few of the prophecies on the Messiah then his skeptics could have easily concluded that those events were just a matter of luck. That was something hundreds of godly men and pagans alike had been able to "accidentally" accomplish throughout the centuries? But what if Jesus were able to match up with five, ten or perhaps one hundred prophecies? Matthew knew without a single doubt that Jesus was the fulfillment of Scripture and, moved by the Spirit of God, he wrote these prophecies down. He hoped, in doing so, that his fellow countrymen would one day willingly surrender to God's appointed Savior.

Perhaps the fulfilled prophecy about Jesus that brought the widest grin to Matthew's face as he penned its beautiful promise was the one found in **Isaiah 9:1-2**:

Land of Zebulun and land of Naphtali. The way to the sea along the Jordan, Galilee of the Gentiles—the people living in darkness have seen a great light; on those living in the land of the shadow of death a light has dawned.

This one was personal. Matthew, a Galilean himself, had been blind and living in darkness for as long as he could remember. Oh, he could see all right, but then again he couldn't. He couldn't see that his quest for money would leave him empty and always wanting more. He couldn't see that his deep desire for power and position would leave him with mostly shallow relationships. He couldn't foresee his constant travel companion named "guilty conscience" walking side-by-side with the earlier promise his boss had made to him about the very slim chance of ever getting caught if he ripped off a client. After all, he was assured by the ruling Romans that they didn't care how much he collected from his fellow Jews, just as long as they got theirs. And most of all, he couldn't see the pit he ended up falling into when he took his eyes off God and focused them instead on pleasing himself while seeking and acquiring the things of the world.

It was cold and dark in his tax collector's pit of despair. His was truly a life that was being lived in the shadow of death. But then there was light. Jesus came by his booth one day and it had never been brighter. Jesus was so different from anybody he had ever met. It was a strange interaction for Matthew, as he could sense that Jesus really wanted to talk to him. It was as though Jesus was actually interested in his life. But then again, he thought, maybe all this attention he was receiving was because Jesus didn't know what he had been doing the last few years of his life while he climbed the corporate ladder of collections. Surely Jesus couldn't be aware of the latest woman Matthew had dumped when she was no longer exciting and fresh. Obviously Jesus hadn't seen him at the local inns drowning his loneliness in expensive wines.

While Matthew raced on the world's fast-track leading to emptiness and despair, hope came speeding around the corner looking to cut him off and force him to stop before reaching the finish line. Maybe somebody finally cared about him. Maybe someone finally could look beneath the surface and see his pain. Maybe someone finally could see how much he hated his life but how he had no faith he could live it out any other way. Maybe. Just maybe.

Then hope put on its brakes, parked in front of the tax collector and made its way behind the booth and into Matthew's heart. Jesus tossed him the rope called grace and truth and Matthew couldn't believe what he was hearing.

"**Me**? You want **me**? You want me to work for **you**? You want me to work for you **now**?"

"You're **what**? You're **coming over**? You're coming over **now**? And you want **my friends** to join us? But, Jesus, my friends are the kind you probably…"

Before he could finish, Matthew caught himself. Then he willingly devoted the rest of his life to catching men. Matthew accepted the lucrative offer and praised God until his death that Jesus never asked for a re`sume` or references.

The Parables

No other Gospel contains as many parables as the Gospel of Matthew. And who better to be chosen to relay them to us than Matthew? No doubt he was a master storyteller himself. He had learned to tell many stories over the years that sounded so believable, such as why Mr. Rabin owed ten thousand dollars in taxes to Rome when it really was only eight. When fellow tax collectors gathered back at the office and recalled their latest revenue rip-offs, surely Matthew chimed in with his best deceiving of the day. He loved a good story, but none compared to the stories he heard flowing from the mouth of Jesus.

How could an ordinary man make dirt and dead seeds come alive and explain all mankind in two paragraphs (**Matthew 13:1-23**)?

How could someone take weeds and wheat and use them to explain judgment and the patience of God (**Matthew 13:24-30, 36-43**)?

Could any average Joe use illustrations of mustard seeds, yeast and fish and get you all excited about God using your life (**Matthew 13:31-35, 47-51**)?

There were the short stories Jesus told about lost sheep that brought tears to peoples' eyes (**Matthew 18:10-14**). Then he would speak a simple parable about an unmerciful servant, causing listeners to become so upset at first about the terrible wrongdoing of the forgiven servant, and so hum-bled by their own lack of forgive-ness for others only moments later (**Matthew 18:21-35**). And let's not forget the wonderful parable of the wedding banquet (**Matthew 22:1-14**). In just this one parable, Jesus taught tons about so many important topics—God's nature, God's patience, the joy of following him, God's anger, God's appeal, God's punishment and probably more than even Matthew himself realized. Who in history had ever cared so much about man and his eternal destiny that they would bring that much meat out of a wedding reception? He told chilling tales of talents, ten virgins and the trouble ahead for the goats, all to better prepare people for judgment day.

> *He told chilling tales of talents, ten virgins and the trouble ahead for the goats, all to better prepare people for judgment day.*

But perhaps Matthew's all-time favorite was the parable Jesus told of the two sons.

"What do you think? There was a man who had two sons. He went to the first and said, 'Son, go and work today in the vineyard.'

'I will not,' he answered, but later he changed his mind and went.

Then the father went to the other son and said the same thing. He answered, 'I will, sir,' but he did not go.

"Which of the two did what his father wanted?"

"The first," they answered.

Jesus said to them, "I tell you the truth, the tax collectors and the prostitutes are entering the kingdom ahead of you. For John came to you to show you the way of righteousness, and you did not believe him, but the tax collectors and the prostitutes did. And even after you saw this, you did not repent and believe him" (**Matthew 21:28-32**).

Consider the following event as a possible personal application Matthew could have made to this simple story told by Jesus.

For as long as Matthew could remember, he had been the first son, the son uninterested in working for God. He was the son most likely to drop out of school, do drugs and demolish his life. He was the son who would have to be threatened with the pain to end all pain before he would finally attend synagogue on Saturday morning, and even then he went with a scowl. He was the son who had been an embarrassment to his entire family ever since he accepted the position with the tax collection company on the sorry side of town. Everybody close to the family had been saying, "I told you so" and "We were hoping to be wrong" and "I think we all knew where he was headed."

Matthew was the one who never measured up to his family's expectations. He was the one who didn't bring home the report card to be framed and hung on the wall. He was the one who didn't manage to find much playing time in the important games. Matthew was the one who always seemed to be rebelling against authority and arrogantly going his own way. Everybody said it was the wrong way. And while many of his actions through the years were definitely due to selfishness, chalk a lot of it up to a refusal to live the life of a hypocrite. Matthew knew all along that his brother, the second son, was merely playing the game. Matthew knew about the bottle of wine under his brother's bed. He knew about his brother's desire to get on dad's good side and ride his coattails to success. Matthew never saw his brother pray alone in the room they shared, but he heard him pray often at the synagogue while many were watching. Not once had his brother apologized to him, but "I'm so sorry" regularly flowed in the direction of mom and dad. Matthew heard his brother memorizing Scriptures on love, but he never saw him come within one hundred yards of a beggar or a Gentile. Sure, Matthew loved his brother. He just didn't want to be like him.

But somehow Matthew, the son most likely to fail, made it first. He got in before his brother. It isn't that hard to believe that the parable could be a simple story about Matthew and his brother, one that applied to him and the many other ugly ducklings who were first to swim to the other side of the pond.

Maybe this parable had more than one meaning for Matthew and he ventured outside his immediate family to make it fit. Maybe this second son was a brother to him in regard to one of his religious relatives. Perhaps he was the valedictorian of his graduating class and a full-ride scholarship recipient to the top scribal school in the land, but one who found himself falling short in God's classroom. Maybe the brother to Matthew was a fellow businessman who was highly respected by his colleagues. He was the one who spent much of his time in successful money making ventures and attending lavish parties for the upper class, but he had yet to receive an invitation to the kingdom party Matthew was enjoying. Believe it or not, those second-son pre-season picks to win it all were still on the outside while many other first-son failures were inside for a change and loving every minute of it.

It was on the inside where Matthew knew he could be real and honest yet still gain acceptance. Inside he could hear what you will be, not what you haven't been. Inside he could ask all kinds of questions and none were considered stupid. Inside he could freely admit he didn't deserve to be there instead of always trying to prove he belonged.

Maybe Matthew gave Jesus the idea for the parable. Maybe Jesus decided to tell it in honor of Matthew's courageous decision to follow him. Even if it didn't have an exact application to Matthew and his life story, surely when he heard Jesus present it for the first time he must have felt a tremendous surge of godly pride about how fortunate he was to have been chosen to be a part of God's winning team after refusing to play for most of his life. When he heard Jesus tell the parable a second time, maybe he felt compelled to visit the "outwardly clean" in Israel and encourage them to get real about the rebellion living in their hearts. When he heard it again, did he decide to accept an invitation to the tax collector family reunion and share the interpretation of the parable with those who were still being duped by the deceitfulness of wealth? And when he wrote the parable down years later to be included in his Gospel, perhaps he took a copy to all of his yet-to-be-saved family and friends, letting them know that the offer of spiritual freedom was still on the table.

Matthew probably never forgot this parable. But more than that, he never forgot its story-teller who, on that most memorable day, happened upon his booth, believed in him and turned him from cheater to champion.

Matthew couldn't help but remember every one of Jesus' parables. Every time a new one was spoken, stronger conviction grew inside of him. It was the conviction so many others in the streets, on the hillsides, in their homes and on the shores shared along with him, that *"no one ever spoke like this man."*

The Power

If the prophecies and the parables still left readers in spiritual limbo, Matthew believed that his written recollection of Jesus' powerful display of miracles would help his people cross over to the Christ.

Matthew was an up-close observer of the supernatural. He wanted people to see with their hearts what he had seen with his eyes. He wanted readers to feel his jaw dropping when the leper went from crusty to crystal clear. He wanted them to feel his heart pounding as he saw the ghost approaching on the water, only to realize it was just Jesus coming for a middle-of-the-night, middle-of-the-sea stroll, skipping across the waves of the Sea of Galilee. He wanted his fellow disciples, and those still contemplating making Jesus their Lord, to picture him shaking his head in utter disbelief and scratching it in wonder while he watched Jesus work a meal-miracle on the hillside. He wanted to transfer his readers back to the time when he and his eleven closest friends delivered a never-ending supply of bread and fish to five thousand listeners without an oven or wagons regularly delivering fresh supplies. He wanted everyone to feel his insides tingle and see his goose pimples appear as he related the amazing story of how a simple touch of Jesus' hand enabled a young boy's heart to start beating again.

Matthew was there with Jesus to witness these and many others miracles. He remembered the stunned look on the deaf man's face as he heard his first words. He remembered the singing and dancing around the bonfire as former paralytics and cripples enthusiastically watched their obsolete mats, canes and crutches disintegrate in the flames. Their dreams of a job beyond begging and dancing before heaven had become reality thanks to the power of a man named Jesus.

And most of all, Matthew wanted his readers to feel the long gasp for breath he took the first moment he laid eyes on Jesus beyond the tomb.

But perhaps the greatest miracle of all was the miracle of Matthew's conversion and his radically changed life. Matthew's story documents the amazing transformation of a cold-hearted man determined to get rich at the expense of others, who became a soft hearted man determined to offer the riches of heaven at the expense of his own life. This amazing miracle of a changed heart moved a man from writing up false reports on people's taxes, to reporting truths of the Son of God. This was the miracle of a man who was transferred from a life of climbing the corporate ladder and walking on even his friends, to a life of lowering himself to serve the needy and allowing even his enemies to walk on him.

In Matthew's opinion, Jesus was so impressive. He was so different than any other religious leader he had ever known and so loving toward all who crossed his daily path. Matthew was quite confident that nobody then, or at anytime in the near or distant future, would ever be quite like Jesus. So Matthew gave his heart that day, and along with it, hope to all tax collectors, prostitutes and sinners (you and me) from that day forward by claiming the possibility that a miracle for them was only a moment away—the moment that Jesus would stop by their booth of sin and offer them employment elsewhere.

It's amazing to me that God would choose someone like Matthew, hated by many and for good reason, to relay the most important truths ever known to man. To put it in perspective, today that would be like God choosing a former high-ranking executive of Enron to go from business to business teaching CEOs and corporate board members the merits of honesty and integrity.

Matthew would be the one most likely to have an impact on the outsiders of today's world. The small groups of people that are shunned by the vast majority of their peers would likely welcome Matthew into their world and would be willing to open up to him more than others who might be trying to "save their souls." Matthew knew their world. It was the world of receiving dirty looks and hearing downright rude comments on a daily basis. It was the world of being stereotyped—past, present and future. It was the world of being unappreciated, unaccepted and unloved at home. It was the world of being forced into a fellowship survival mode and searching for approval and a sense of belonging from any individual or group, no matter how strange or set apart from the normal environment.

Matthew would have loved an opportunity to spend time with those caught up in the dark Goth culture and present the real Jesus to them. He would long for a few minutes alone with the inner city gang member who was never taught righteousness and honesty as a means of survival. He would spend time with the gang leader who never had a father, or the one who would have been better off without the one he had. He would try to get involved with the angry 15-year-old girl who just found out she was pregnant, the same girl who spent most of her nights alone at home and who never got a real shot at enjoying her youth. Matthew would proudly introduce all of these young men and women to the Jesus they never knew. He would look to join the chess club at school and meet a few nerds of the 21st century, those who were regularly persecuted for their clothing selection, visible pencils and pens and honor roll status. He would want a turn with the students sporting the bright, multi-colored hairdos, not to change their hairstyles but to change their perceptions of his friend Jesus. He would cherish an opportunity to talk with the multi-tattooed crowd and those with more body piercing than body parts, not to condemn and call them crazy but to tell them the story of Jesus, an outsider in his own right whose body piercing was the means to their salvation.

Matthew, the man with a big heart for the "rejects" of the world, told as much in his Gospel as God intended for him to tell. His primary focus centered on the prophecies, the parables and the power of the Son of God. True treasure was contained within his Gospel and available to be discovered by anyone willing to search, outsider or in. Thankfully, Matthew's masterpiece has been perfectly preserved for two thousand years so that everyone can grab hold of the most precious gem of all—Jesus and a personal relationship with him.

❧ Chapter Twelve ❦

Romans, Lend Me Your Ears
✦ ✦

The beginning of the gospel about Jesus Christ, the Son of God.
— Mark 1:1

While Matthew left a lasting impression on his conservative Jewish readers, Mark went in search of a different audience. First and foremost, Mark would focus his efforts on reaching those living in and around Rome, the commercial and political center of the first-century world.

What could impress these Romans? What information would be helpful to the Christians there to pass along in their efforts to bring family, neighbors, co-workers and strangers into a relationship with Jesus? What should he write down in his compact thesis on Jesus so the busy with loving the world Romans would get busy with loving the Lord? How could he get the minds of young men and women there away from the pursuit of a good education and onto the pursuit of a great eternity? How could Mark inspire the sexually promiscuous in Rome to pay more attention to the oracles of God than to the next orgy? What information could he possibly present to the star athlete and the confident soldier to convince them both that Jesus was the ultimate gladiator and his methods of fighting would lead to victory every single time? What could Mark tell the Roman businessman about Jesus to encourage him to pursue spirituality and not just a well-established and great-paying career? What could he share that could be more exciting to an entertainment-crazed Roman citizen than the latest theatrical presentation or championship chariot race at the Coliseum?

Mark wasn't overly concerned with the initial cold response to the truths of the Son of God on the part of many in the world capital. Despite most people's refusal to acknowledge the ultimate lordship of Jesus, hundreds of residents in Rome had already made the decision to confess Jesus as Lord. Yet millions still needed another opportunity and Mark was all about second chances. He had looked forward to doing something significant for

God's kingdom ever since he had been convinced of his usefulness by the apostle Paul despite a lapse in good judgment earlier in his life that had led to his departure from the mission field (**Acts 13:13, 15:36-38, 2 Timothy 4:11**). And why not target Rome. Nobody thought too much about the possibility of Rome being a place where the gospel message would spread like wildfire, especially in the midst of intense persecution that was being promoted by the various emperors who considered Christianity and its King a threat to their sovereign rule. But then again, nobody thought much of Mark's chances to make a great impact for God after his disappointing self-dismissal from a most important ministry responsibility. So the man who knew the power of an extra opportunity was inspired to take another shot at the stubborn Romans.

God gave Mark all the ammunition he would need for victory as he waged war on perhaps the most difficult stronghold to dismantle in Satan's domain, penning sixteen straightforward chapters about the life and times of Jesus Christ. He totally bypassed the details of Jesus' birth. He completely skipped over his unusual pre-teen temple scene. Mark didn't include anything about the life of Jesus until he turned thirty and started turning up the heat.

"*At once…*"

"*Without delay…*"

"*As soon as they left…*"

"*Very early in the morning…*"

These introductory words immediately captivated those in Rome who had been privileged to receive a copy of Mark's Gospel, or those who heard it being read for the first time after saying "Yes" to a disciple's invitation to a worship service. Jesus was a man on a mission. He had important business to take care of and nothing would keep him from it. He appeared to have other-world energy and the typically workaholic Roman wouldn't have it any other way. Most of those in Rome who heard these opening remarks or were reading about it on their own felt that Jesus was worthy of a fuller investigation and decided to pay close attention to the material that would follow.

"*Repent…*"

"*Be quiet…*"

"*Be clean…*"

"*See that you don't tell anyone…*"

Unbelievers in Rome would continue to be impressed with this ***supposed*** king. After all, he certainly didn't lack confidence. He didn't seem to be afraid to say what needed to be said and he didn't seem to care what

people thought about it afterwards. Jesus reminded them of Rome's powerful war generals of the past. These were the courageous men who had
paved the way for their luxurious lifestyles and the ones responsible to keep
watch for any uprising nation in revolt who might try to take it from them.
So they continued to closely monitor the man named Jesus.

"So many gathered…"

"A large crowd came to him…"

"Many tax collectors and sinners were eating with him…"

"A large crowd followed him…"

"Because of the crowd he told his disciples to have a small boat ready…"

Now it was getting exciting!

"Not only does this guy tell it like it is, but he fills the seats," they remarked.

*"He may just be a fascinating "traveling salvation show," but anybody who
can get crowds to come to him, and even better than that, to follow him, at the least
deserves my attendance at one of his performances."*

And few, if any, were bothered by the ***sinners eating*** with him revelation. The Romans were world renowned for both! Belief in Jesus was
quickly growing in the hearts of the men and women who were hearing
about this amazing man for the first time.

"He is out of his mind…"

"He is possessed by Beelzebub…"

"He has an evil spirit…"

"And they took offense at him…"

Mark's revelation of how Jesus encountered opposition in his efforts
to propagate his beliefs didn't seem to bother the Romans. They, too, had
crossed paths with their fair share of enemies and had remembered hearing very few words of encouragement or congratulatory remarks coming
from those on the outside. They dominated the world and the world didn't
like it. Rome had all the power and most of the other nations were power-
less to do anything about it. Rome had all the money so nobody else could
cash in on any opportunities. Rome had all the modern conveniences and
luxuries and other nations under their powerful rule were embittered about
being well past due on the promise made by the ruling body in the great city
to bring their behind-the-times cities up to speed. The Romans were well
aware of the jealousy and anger prevalent among the many nations who
had been assimilated into their regime. So Jesus' lack of popularity and
prestige with those inside of Israel did little to tempt these readers to quit
their investigation. If anything, it aroused their curiosity as to the power
this man possessed to stir it up the way he did. And, like any good story, it
kept them wondering about what would happen next.

"Then the wind died down and it was completely calm…"

"They saw the man who had been possessed by the legion of demons, sitting there, dressed and in his right mind…"

"Immediately her bleeding stopped…"

"Immediately the girl stood up and walked around…"

They weren't even a third of the way through the Gospel and thoughts of "I'm thoroughly impressed" were impressed on their minds. Most of those living in Rome loved to be regularly entertained and the magic and illusion shows were sold out on a regular basis. Those who attended these popular presentations of wizardry knew that the re-appearing rabbits and disappearing doves didn't really happen. But, they concluded, just having the ability to make it look so real and fascinating was a sign that the performer had special powers granted to him as a gift from one of the many gods worshipped there.

Yet no magician they were aware of had ever messed with altering weather patterns (**Mark 4:35-41**)! Women from the magic show's audiences had appeared to be sawed in two before, but no magician in his right mind had ever asked a mental patient to be a volunteer for one of his acts and then proceed to put him in his right mind (**Mark 5:1-20**). Handkerchiefs had mysteriously disappeared, but never internal bleeding or blindness (**Mark 5:25-34**). Master illusionists of the first century had been observed escaping from locks, handcuffs, ropes and chains, but never had anybody caught sight of a real corpse waking up and coming out of his coffin (**Mark 5:35-43**).

Much more of the same information on Jesus lie ahead. Much more would be uncovered about the determination and passion of Jesus. People would notice the same confidence, the same crowds, the same controversy and the same "come out of nowhere" miraculous abilities. Initially, these were the things about Jesus that made the biggest impression on those living in Rome.

Then they came to the end of the gospel story and it didn't make sense to most of them.

"Why would a man with all that passion become a pushover at the prime age of thirty three?"

"Why did someone with so much confidence to speak in the beginning become so silent in his final hours?"

"Why would someone who had the support of thousands not rally them to his side for his biggest battle?"

"Why should the negative remarks and controversy he calmly disregarded in the beginning get under his skin now and cause him to cower?"

"And where are the miracles? Start a storm, Jesus! Change the enemy's demeanor like you did with the demon! Lead them to the sea and out into its deepest waters, then walk away and taunt! For God's sake, Jesus, do something!"

It wasn't supposed to end this way. So they decided to go over it again, only this time they would listen more carefully or read through the Gospel just a little bit slower. Perhaps they missed something crucial the first time through.

"I'm going to forget the crowds, the miracles and everything else and instead look for signs in Jesus to make this ending make more sense."

Everyone who chose this course of action would later fill the pews in the Rome Christian Church. For most of them, their conversion to the belief that Jesus was their one and only king came as a result of the never-seen-before way he treated his fellow man. Like the Roman Christians did, let's take a look at the unique way Jesus treated the people he came in contact with on a day-by-day, hour-by-hour, minute-by-minute basis.

Uneducated, unrefined and unimpressive fishermen: These were the men who were typically treated with disdain by the educated crowd and considered by many to be important only for securing food on a family's table. But Jesus said to them, *"Come follow me, and I will make you fishers of men"* (**Mark 1:16-18**), looking to these ordinary types to take the lead in the greatest revolutionary movement in the history of mankind.

Diseased lepers: These outcasts were to be completely avoided, kept secluded from the "normal" population and considered, by many, to be akin to the animal world. When encountered by Jesus, however, they were touched and always treated with tremendous respect. *"Filled with compassion, Jesus reached out his hand and touched the man. 'I am willing,' he said. 'Be clean'"* (**Mark 1:40-42**).

Paralytics: These handicapped individuals were considered a bother, a burden and better off dead. But while they were in the presence of Jesus, he gave each of them his very best: *"When Jesus saw their faith, he said to the paralytic, 'Son, your sins are forgiven.'… "He (also) said to the paralytic, 'I tell you, get up, take your mat and go home'"* (**Mark 2:1-12**).

Tax collectors: These highly deceitful Jewish employees of the Roman government were hated, despised and avoided by the vast majority of Israelites. But Jesus offered them his full love and support and gave them equal time and attention: *"While Jesus was having dinner at Levi's house, many tax collectors and 'sinners' were eating with him and his disciples, for there were many who followed him"* (**Mark 2:15**).

A man with a shriveled hand: This individual was classified as a freak and rendered useless for service to his fellow man. But Jesus showed him his "ordinary" kindness: *"Stretch out your hand," he said. He stretched it out, and his hand was completely restored"* (**Mark 3:1-5**).

A man possessed by many demons: This frightening "semi-human being" was shunned by those in his hometown and deemed worthy only for solitary confinement. But Jesus approached him one day in the cemetery and unlocked his potential: *"What is your name?"... "Go home to your family and tell them how much the Lord has done for you, and how he has had mercy on you"* (**Mark 5:18-20**).

A woman suffering from bleeding for twelve years: This unfortunate woman was considered a sub species by most men and she would have been questioned by many as to her right for basic medical treatment. But Jesus set up an immediate appointment with her and gave her some special attention: *"He said to her, 'Daughter, your faith has healed you. Go in peace and be freed from your suffering'"* (**Mark 5:34**).

Those in a crowd who were hungry and heading home: This congregation of hungry humans would probably have been sent away with nothing but growling stomachs and simple "best of luck" wishes by most prominent speakers. But Jesus directed them to find a comfortable spot on the hillside grass and he quickly became their four-leaf clover: *"Then Jesus directed them to have all the people sit down in groups on the green grass. So they sat down in groups of hundreds and fifties. Taking the five loaves and two fish and looking up to heaven, he gave thanks and broke the loaves. Then he gave them to his disciples to set before the people. He also divided the two fish among them all. They all ate and were satisfied..."* (**Mark 6:35-43**).

A nagging but persistent Gentile woman: This woman would have absolutely annoyed most people to the point of anger and frustration. But Jesus politely said: *"For such a reply, you may go; the demon has left your daughter"* (**Mark 7:24-30**).

A high-ranking officer under his immediate leadership who had made a big mistake: Most men in positions of absolute authority would have responded to their subordinate's blunder by gracefully dancing around the real issues, afraid of losing a top official. But Jesus smashed the sin of sentimentality and rebuked his lead apostle: *"Get behind me, Satan. You do not have in mind the things of God, but the things of men"* (**Mark 8:31-33**).

A rich young man who could have provided him with complete and long-term financial support: Most candidates for office on a fund-raising mission would have cared very little, if any, about a donor's morals and character just as long as they were able to secure a much-needed donation from them. But Jesus declined the easy opportunity for cash and instead demanded change: *"One thing you lack. Go and sell everything you have and give to the poor, and you will have treasure in heaven. Then come, follow me"* (**Mark 10:17-22**).

Little children: Most adults considered these young people to be a nuisance and a hindrance from having better opportunities and sufficient time to be able to move ahead in life. But Jesus slowed down his fast and furious pace and gave the toddlers top priority: *"People were bringing little children to Jesus to have him touch them, but the disciples rebuked them. When Jesus saw this, he was indignant. He said to them, 'Let the little children come to me, for the kingdom of God belongs to such as these. I tell you the truth, anyone who will not receive the kingdom of God like a little child will never enter it.' And he took the children in his arms, puts his hands on them and blessed them"* (**Mark 10:13-16**).

Potential followers: Most religious recruiters would have over-looked any weaknesses in character or compromises in the heart and carefully looked for a better time to point them out. But Jesus met these blue-chip prospects and the condition of their hearts head-on: *"On reaching Jerusalem, Jesus entered the temple area and began driving out those who were buying and selling there. He overturned the tables of the moneychangers and the benches of those selling doves, and would not allow anyone to carry merchandise through the temple courts. And as he taught them, he said, 'Is it not written: My house will be called a house of prayer for all nations? But you have made it a 'den of robbers'"* (**Mark 11: 15-17**).

A widow offering two coins in the temple treasury: Most people in charge of financial affairs for the glorious temple would have said to the widow, "No thanks, we really only take paper." But Jesus acknowl-edged the offering and gave her the proper praise: *"I tell you the truth, this poor widow has put more into the treasury than all the others. They all gave out of their wealth; but she, out of her poverty, put in everything—all she had to live on"* (**Mark 12:41-44**).

Those who mocked him, spat upon him, cursed him and shouted out boldly in agreement of his crucifixion: Most who were being ridiculed or wrongly accused would have retaliated by unleashing a fury of foul language: But Jesus said nothing (**Mark 14:53-15:39**).

Sure, the teachings of Jesus were still impressive on their second trip through the Gospel. They were simple and sensible. They were common sense and clear. They didn't leave them with more questions than when they started, much like the teachings they had heard in the latest brand of philosophical jargon for sale in the local marketplace. They could see themselves not only believing the teachings of Jesus, but also doing them. But without a doubt, the clincher for most of these Romans had to be how

Jesus treated people. This was the truth that turned them from simply being aware of the story to becoming hard-line followers of the main character.

The competition wasn't even posing a challenge. The many pro-claimed gods of the Roman Empire all seemed to played favorites. There were gods for the poor, gods for the rich, gods for the educated and gods for the peasants. It seemed as though there was one brand of god available for every brand of Roman resident. Some gods claimed power over the sea. Others claimed power over the sun. There were animal gods, mountain gods, beach gods, love gods and sky gods. Why, if you couldn't find the god of your liking, you could invent one, create an idol of worship, sell it on the street corner and probably make a killing. But most of these gods were known to be all about exercising punishment options long before patience options.

"Tell me, what have any of these so-called gods done for the benefit of the people in Rome?" many began asking themselves.

*"Even more important, what have they ever done for **me**? And what has all this religion in Rome done to change the hearts of Roman citizens?"*

More questions began to surface in the minds of many readers.

"If our Roman god of love is for real, then why do so many of the married men who worship him get divorced when their wives gain weight?"

"Why are some of his followers not bothered in the least when they abandon their babies in a field and leave them to die just because they were born with a defect?"

"Why do I feel so full of hope on my way to the latest and greatest party, have the time of my life with a number of women, but afterwards I feel so empty and uninterested in any of them?"

"Why do I worship Caesar when I've known all along it was either birthright, big bucks or brawn that brought him to the throne?"

"Why are people so cold-hearted here? Why are women considered second rate? Why do the ones with the biggest bank accounts always get their way? Why are people who are born with physical flaws blamed for their womb adventure? Why is the divorce rate skyrocketing? Why are so many top prospects for empirical advancement drinking poison to end it all? Why? Why? Why?"

Then they remembered Jesus and their questions were answered.

*"We have all these problems because we're **very** interested in these gods, but these gods don't seem **very** interested in us."*

They concluded that their present gods had failed to teach them many ***things***. Things like the incredible value of every human being regardless of gender, generation or gross income. Things like showing sensitivity toward people and listening to them completely before laying things out completely. Things like considering where down-and-out residents had been in life before telling them where they needed to go in life. Things like equality and how Caesar is no better than his cook and a soldier is no more important than a schoolboy. Things like concern and how the weak need to be in our hearts and not in our institutions. Things like unselfishness and how your kids are more important than your career and the widow more important than your wages. Things like sacrifice and how glory is attained in giving up your rights more than in going to battle. Things like love and how the amount you give is not to be based on the amount you get. Things like heaven and how downsizing and simplicity really aren't bad ideas for now if it will help you to secure true treasure for later on.

When those in Rome were presented with the truths of Jesus in the Gospel of Mark, these were the ***things*** they noticed. They were seeing the true, one and only God for the first time. They were watching him in action. At the end of Mark's Gospel, they were informed of the amazing and unlikely conversion of one of their own. When they realized that a respected Roman centurion had come to understand the truth about Jesus while watching him die on a cross, they, too, were convinced—*"Surely this man was the Son of God"* (**Mark 15:37-39**).

Mark brought God and his message of Jesus to the city of Rome. Once again, God used someone we may not have picked for this highly important job. But God knew the impact that this man, acquainted with failure, would have upon his audience. If Mark were here today and telling people about Jesus, he would be the disciple most likely to look for those looking for a second chance. He would try to gain the qualifications necessary to teach a high school GED class and make his students feel like it was their first time. He would stand outside an abortion clinic and put his arm around the women who came out weeping. He would set up a meeting with the parole officer to find out which of the recently released prisoners would need some extra help to avoid a return visit. He would frequent the businesses of the owners he knew had taken out a second mortgage on their home to take a second and final shot at being their own boss. He would be found speaking at drug rehabilitation centers, hovering outside of divorce courts, appealing to a convicted drunk driver who had been involved in a fatal accident and talking to a death row inmate who had only a few days of life remaining.

If Mark were playing golf in your foursome, he'd be the one most likely to offer you another mulligan so you could break 90. If you missed the first question while a contestant on ***Who Wants to Be a Millionaire?***, you could probably count on getting a "That's okay" call from him. And he would have been thrilled with the 2004 Boston Red Sox World Series victory (wow, that was hard to type), a long-awaited title for one of the best-known losers in the baseball world.

Mark, a man who knew the meaning of a second chance, came to Rome with the amazing message of Jesus and his much-needed and much-welcomed announcement about a second chance. And third. And fourth. And—you fill in the rest!

This was the message of a most unusual leader and his most unusual method of conquering the world. It was a message of treating people right and giving people grace. Only one had ever been able to accomplish this daunting task and maintain this perfect standard throughout his entire life. So thousands in Rome discovered Jesus and concluded that he was Lord. For some, this came with a huge price. But even if a proclamation of "Jesus is Lord" at their baptism might mean that the following day would be their last, they would still follow him. If their final hours were to be spent in intense suffering on the Roman Coliseum floor while being devoured alive by hungry lions or starving dogs, they still believed that following Jesus was their only option. For to finally understand that they were loved, respected, valued, cherished and deemed important by their Creator, even for a mere twenty-four hours—that would be worth more to them than the many years they had lived in "I'm not important" ignorance.

❧ Chapter Thirteen ❧

Doctor, Doctor
Give Me the News
❧ ❧

Many have undertaken to draw up an account of the things that have been fulfilled among us, just as they were handed down to us by those who from the first were eyewitnesses and servants of the word. Therefore, since I myself have carefully investigated everything from the beginning, it seemed good also to me to write an orderly account for you, most excellent Theophilus, so that you may know the certainty of the things you have been taught.
— Luke 1:1-4

If you had lived in the first century and needed to hire a good private investigator, Luke, the author of this Gospel of Jesus, would have been a great option. He was always careful and orderly. If he were working on a case, he would have been certain about the level of importance for everything he set out to do. He was not one to waste valuable time and he would have made sure every piece of data he collected was destined to help him solve his ongoing investigation.

Whether Luke ever meddled in detective work is uncertain. We do know, however, that he worked in the medical field (**Colossians 4:14**), and if anyone were searching for a caring and trustworthy physician, they probably wouldn't have been disappointed in an appointment with him. Like any good doctor, Luke wanted to do whatever he could to make sure his patients had access to the greatest of care. He would take a second look. He would have a patient in his office the next day for a follow-up visit to see if his fever had broken. He would run the test for scurvy one more time just to make sure he hadn't missed anything or administered it incorrectly the time before.

More than likely, Luke had studied for years to pursue his dream of being a physician. He greatly valued physical life and wanted to do whatever he could to make people's time on earth as pain-free and pleasant as possible. Then he discovered Jesus. The Great Physician performed heart surgery on the general physician and Luke would never be the same. Oh, he still helped those who were physically harmed and hurting to heal. He still made his rounds and kept his office hours. But Luke had a greater purpose now. As he treated his patients, he no longer only cared that their physical pain would cease and comfort would follow. Now he also cared that they might become aware of the pain Jesus felt on a cross and realize that comfort could come from following him.

What an honor it must have been for Luke to be selected to communicate the Gospel of Jesus to the Gentile world. He had to be thrilled with the opportunity of gathering facts from those who were eyewitnesses to his majesty (**2 Peter 1:16-18**). He was familiar with some of the men and women who had followed Jesus throughout his days on earth, but now he looked forward to meeting more of them during his many days of intense research that would help to prepare him in writing his gospel account.

Certainly Luke set out to be more committed to this project than he had been to any project assigned to him during his days of training at medical school. He would look into this one life more closely than he had ever looked into the history of one of his patients to diagnose their problem. He could anticipate the skeptic's questions because they would probably be many of the same ones he posed to his teachers of the Christian faith. It was the Gentiles who Luke was primarily aimed at convincing. He knew the many "wisdom-seekers" in the Gentile world would need to be convinced through different means than the Jews had been. Most of the Jews who had become disciples did so, in large part, due to the many prophecies in their sacred Scriptures describing the Messiah that fit perfectly with Jesus. For the Gentiles, though, it had to go beyond that. They would need more than the prophecies, and more than just another promise of a better way of life for their future. They would need philosophical proof. Jesus had to make sense. His teachings would have to challenge them, but not be confusing. His messages would have to be meaty, but not too tough. His sermons would have to be interesting, but also intelligent. Most of Luke's Gentile readers would agree upon a clear philosophy of, *"We'll take it slow, but it better flow!"*

Most Gentiles who would read Luke's Gospel had studied in school at some point in their lives and some were probably still attending. He knew his readers would be constantly comparing and contrasting what they saw in Jesus with what they knew about the famous philosophers, both past and present. Whoever was reading Luke's account probably had a favorite philosopher or two and their all-important question for Luke was this—can this Jesus persuade me to believe that his wisdom is out of this world and far above anything I have ever, or will ever, study? Luke welcomed the challenge.

With these challenges in mind, and with the task before him of in-troducing Jesus to the Gentile world, the good doctor packed his bags and started on this gospel trip. He would travel throughout Israel and interview those who had come in contact with Jesus and his disciples. He knew others had already written of Jesus, but Luke had a new audience in mind. Or, more properly, God had a new audience in mind—Theophilus—***lover of God***.

Much has been written and debated concerning the exact identity of Theophilus. Many believe Theophilus was a reference to an individual in the Christian faith. Perhaps he was a top leader amongst the Gentile churches and he would be a key to helping thousands of new Gentile dis-ciples cling to their faith in spite of severe opposition. Or, he might have been a long-time disciple of Jesus who had recently begun to waver in his faith and commitment. Perhaps Theophilus was one of Luke's fellow phy-sicians, someone he had convinced to follow Jesus but who had recently become too humanistic in his medical practice and too casual in his pursuit of God. This gospel account could help to bring back the spiritual focus he would need to cling to his faith in the midst of all the worldly wisdom that surrounded him. Maybe Theophilus was a good friend of Luke's who had reached a plateau in his discipleship and was stuck in his faith. Luke's Gospel could be the glue remover. His words would be used to call his friend back to the original zeal and joy he displayed upon his decision to follow Jesus.

If Luke's investigative work and the writing that followed were sim-ply to move the heart of one man, he must have thought that writing this biography of Jesus was well worth all the time and trouble. He was sure the true and powerful message of Jesus wouldn't stop after that one individual had finished reading his Gospel. If this Theophilus captured the message and the heart of Jesus, he undoubtedly would pass it on to as many as pos-sible and the "Jesus-fire" would rapidly spread to those under his sphere of influence.

Luke probably envisioned the need, at some point in his near future, for many more copies of his Gospel to be transcribed. With his generous income from being a doctor, he could hire scribes to carefully create ad-ditional Gospel accounts. Luke would do everything within his power to get the word out. He firmly believed that his message of Jesus would find its way off the written page and into the heart of Theophilus, the lover of God. His convictions would then be strengthened and, as a result, he would help to bring abundant fruit to God from the Gentile world.

Others believe the term, Theophilus, refers to "lovers of God" in a general sense, or members of God's first-century church who would soon have access to this orderly account of Jesus. Certainly it would be a great help to any of the Gentile brethren who needed more hard facts about Jesus in order to help convince their non-trusting friends. Maybe a large number of disciples in the Gentile churches were discouraged or being persecuted. Perhaps they had been tempted to return to their empty, but much easier, philosophical ways and Luke felt compelled to take one last shot at help-ing them to stay put with Jesus. Whoever Theophilus was, God knew. God knew who would read Luke's Gospel first, second and third. God knew you would read it someday and, in a sense, that makes you Theophilus!

So what does Luke have to say about this most amazing man? What impressed this intellectual and well-respected man of his community about the one called Jesus? Why did his work as a doctor, the very thing he had dreamed of doing since he was a young boy, no longer occupy first place in his heart? Why were life-saving surgeries now considered just silver medals to Luke and serving Jesus was the gold?

Luke is the only Gospel writer who records the incident in the life of Jesus when he was twelve years of age, talking to the elders in the temple of Jerusalem (**Luke 2:41-52**). Did Luke strongly sense the need to include this information, knowing something about the people who would be reading his Gospel first? Did he anticipate his predominantly Gentile audience say-ing something like, *"Wait a minute, all the great teachers and philosophers we know about started their careers at an early age and were seen to be shoe-ins for a successful future. So when did Jesus get his start?"*

At the age when most boys were asking about girls, Jesus was asking about God. While most twelve year-olds were looking for the nearest game of kickball, Jesus was looking for the nearest teacher of the Torah to dis-cuss the most difficult Scriptural questions. While most adults in those days seemed bored and bothered by the immaturity and lack of understanding that a typical pre-teen displayed, Jesus' maturity and "wisdom beyond his years" were causing elders to shake their heads in disbelief.

"How did he know that?"

"We've never seen a college graduate quite that smart!"

"No, that's not totally accurate. We've never seen anybody quite that smart!"

"By the way, what's the minimum age for employment in the temple?"

God was growing up and it was obvious!

Now it was on to eliminating other possible hang-ups his audience might have. Similar to every other up-and-coming philosophy protégé, Jesus had also been announced. Somebody who was already well respected amongst his peers had both predicted and proclaimed the arrival of Jesus. Luke felt driven to record the ministry of John the Baptist to help eliminate the possible Gentile stumbling block of someone being considered "great" without excellent references and a few forerunners (**Luke 3:1-18**).

As Luke continued to be fed by the Spirit of God, he anticipated more tough questions from the Gentiles.

"Okay, but is he from good stock and can you show me proof?"

Luke was eager to share all about the family tree of the man from heaven.

"Have you ever heard of King David?" he replied (**Luke 3:31**).

Even the Gentiles liked David and admired his many accomplishments. He was a legend, not just to the Jews, but his military might and poetic psalms were world-renowned.

There were other names included in Jesus' family tree that would have impressed the Gentile reader, but with the mere mention of David, most of Luke's readers had more than enough information to satisfy their curiosity about the lineage of Jesus. For those who needed more, Luke wrote down specific names of Jesus' distant relatives all the way back to the very beginning of time. Anybody who doubted Luke's recorded genealogy of Jesus could have visited the Jewish temple in Jerusalem where official documents could supply positive proof.

Most Gentiles would continue reading Luke's Gospel beyond this point, but not without searching for more answers to their key questions.

"But was Jesus tough? Could he take a punch? He wasn't a pushover was he?"

Luke provided the answer: *"Jesus full of the Holy Spirit, returned from the Jordan and was led by the Spirit in the desert, where for forty days he was tempted by the devil. He ate nothing during those days, and at the end of them he was hungry"* (**Luke 4:1-13**).

*"But that's impossible, Luke. No **man** could live that long in the desert without food."*

And through the pen of Luke and the power of the Holy Spirit, God was moving the unbelieving Gentiles in the exact direction he had intended.

"So what kind of an orator was he? We've heard some pretty good ones in our day you know."

Again, Luke obliged: *"All spoke well of him and were amazed at the gracious words that came from his lips"* (**Luke 4:22**).

"You mean every last one of them? So, what you're saying is, he had no problem in the pulpit? Move along then! I'm still listening."

But more of their questions still needed to be answered.

"Now Luke, every great philosopher, both past and present, has had the ability to gather a substantial following. Some of them seem to spellbind their candidates. What about Jesus?"

Luke responded: *"Then Jesus said to Simon, 'Don't be afraid; from now on you will catch men.' So they pulled their boats up on shore, left everything and followed him"* (**Luke 5:1-11**).

*"You really mean they left **everything**? Okay, I'm still listening, but did all that attention get to him? You can always spot a true teacher from above by whether or not they get caught up in all the hysteria or whether they're able to escape and keep their lines of communication open with the gods. Sometimes we look for days before finding our favorites."*

Luke brought more needed information to those Gentiles needing more proof: *"Yet the news about him spread all the more, so that crowds of people came to hear him and to be healed of their sickness. But Jesus often withdrew to lonely places and prayed"* (**Luke 5:15-16**).

"But could he handle his critics?" future readers might ask. *"The best we've seen can keep on preaching even when the heckling starts."*

Luke put more of their doubts to death with the sword of the Spirit: *"Jesus knew what they (the Pharisees) were thinking and asked, 'Why are you thinking these things in your hearts? Which is easier: to say, 'Your sins are forgiven,' or to say, 'Get up and walk'? But that you may know that the Son of Man has authority on earth to forgive sins'… He said to the paralyzed man, 'I tell you, get up, take your mat and go home.' Immediately he stood up in front of them, took what he had been lying on and went home praising God. Everyone was amazed and gave praise to God. They were filled with awe and said, "We have seen remarkable things today"'* (**Luke 5:17-26**).

"So you're telling me that if I keep reading I'll see him silence his critics in more astounding ways? This I have to see!"

Seeds of faith had been planted in the Gentile hearts as they continued to read Luke's account of Jesus. And, as usual, Satan continued his tireless efforts to dig up and destroy every last one of them (**Luke 8:11-12**).

"Okay, but what about bringing big points to the little guy? You need to make this stuff simple and understandable even to those with the lowest IQ's."

Luke stood watch over the hopeful harvest and continued watering: *"Jesus answered them, "It is not the healthy who need a doctor, but the sick. I have not come to call the righteous, but sinners to repentance"* (**Luke 5:31**).

*"Hey, that's good! Luke, did you put that **doctor** stuff in there or did Jesus really say that? Okay, okay! Keep talking. I'm listening."*

Much progress was being made, but the task of showing off Jesus to the Gentile world was far from finished.

"Luke, I need to hear his eloquence. Give me some good poetic points. Let me hear the ebb and flow of this so-called Son of God."

Luke must have been thrilled to offer the following: *"Looking at his disciples, he said: 'Blessed are you who are poor, for yours is the kingdom of God.*

Blessed are you who hunger now, for you will be satisfied. Blessed are you who weep now, for you will laugh. Blessed are you when men hate you, when they exclude you and insult you and reject your name as evil, because of the Son of Man. Rejoice in that day and leap for joy, because great is your reward in heaven. For that is how their fathers treated the prophets. But woe to you who are rich, for you have already received your comfort. Woe to you who are well fed now, for you will go hungry. Woe to you who laugh now, for you will mourn and weep. Woe to you when all men speak well of you, for that is how their fathers treated the false prophets" (**Luke 6:20-26**).

"Could you do that again, Luke? I'm really beginning to like this guy!

The seed was now a growing plant, ready to make an appearance above the soil. Gentile truth seekers would continue reading Luke's Gospel and find more convincing proof that Jesus was in a class all by himself and that nobody else in history had even bothered to enroll.

What else about Jesus convinced the Gentiles to drop the philosophy gig and go to work for Jesus?

Maybe it was the "love your enemies" lingo or the blueprints for a "house built on the rock" (**Luke 6:27-49**).

Maybe it was Jesus' uncompromising willingness to accept any and all outcasts into his inner circle (**Luke 7:36-50**).

Maybe it was his bright-as-lightning transfiguration and the ensuing conversation he had with a couple of reputable dead men (**Luke 9:28-36**).

Maybe it was his hard-line expectations and his refusal to let people play by their own set of rules (**Luke 9:57-62**).

Maybe Jesus' moving account of the Good Samaritan tugged at the heartstrings of the social reformers who were reading Luke's Gospel account (**Luke 10:25-37**).

Maybe the close-to-home story about Martha's panic and paranoia gave the frantic housewife some much-needed conviction regarding her own obsessive behavior that kept distancing her from members of her family (**Luke 10:38-42**).

Maybe the "woes" Jesus warned people about in the middle of Luke's story made some Gentiles say "whoa" to their hypocritical behavior (**Luke 11:37-52**).

Maybe the many words Jesus spoke on the dangers of money and greed finally made sense to the rich but run-down business owner (**Luke 12:13-21**).

Maybe some of the Gentiles were convinced when they read about Jesus crying out to God rather than becoming bitter when large numbers of people refused to answer his call to discipleship (**Luke 19:41-44**).

Maybe a few Gentile farmers who truly loved their sheep finally opened up their hearts to spiritual truths when Jesus told his wooly parable (**Luke 15:3-7**).

Maybe a desperate teenage boy, one who had been recently separated from his father due to his own arrogance and a determination to prove he was responsible enough to be out on his own, stumbled upon a copy of Luke's Gospel. Perhaps, after reading the parable of the prodigal son, he gained his senses then gained the necessary confidence to take his first steps toward returning home (**Luke 15:11-24**).

Maybe it was the story of Lazarus and the rich man that softened the heart of a wealthy Gentile who always turned a deaf ear to the homeless beggar outside his mansion who was damaging his reputation. Perhaps after reading the story for the third or fourth time he finally admitted to himself that it had to be a message from God sent directly to him (**Luke 16:19-31**).

Could it have been the story of Zacchaeus that gave hope to both the "big shot" and the "little squirt" (**Luke 19:1-10**)?

Maybe, for some Gentile physicians and anatomy experts, it could have come from reading about the sweat on Jesus' brow that fell like drops of blood while he agonized in prayer in the garden of Gethsemane. Was it this exact moment in the life of Jesus that conveyed to them the intense struggle of a despondent man, but even more, the intense love he had for mankind that enable him to push through the awful ordeal (**Luke 22:39-44**)?

Was *"Father forgive them, they do not know what they are doing"* a wake-up call to the misguided zealot who had been attacking the name of Jesus (**Luke 23:32-34**)?

Did the amazing grace allotted to the thief on the cross prove that it wasn't too late for the person who had been told by everybody else that it was (**Luke 23:39-43**)?

Or, did the resurrection of Jesus convince the majority of the Gentile hold-outs? They knew the exact location where all the great philosophers, scientists and other highly respectable people had been laid to rest, and none of them had ever pushed up dirt or claimed to even try (**Luke 24:1-7**).

We may never know what segment of Luke's writings made the biggest impact on his individual audiences. But we can be confident that his vivid portrayal of Jesus was a highly effective tool in the evangelization of the Gentile world. Luke used a powerful combination of his worldly skills and his love for Jesus to astound the intellectuals of the first century.

If Luke were to make a 21st century appearance and share his thoughts on Jesus, college professors might be on his list of people to approach and he might even enroll in a few classes just to have additional opportunities to introduce them to Jesus. He'd probably fare well leading a Bible study with a group of medical students and resident physicians, helping them to deal righteously with their maddening schedules and humbly in regard to their future wealth and positions of vast importance. He would set up some time to share his insights at a meeting for members of a high school's honor society. He would look for opportunities to discuss truth with Nobel Prize winners, Fortune 500 CEOs, Ivy League graduates and members of Congress. It wouldn't be surprising to find him at a presidential debate, in a corporate board meeting of a top theological seminary, in a library's research section, at Border's reading a book and looking for a fellow bookworm to strike up a conversation with, or just watching Jeopardy with a few friends to have a little fun and engage in a battle of the brains when it comes to useless knowledge. Whoever ended up crossing Luke's path would get a terrific opportunity to be introduced to the greatest man who ever lived.

Many of the Gentiles in the first century saw Jesus from Luke's perspective and they finally understood the vast supremacy of his life compared to all others. Keep your eyes on Jesus and you'll understand it, too.

🌿 Chapter Fourteen 🌿

Bonus Coverage
From a Best Friend
✍ ✍

This is the disciple who testifies to these things and who wrote them down.
We know that his testimony is true.
—John 21:24

John's Gospel account of Jesus might just as well have been entitled, *The Inside Edition.* Of the four Gospel writers, it appears from Scripture that John knew Jesus better than the other three. He was there in a gloom-filled bedroom with fellow apostles Peter and James and watched Jesus revive a dead girl without CPR (**Mark 5:35-43**). John stood on the mount of transfiguration with those same men and overheard the amazing conversation Jesus had with two men who had been dead for hundreds of years, then listened carefully as God told him to listen to the one who had been alive forever (**Mark 9:2-8**). There were undoubtedly many other times when that small group of disciples received special teaching and training from Jesus. More than likely, John also had a number of one-on-one encounters with Jesus. From the Gospel accounts, it seems as though John was the only one of the twelve apostles who actually witnessed some, if not all, of the crucifixion. Some believe, because of some of the language found in this fourth Gospel, that Jesus and John were best of friends. Whatever the relationship was in comparison to the other eleven apostles, one thing was obvious—John felt loved by Jesus (**John 13:23, 21:7, 21:20**).

He felt loved when he wanted to unfairly exclude others from the group but, amazingly, Jesus refused to exclude him (**Luke 9:49-50**).

John felt loved when his idea of aiming some lightning directly at the stubborn Samaritans wasn't followed up by a bolt to his backside (**Luke 9:51-56**).

He felt loved especially when he wasn't forced to take a demotion after selfishly asking for a special seat next to Jesus (**Mark 10:35-45**).

Maybe it was the foot washing he received from Jesus that ultimately cleaned out his heart (**John 13:1-17**).

Maybe John realized how much he was loved when Jesus, while dying in pain on the cross, met his personal and most pressing needs by requesting that his mother, Mary, continue in that important role with him (**John 19:25-27**).

Maybe the love he felt reached its apex when John first realized his sin was being painfully fastened to his best friend, the one who had never let him down or treated him unfairly (**John 19:17-30**).

Whatever it was that thrust John securely across the Jesus-is-Lord line, all the possible options come out magnificently in ink through twenty-one chapters in his Gospel. Like all those chosen to tell the story of Jesus, it must have been an unbelievable honor for John to write about him. Surely he couldn't wait to show off his friend. John welcomed the opportunity to go toe-to-toe with the Gnostic troublemakers and reveal the Jesus of the earth and the Jesus of eternity. After all, he had spent three unbelievable years with the man. He had touched him, talked with him and taken trips with him. Jesus wasn't a ghost or a figment of his imagination and John jumped at the chance to make Jesus real and relatable. He also looked forward to silencing the "he wasn't anything special" critics by recounting those startling revelations of *"I and the Father are one"* and *"If you've seen me, you've seen the Father"* and *"Before Abraham was born, I am."* He relished the opportunity to provide even the newest of Christians with an effective tool for teaching. His Gospel would be a dagger for the sword-less, an absolute for the maybes and an "it's in the bank" for those afraid to make a deposit.

Little did John know that his recollections of Jesus would contain the most popular passage in the entire Bible during the twentieth century— *"For God so loved the world that he gave his one and only Son, that whoever believes in him shall not perish but have eternal life"* (**John 3:16**).

Little did he know that his simple observation of a man in love with people would become the shortest verse in the entire Bible, *"Jesus wept"* (**John 11:35**).

Without John, we wouldn't have known how Jesus embraced the social scene as we watch his willingness to not only attend a wedding but help with the drinks (**John 2:1-11**).

Without John's Gospel, we never would have met Nicodemus and been briefed on being born again, all the while contrasting the wealth of wisdom Jesus possessed compared to a respected Jewish leader (**John 3: 1-21**).

We never would have known the woman at the well and understood how Jesus could turn a simple "I'm thirsty" request into a sensational "I'm the Messiah" revelation. We wouldn't have been able to marvel at Jesus sailing smoothly past the many prejudices of his day, caring more about the sinful Samaritan woman's soul than the status quo (**John 4:4-27**).

We wouldn't have witnessed the healing of an invalid and a later discussion with him in the temple, proving that Jesus cared more about clearing up the big picture than healing the body (**John 5:1-15**).

Without John's Gospel, we would never have discovered the absolute best method of crowd control in the recounting of a narrow escape made by a woman who had been caught in the act of adultery—*"If any of you is without sin, let him be the first to throw a stone at her"* (**John 8:2-11**).

Thanks to John, we get a detailed account of a blind man receiving sight and find out Jesus is a friend and not just a faith healer (**John 9:1-38**).

We see the ever-popular Psalm 23 become flesh as John records the mission of Jesus, reminding us all that God was not misrepresenting himself to David a thousand years before his physical arrival on earth. *"I am the good shepherd. The good shepherd lays down his life for the sheep"* (**John 10:1-18**).

In this fourth and final Gospel, we watch Lazarus being called back from Paradise and called out of his tomb by the power of Jesus, accomplished even after Lazarus' body had lain completely lifeless for four days. The real tears of Jesus and the real resurrection of Lazarus show us both man and God, totally together, totally one in Jesus (**John 11:1-44**).

Throughout the Gospel of John, we see God doing in Jesus what he had been doing for thousands of years, only this time in the flesh—cleaning up the dirt mankind had accumulated in his walk through life. *"After that he poured water into a basin and began to wash his disciples' feet, drying them with the towel that was wrapped around him."*

No anger. No accusations. No attitudes. Just a bowl of water, a towel and a message saying, "There's nothing I won't do for you" (**John 13:1-5**). God was doing his absolute best (as always) through John's Gospel to attract as many people as possible to Jesus–the Revealer.

To the faithful Jew who looked forward to the yearly Passover celebration like many of us look forward to Christmas, Jesus was the Lamb of God (**John 1:29**).

To those whose lives were basic and bland, Jesus changed water into wine and encouraged people to start living again (**John 2:1-11**).

To the Israelite man who hated hypocrisy and was ready to abandon any call to follow his nation's current religious leadership, Jesus cleared the temple and cleared the way for him to stick around until the right leadership could be installed (**John 2:13-17**).

To sinful and emotionally scarred women, those who were often seen as inferior to the good and regular crowd, Jesus conversed for a long while with a five-time divorcee who was currently shacking up with her hopeful sixth, giving them hope that, if they could find one of his disciples, they might just find some dignity as well (**John 4:4-27**).

To all the half-breeds of the known world who were looked upon as half-human, Jesus converted a large quantity of despised Samaritans in the town of Sychar and convinced them that who their mom and dad were had nothing to do with their value in God's eyes (**John 4:39-42**).

To the baker who found pride in knowing his job was helping to keep people alive and satisfied, Jesus was the Bread of Life who could do the same for him (**John 6:35-40**).

To those who lived with the guilt of adultery but hadn't been discovered in their sin, Jesus forgave the adulterous woman and gave them courage to come forward without the risk of rocks nearby (**John 8:2-11**).

To any parent or child who had lived for the longest time with unwarranted guilt about a birth defect, Jesus put out a warrant for the Accuser's arrest by proclaiming, *"Neither this man nor his parents sinned, but this happened so that the work of God might be displayed in his life"* (**John 9:1-5**).

To hardworking shepherds, who for years had guided their flocks to greener pastures with an uncompromising care and commitment, Jesus was the Good Shepherd who painted for them a poignant picture of a God who loved his creation and who would commit his life to protecting them from their enemy (**John 10:1-18**).

To the emotional male who had often been told to get tough and get a grip, Jesus wept and freed him from the guilt he had carried for years thinking that he was too effeminate and an insult to the male species (**John 11:33-36**).

To the gardener overlooking his vineyard who knew that his fortune and his future were in the vine, Jesus was the true vine offering him a life of true riches from that moment on, and even greater rewards in the life to come (**John 15:1-8**).

To the young woman who had been abused and discarded by her parents, still somehow convinced that she was the biggest cause, Jesus revealed, *"They hated me without reason,"* giving her courage to silence the suicide demons who had been attacking her for years (**John 15:18-25**).

To those who thought trouble in life meant being in trouble with God, Jesus said, *"In this world you will have trouble,"* and in one short sentence rescued them from their make-believe doghouses and welcomed them into the house of God (**John 16:33**).

To those who had displayed too many moments of sinful and embarrassing rage, discouraging them from having any hope of ever removing a bad reputation, Jesus stuck with Peter after he stuck it to Malchus' ear, encouraging them to make amends and move on in life (**John 18:10-11**).

Of the four Gospel writers, John was the one who would have been most likely to make an impact on the common man, the blue-collar worker and the good ole' boy. As a fisherman by trade, he knew all about working weird shifts, putting in a hard day's work, long hours with little pay, on the job injuries and the feeling of being disrespected by the educated crowd. If John were making his appeal today, he would find great pleasure in studying the Bible with the intellectual crowd, but he would feel most comfortable opening up the Good Book with those he could relate to the most. He would travel to the coasts and look to land a job with an offshore fishing company for a few months of fishing and catching men. He would have no problem finding employment with a construction company. He would win the respect of the other bridge builders by his hard work and helping hand, thus building a bridge for them to come to Christ. He would sympathize with the janitor working the swing shift and help him to come up with a plan to find enough fellowship to help reverse the trend of his weakening faith. He would hop on board with a long distance truck driver and help him deal with family management and purity struggles. He would be one of the first in the church to spot favoritism toward the upper class and those of higher education. Then he would preach a sermon to make sure the garbage collector and the grocery store stocker knew that God was equally proud of them. John would do for people now what he did in the first century—make sure everyone came away with the right impression of Jesus.

> *He knew there was so much more to tell about Jesus, but where would he stop? How many more books could he have published?*

John had so much to say about his best friend and his Savior. He could have carried on in writing his Gospel, but what he recorded was more than enough. He knew there was so much more to tell about Jesus, but where would he stop? How many more books could he have published? How many libraries would have to be built if he told everything of his time with Jesus? So God said stop. If John's readers couldn't comprehend that Jesus was undeniably unique from these twenty-one chapters, would anything else convince them? If the teaching, the miracles, the impact and the love displayed by Jesus didn't convince readers of this Gospel that the Word had become flesh, what could? If doubters and unbelievers didn't agree with Thomas' assessment of Jesus, "My Lord and My God", after they had taken the time to read John's Gospel, would they ever agree?

There wasn't a need for more information. John recorded just the right amount of miracles. He displayed in Jesus just the right amount of love. There was a perfect record of his teachings for potential students. There was just enough information to make it obvious that Jesus wasn't just another messenger of God, but that God himself had done what no man thought could ever be possible—he had made a personal visit to the planet in the person of Jesus Christ.

John showed us it was possible. Matthew, Mark and Luke gave us essentially the same message about Jesus, only their accounts were originally directed at different audiences. Praise God we have all four. Put them all together and this is the conclusion—none of us can say that we haven't had an incredible opportunity to see the one and only God Almighty in human form. Jesus Christ—all God and all man, and all we need for this life and the life to come.

❧ Chapter Fifteen ❧

The Arrival
❧ ❧

*While they were there, the time came for the baby to be born, and she gave
birth to her firstborn, a son. She wrapped him in cloths and placed him in
a manger, because there was no room for them in the inn.*
— Luke 2:6-7

It all started in a stable. That busy night in Bethlehem when "No
Vacancy" signs hung everywhere, in a delivery room full of dust and hay a
godly young woman brought forth a baby boy destined to be king.

The unpleasant stench of manure lingered throughout the barn as
most of the farm animals had been herded into the stable's warmer and
safer quarters for the night. Tired from their journey to Bethlehem in order
to comply with Roman requirements for a census, and exhausted from
staying up through the night to bring their firstborn into the world, Joseph
and Mary still found the energy to praise the God who had heralded this
unusual birth, expressing gratitude for the roof over their heads and the
safe birth of their son.

No immediate relatives were nearby to offer congratulations and
compare the newborn's facial features to that of mom and dad. No nurses
or doctor made their regular rounds to ensure that mother and child were
both doing fine. It was simply mom and dad, some donkeys, horses and
cows, the occasional mice that scurried across the dirt floor and an infant
who had been gently wrapped in swaddling clothes and placed in a spare
feeding trough found in the barn's rafters.

The makeshift outer garments kept the baby king plenty warm and
Mary's milk and tender touch kept him satisfied through most of the night.
And though trumpets weren't sounded in recognition of his safe arrival and
most of the world remained completely clueless about the miraculous coming, God had finished his personal nine-month project in Mary's womb and
was now ready to enact the plan that had been drawn up for all eternity.

"In the beginning was the Word. And the Word was with God. And the Word was God" (**John 1:1-2**).

"And the Word became flesh and made his dwelling place among us" (**John 1:14**).

Can you believe it? God came to live on the planet he created and his first place of residence was a rickety old barn. His first roommates were animals. His first smell was that of donkey dung. His first crib was a trough. His first visitors were shepherds from a nearby field. It's not the most likely of beginnings for the King of Kings. Unless, of course, you already knew how later on as an adult, and in the religious spotlight, this king would have absolutely no desire for the better life or the best things. Jesus embraced simplicity from breath one and hugged it tightly for thirty-three years. He expected nothing and gave everything (**Philippians 2:5-8**). He had nowhere to lay his head as an adult, so why start now as a baby (**Luke 9:58**). And why shouldn't some lowly shepherds be the first to see God's arrival? It was merely a sign of things to come. Most of the religious leaders at the time of Jesus' birth arrogantly concluded that the shepherds, those low-life, dead-end field observers as they were often described, weren't fit for lofty matters. Sure enough, Jesus would grow up to associate with tax collectors, prostitutes, drunks and other sinners, the same sorry souls the religious leaders of his day would deem useless and unfit for spiritual matters. Thirty years after his birth, those same outcasts were the low-life, dead-end losers who Jesus loved to spend time with and save on a regular basis (**Matthew 9:9-11**). And why shouldn't a humble manger accommodate the king for his first night's sleep? It would be two simple pieces of wood that Jesus would be fastened to on his final day. And why shouldn't he be surrounded by the stench of manure? He would physically depart from the world with the harsh odor of man's spiritual refuse all around him as he bore every human's most hideous deeds while dying on a cross (**2 Corinthians 5:21**).

After the birth of Jesus, Bethlehem became a city with a constant buzz for a number of days. The shepherds, usually shy and wanting to keep mostly to themselves and their sheep, had stirred the city with what they termed angelic adrenaline, convincing hundreds of Bethlehem's residents to go and take a peek at the little one. People would come to a small room at a local inn a few blocks away from the stable where Jesus was born. Joseph and Mary had rented out the room, finally finding an opening after a large portion of the out-of-town census crowd left for home. It was a palace compared to those first few days of parenthood in the barn, and Mary always had bread and water ready for the curious visitors who happened by.

"So, are you sure that's how you got pregnant?" many were asking.

"So, do you think your son really is the Messiah?"

"When do you suppose you'll move to Jerusalem to start his training?"

"Could you tell us again exactly what Simeon and Anna said about Jesus? Were they really sure" (**Luke 2:25-38**)?

"Wait a minute! Could it be the shepherds had a few too many, or perhaps they were just dreaming about the angel choir" (**Luke 2:8-18**)?

The baby-born-to-be-king novelty died down after a short while and people in Bethlehem went back to their regular lives. Back to their normal every day existence and back to their superficial, religious ways. Back to their sin and shallow relationships. Back to everything the baby they had been visiting would promise to release them from when it came time for him to preach.

The young family settled in Bethlehem and Joseph found carpentry work with one of his father's former co-workers who had recently moved to the small town about 50 miles southwest of Nazareth. About a year later, the young family was back on the front page of the Bethlehem Gazette.

"*Caravan of Eastern Magi Arrive,*" was the headline.

It wasn't often that wise men from distant nations entered their town. Nobody could really even remember the last time it had happened. But they were in the city now for some reason and saying something strange about an unusually bright star—and that this child they were visiting would grow up to be a star. So once again, Jesus became a controversial figure—and he's wasn't even two years old. But that's not surprising when you consider that's all Jesus would ever be. And didn't Simeon say this would be so?

This child is destined to cause the falling and rising of many in Israel, and to be a sign that will be spoken against, so that the thoughts of many hearts will be revealed (**Luke 2:34-35**).

Jesus was still learning to utter his first words, couldn't even form a whole sentence yet, and people were already arguing about him. But that's not surprising either since, whether Jesus spoke or remained silent as an adult, controversy followed him everywhere.

Then life took a sudden and dramatic turn for the young married couple. After Joseph went to sleep one night, God went to work on Joseph revealing specific plans about a different location for him and his family to take up residence (**Matthew 2:13-15**). Upon awakening from his dream, Joseph and Mary immediately began laying out plans to turn the dream into reality. But how were they going to manage the move to a neighboring country with no money saved and living on such a small income? Yet they had to go. Joseph's dream had been so abundantly clear and the message he heard was a matter of life or death.

Get up, take the child and his mother and escape to Egypt. Stay there until I tell you, for Herod is going to search for the child to kill him (**Matthew 2:13**).

Staying in Bethlehem wasn't an option that Joseph and Mary considered. They had always honored God's word despite any difficult implications, and it would be no different with this current challenge.

Then the idea was mentioned. Neither of them could decide whether or not the proposal was appropriate. The items weren't really even theirs, but unless they sold them they could see no other way to afford the move to Egypt. After a few more minutes of wrestling in prayer about the wisdom of the plan, they reasoned that God had allowed the magi's recent visit, in part, to fund their upcoming journey.

So they did it. In the middle of the night they knocked on the door of the synagogue leader's house and boldly requested of him to buy the gold, frankincense and myrrh left by the magi as gifts for their son. They couldn't risk the chance of not finding an interested buyer along the way, and they needed some immediate funds for the first few days of their travel. Sensing the couple's panic and resolve to leave Bethlehem immediately, he offered a purchase price that Mary and Joseph knew wasn't fair, but they really had no choice. There was no time to waste and the money from the sale was still a sufficient amount to make it to Egypt and plenty extra for the first few months to pay for food and rent while Joseph searched for permanent carpentry work.

Joseph and Mary left for Egypt that night with a pit in their stomach after a few sad farewells to the families they had grown close to in their nearly two years of living in Bethlehem. Little did they realize that the little boys Jesus played with would be brutally murdered within a few weeks when Herod would unleash his ferocious wrath in the streets of Bethlehem looking to kill his competition. Jesus would narrowly escape the massacre. But this shouldn't be surprising either when you consider how often Jesus, in his three years of public ministry, escaped at just the right time from those looking to end his life (**Luke 4:28-30, John 7:30**).

Now exiled, and like their ancestors, stuck in Egypt, Joseph and Mary waited for the moment they could take their family to familiar turf. Another deep sleep produced the plan.

Get up, take the child and his mother and go to the land of Israel, for those who were trying to take the child's life are dead (**Matthew 2:19-20**).

One more dream and Joseph and Mary were finally back in Nazareth (**Matthew 2:21-23**). So much had happened in those few years away from their hometown—the census; the trip from Nazareth to Bethlehem;

the stable; the birth of Jesus; the shepherds; the excitement; the wonder; the worry; the gossip; the magi; the dreams; the escape; the wait and the return. If all of this had happened in a span of approximately three years, what additional excitement and drama could they expect from this point on? But that's not surprising, either, since Jesus would live a more intense and exciting last three years of his life than anyone else in the history of the world.

Nazareth hadn't changed much. The old buildings on the corners that should have been torn down by now were still standing. Unemployment was still soaring. Prostitution was rampant and fewer and fewer people were attending the synagogue. Not many had moved to Nazareth since their departure but a few of the local businessmen had managed to take their bright futures to neighboring towns. The sinful behavior of the Nazarenes was still severe and gossip and slander lingered close to the top of the list.

"Guess who's back?"

"They can run but they can't hide!"

"When will they just admit the truth about their pre-nuptial no-no? He looks just like his father."

"Hey, Nazareth's reputation is bad enough without this family being added to the rolls."

"Did you hear about all that stuff they said happened in Bethlehem? But you know what they say? If they lie to you once, they'll lie to you a million times."

There he was, a pre-school lad and people are already saying awful things about him and his family. Jesus was only three and his reputation was already being smeared. But as God sees it, something of great importance is beginning to happen to his Son at an early age. Before he is three years old, Jesus is being taught the value of family. He's being groomed to focus on what his Father thinks, not what people think. As a child, he's beginning to be trained in the wisdom of listening to the voice of God, not his feelings. At this early age, he's only a few years away from experiencing the harmful effects of slander and sarcasm that will rapidly spread in his school and around the entire town. And he will soon learn how the public's misinformation concerning his personal life and their mean-spirited campaign to keep on proclaiming it will make him feel horrible on the inside.

While still in need of daily naps, Jesus is nearing the time when he will learn the value of a few true friends. As a small child, his parents will teach him about turning the other cheek and he will begin to learn the daunting challenge of loving his enemies. He will begin to be taught about how to patiently deal with people's doubts, and he will begin to understand exactly how it feels to endure disappointment and discouragement.

As one who was only recently potty-trained and still on the far left side of the being polite learning curve, Jesus was beginning to learn how to be the Sympathizer of our individual weaknesses (**Hebrews 2:17, 4:15**) and the Savior of the entire world.

Yes, God had put Jesus in just the right family. Jesus would grow up just like you and me, and Joseph and Mary would bear the responsibility of guiding him every step of the way. A carpenter who made a living on hammer and nails and an absolutely pure young woman who was deemed a whore were selected for his earthly arrival. But that's not surprising either, since false accusations and a hammer and nails were also selected for his departure.

❧ Chapter Sixteen ❦

From Three to Thirty
❧ ❦

And the child grew and became strong; he was filled with wisdom,
and the grace of God was upon him.
— Luke 2:40

Then he went down to Nazareth with them and was obedient to them…And
Jesus grew in wisdom and stature, and in favor with God and men.
— Luke 2:51-52

Due to the limited amount of information found in the Scriptures that documents the activity of Jesus from age three to thirty, most of us rarely consider some very important moments or situations that could have occurred in the life of Jesus. In my opinion, this is an unfortunate oversight, robbing us of a way to see Jesus that could draw us closer to him, giving us a better understanding and appreciation that his upbringing was probably a lot like ours. Granted, the following material is only based upon **probable** occurrences in his life, not **actual**. But see if you don't agree—any or all of these events could have been valuable lessons in God's training and instruction manual, designed to help the young boy Jesus grow up in the ways of God and then go on to become the most incredible man to ever live. And if they're true, each of them could also help us to better understand the incredibly beautiful mystery that seems so difficult to grasp and accept—that, while Jesus will never deny he's our boss, he'd rather be remembered as our big brother (**Hebrews 2:10-12**).

We're aware of one event in the life of Jesus during these years that took place when he was twelve. Luke relates the story of a typical pre-teen boy spending a not-so-typical amount of time in the sacred temple in Jerusalem. We'll touch on that episode later on in the chapter, but first let's imagine for a few pages what might have been for Jesus from three to thirty.

Let's make him as real as we possibly can. Let's see if some of the mundane, but most necessary, ingredients in growing up could have made a major impact on him and, eventually, an impact on you and me. Let's look at more than a quarter of a century of ordinary and see how it could have helped in preparing Jesus for three years of extraordinary. Here are some questions I have about these times.

Do you think Jesus ever got spanked? Did Joseph and Mary ever experience the terrible twos with their firstborn son? Did Jesus ever hear the ever-famous, "This is sure going to hurt me much more than it's going to hurt you," from either of his parents? Did he ever have to write 100 times, "I will do my chores without being reminded?"

Did Jesus attend school like most other kids his age? If so, did he have much homework? Was he always able to finish his assignments in the classroom or did daydreaming get the best of him on occasion? Did Mary ever call out to him and catch him off-guard during a time with his buddies in the backyard: *"Jesus, have you finished your history worksheet yet?"*

Did Jesus ever hear his mother make any of these important reminders?

"Jesus, eat your vegetables. You want to grow up big and strong don't you?"

Did mom's healthy hint become his habit as an adult, giving him the necessary physical stamina to make his many climbs up the mountain for all-night prayer (**Luke 6:12**)?

"Now Jesus, what do you say to the nice lady?"

Maybe he remembered to honor his mother's admonition when the widow left her mite in the offering plate and nobody else thought such a measly amount was worthy of even a "thank-you" (**Luke 21:1-4**).

"Jesus, are you still up? You need to go to sleep right now!"

Was this the early training for a disciplined life that later allowed Jesus to rise before the sun and spend quality time with God before the rest of the world rolled out of bed (**Mark 1:35**)?

"Jesus, you need to be a big boy and take your medicine, son. I know it doesn't taste good, but you won't get better unless you do."

Did the strategy that worked on him as a child continue to work on him as an adult while he agonized in the garden of Gethsemane, and later when nails were hammered into his flesh and onto the wood of the cross (**Matthew 26:36-46, 27:31-35**)?

"Now Jesus, be very careful. Make sure you look both ways before crossing the busy street and don't talk to any strangers."

Did this early and excellent life-saving advice serve Jesus well as an adult as he constantly stayed one step ahead of those looking to trap him with his words or kill him before his time (**John 7:1-9**)?

*"Jesus, remember what your father said! Whenever **anybody** comes over to the house you need to get up and give them a hug."*

Did a leper, twenty years later, receive the loving touch of Jesus as a result of the solid teaching he received at home (**Mark 1:40-42**)? Did tax collectors and prostitutes get a good welcome from him in his later years simply because God had programmed him to do it before the beginning of time? Or, was it more because God had placed Joseph and Mary as Jesus' earthly overseers to teach him about unconditional love (**Matthew 9:9-12**)?

"Son, always remember you're stronger if you walk away than you are if you fight."

Did this valuable piece of parental advice form the key element of his first recorded sermon and did it help him to possess the toughest and reddest cheeks ever known to man? *"Do not resist an evil person. If someone strikes you on the right cheek, turn to him the other also"* (**Matthew 5:39**).

What other childhood and growing-up experiences could have contributed to his training to become our advocate and role model (**1 John 2: 1-2, Hebrews 4:15**)?

How often did he get to say grace at the dinner table and how did Joseph and Mary teach him to take it deeper than a legalistic offering of thanks? When did he realize the Provider was much more important than the provision?

Did he get an allowance and, if so, did he tithe it or give it all?

What did he do for fun with the neighbor kids? Did they play together with plastic farm animals and, if so, did Jesus always have the most fun when he had the white horse?

When playing a first-century version of Red Rover-Red Rover, did he secretly let the other kids break through his portion of the wall of locked arms to illustrate what would occur one day when his outstretched arms would be the breakthrough to victory in the game of life?

Did he ever play follow the leader? When he was picked to lead, did he only act out things he knew the other participants could also accomplish because that's how he would be one day as their Lord? Did he love to play the game mostly as a follower so he could learn the feeling of facing obstacles with courage?

Did Jesus and his childhood friends enjoy playing anything similar to our version of Cowboys and Indians? Maybe it was called Jews and Samaritans. Did he insist on being the Samaritan to feel what it was like to be targeted and mistreated for no apparent reason? Or, did he refuse to play the game altogether because he hated to take sides?

Did he ever stay up late with his friends or family playing a first-century version of Risk? Did he change the wording of the game's ultimate goal from take over the world to save the world (**Matthew 28:18-20**)?

Did he love stuffed animals like most children do? Perhaps his personal favorites were the lion and the lamb. Did he ever pretend they were fighting and each time the lamb would come out on top (**1 Peter 5:8**)?

Did he ever paint a picture of a tree or draw the sky in a coloring book and have a moment of de`javu (**Colossians 1:16**)?

Did he ever perform in a school play? Did he get the lead for *King David* or was he not striking enough in appearance or believable enough when delivering his lines (**Isaiah 53:2**)?

What was his life like at home with all his siblings? We do know that four little brothers and at least two little sisters were a part of his upbringing (**Mark 6:3**). When did he first gain enough trust from his parents to baby-sit for them so they could get away for a needed date? Maybe the many opportunities to keep his six siblings from warlike behavior prepared him for similar moments of "break-it-up" with the twelve (**Matthew 20:20-28**).

How much did his brothers and sisters struggle with jealousy and envy when they heard their parents share about Jesus' exciting beginning and his destiny for future success? Did they ever believe in Jesus as more than a big brother before his death (**John 7:1-5**)?

How much interaction through the early years did Jesus have with his cousin, John the Baptist? Did they ever challenge one another in Bible Jeopardy? Did they ever argue over who was the most radical? Did they take turns preaching and afterwards offer each other input?

Did Joseph and Mary ever take Jesus on a trip to rediscover his roots? Did they go back to Bethlehem and walk through the stable on occasion? Did Jesus ever get to meet the shepherds who witnessed his first hours of life? Did they take time to mourn at the cemetery built for all the children who died as a result of the massacre they missed (**Matthew 2:16-18**)? Did they reconstruct the hurried trip to Egypt to show Jesus how God had protected them along the way?

When Jesus studied the history of Babylon in school, when did it occur to him that he had been there? Did the lesson about Shadrach, Meshach and Abednego bring a smile to his face while the class debated the identity of the fourth individual who fellowshipped in the fire with the non-flammable boys (**Daniel 3:19-25**)?

Did Jesus play sports? Was he on any athletic teams? If so, and the weather was bad for one of his games, did he ever calm the storm and dry the field without anyone knowing about it so the show could go on? Perhaps he was the team manager or water boy. No doubt he would gladly carry the equipment since later he would gladly carry his cross.

What kind of student was Jesus? Did he get straight A's? Did he ever get a B due to a teacher's pride and unwillingness to accept the fact that one of his students had more information than him? Did he ever know what the test questions would be before they were written?

Did a girl ever pass him a love note in class? If so, what did he say to her when class was done? How did Jesus keep his hormones in check? Did he ever go on dates just to keep the rarely-asked-out-girls encouraged?

Did he get teased or picked on at school? Did the bullies ever gang up to get him? Did he experience at school what he would one day encounter with the Sanhedrin (**Matthew 26:57-68**)?

What did Jesus do when he saw others being picked on at school or in the neighborhood? Did he ever befriend a labeled loser at his locker, much like he did the woman at the well (**John 4:4-26**)? Did he ever decide to eat lunch with the homely looking boy who had just moved into the school district because all the other students were mocking him? Did the reminder of that boy's beaming face stick with Jesus throughout his life and inspire him to take a shot at spending the day with Zacchaeus (**Luke 19: 1-10**)? Did Jesus take the risk of being ridiculed for his association with the tax collector, remembering the complete change which took take place in a young boy's heart when love and acceptance met him at the lunch table?

Did Jesus have perfect attendance or were there sick days for the Son of God? Did he have pimples or crooked teeth? Did he have big ears or a high forehead? What kind of childhood accidents did he get into? Did he ever break a bone jumping out of a tree? We know there were none broken later in his life when he was on the tree, but what about during the many days that came before (**John 19:31-37**)?

Did he ever have to be shaken to wake up from a deep night's sleep? Did he have a curfew? Were the local police ever called when Jesus didn't come home for dinner and was still a no-show at bedtime? Did they finally find him on a mountaintop in the middle of the night and feel the need to give him a few sobriety tests (**Luke 6:12**)?

Did Jesus have a savings account? Could he have anticipated the difficult days ahead and saved it for a rainy three years?

If there were tough times at home when there was little food on the table, did he ever remember the nearby location of any gold he created, go get it, then go buy a few groceries for the family? Was there ever a secret bread and fish miracle that led to an unexpected special-delivery by Jesus to some poorer families in the country?

Were there other silent miracles he performed to bring comfort to people before he went public with them?

Did he ever walk on water when no one was watching just to have some fun with board-less surfing?

What was his favorite color? Perhaps it was a tie between blue and green since those were the two he used the most in the creation. Or, maybe it was dark red because it was the only color that mattered when it came to salvation. Or, maybe he refused to have a favorite one, knowing man would way too easily get hung up on things like color.

How many times did he go to Jerusalem for the regular Jewish feasts? How many Passover lambs were slain in his presence before he realized he would be the final one?

Did he ever take a job as a fisherman just to make himself more relatable to the four men who would choose to follow him first (**Mark 1: 14-20**)? What other odd jobs did he have, if any, besides carpentry? Could he have spent a few years as the first honest tax collector to teach Matthew that it really was possible?

When Jesus attended funerals, was he tempted to show off too soon?

When he watched a wedding, did he feel saddened he would never get to say, "I do?" Did he have to hear some of the following words in regard to his extended term of single living?

"Jesus, when are you planning to tie the knot?"

"Jesus, everyone in your family is hitched but you."

"Why Jesus, I know the nicest girl…"

When did he start helping his dad in the carpentry shop? While sweeping up the wood shaves, did he see it as an opportunity to rejoice as he anticipated sweeping away the sins of the many millions who would one day follow him? When his hammer would strike a nail, would he ever shake or shiver?

Did he help with the business side of the board business? How much work did he and his father do that was never paid for? Did he begin to understand in his teens from those who took unfair advantage of a job well done what many would do to him after he completed the finest work ever accomplished?

At what point in his life did people his age begin to dismiss the negative remarks their parents had voiced about that fellow classmate of theirs? Did any of those parents start seeing the light before he announced he was the Light?

When did Jesus himself discover who he was? Did he grow into it or was there an earlier transfiguration settling it once and for all?

Was the event recorded in **Luke 2:41-50** a sign he already knew what others much older than him would take years to figure out? Or, was that episode in the temple merely a single thread in the tapestry of a young man slowly but surely coming into his own?

It's fun to conjecture about these things and more, but only one thing is for sure—Jesus was simply amazing from three to thirty. He was, at the very least, submissive and obedient to his parents, and that speaks volumes, whether today or two thousand years ago (**Luke 2:51-52**).

I hope you enjoyed your time on the paths of perhaps and probably. But remember, they are only that. If there were more crucial pieces of information on Jesus, God would have told us tons about the toddler, the ten-year-old, the teen and the man in his twenties. But all we have is a few days when he was twelve and we'll have to be satisfied with that. Because for Jesus, life really began at thirty!

✺ Chapter Seventeen ✺

No One
Ever Spoke Like This
ↄ ↄ

*When Jesus had finished saying these things, the crowds
were amazed at his teaching, because he taught as one who
had authority, and not as their teachers of the law.*
— Matthew 7:28-29

Whether he was delivering words of encouragement to a group of
ten, teaching a parable to a medium-size gathering of a hundred, announcing a call to discipleship to a thousand curious observers or proclaiming a
"You're either with me or against me, count-the-cost" sermon to a crowd
of ten thousand, Jesus made an eternal impact on listener's hearts like no
other teacher before. His words were often poetic but always powerful. The
messages brought forth from his lips were pure and precise. And one thing
quickly became predictable when he preached—that his words would not
be predictable! Sermon after sermon, listener after listener left shaking
their head in disbelief, wondering exactly what it was they had just heard.

"Did he say what I thought he said?"

*"I didn't think you could say **that** in a sermon!"*

"I had no idea he was heading in that direction when he started."

"He's not messing around, is he?"

Even those who hated what Jesus was saying, or refused to accept
it as binding, knew his message and method of delivery were not common or customary compared to others who claimed to channel truth
from above. The messages given by Jesus were straightforward and always
delivered with a seriousness that religious audiences had seldom, if ever,
witnessed. He spoke with great authority, as if to say, "All of you need to
be taking careful notes and carefully taking this to heart." Jesus spoke in a
much different way than most Israelites had been accustomed to hearing
throughout their religious lives. Sure, they had heard lesson after lesson
Saturday after Saturday in their synagogues, but much of it was diluted
with tradition. Most of them couldn't remember the last time any religious

speaker had ever held them accountable to upholding any of the ideals presented in the lessons they taught. The Jews had listened to many expositors declare "I think" but had heard very few with the guts to say "I know." They were familiar with "You should" but unacquainted with "You must." They were regularly being soothed with "Relax!" yet rarely being spurred to "Repent!" Then along came Jesus!

The Sermon on the Mount, the first recorded words of Jesus to a listening audience, contains the essence of Jesus—who he was, how he lived, what he taught and what he expected from his followers. Similar to every sermon Jesus preached, he displayed an eagerness to make sure his listeners were clear about his standards. He didn't want anyone claiming to be his follower who had little or no idea about what he taught. If Jesus were to preach at your church next Sunday, he would express the exact same concern. Two thousand years ago it happened and the temptation is just as powerful today—to call yourself a Christian and claim allegiance to Jesus, all while having very little idea, if any, about what he taught.

While many people have never been familiar with Jesus' teachings, others have had access to his message at one time or another but, over time, they've forgotten much of it. Some have heard the wrong message to begin with and need it replayed for clarity. Some who have heard his message have filtered it to fit their lifestyles. And there are some people who know it all, but don't want to do it all. Where are you when it comes to the teachings of Jesus? Wherever you may find yourself at this very moment, it will be good for you to consider once again the sermon that shook the foundations of the first-century religious world.

Most of those who came to hear Jesus that day brought some extremely heavy baggage with them. People had their religious suitcases filled with tradition, family theology, "But it's always been this way" and "But my rabbi told me." Their bags were closed and securely locked, hugged tightly next to their chests. Jesus didn't ask anybody to check their bags with him when they entered, but he would expect them to be left behind when they exited.

The problem wasn't that those in the audience hadn't heard enough teaching. They had heard way too much—too much of the wrong teaching and too much teaching with too little context. Simply put, there was too much talk of the day and not enough truth of the hour. So their suitcases were stuffed. Many had been sitting on theirs for years just to get them to stay closed.

So what did Jesus say that day that led to such a rousing response from those who heard him for the first time (**Matthew 7:28-29**)? What message did he deliver that caused listeners to wish they had taken the time to inscribe every last word of it on stone? What did Jesus say to bring him from nowhere to be seen in the race of history's greatest heralds to being out in the lead by a full lap?

"Blessed are the poor in spirit, for theirs is the kingdom of heaven. Blessed are those who mourn, for they will be comforted. Blessed are the meek, for they will inherit the earth. Blessed are those who hunger and thirst for righteousness, for they will be filled. Blessed are the merciful, for they will be shown mercy. Blessed are those who are pure in heart, for they will see God. Blessed are the peacemakers, for they will be called sons of God. Blessed are those who are persecuted because of righteousness, for theirs is the kingdom of heaven. Blessed are you when people insult you, persecute you and falsely say all kinds of evil against you because of me. Rejoice and be glad, because great is your reward in heaven, for in the same way they persecuted the prophets who were before you" (**Matthew 5:3-12**).

In baseball terminology, this would be recorded as a leadoff home-run. In football, it's an 80-yard bomb for a touchdown on the first play from scrimmage. Jesus did what almost every other preacher of the day was unwilling to do—he told people to take their eyes off their problems, to quit wallowing in self-pity and to look to God instead of the world to reward them for faithful living. They had often heard just the opposite.

"I'm so sorry to hear about how hard it's been for you lately. You really deserve so much better than that."

"If you want anything out of life, you must fight fire with fire!"

"Don't be such a pushover. Stand up for your rights and let your voice be heard."

"You have every reason in the world to be mad. Why, I'm mad about that, too."

Jesus expected his listeners to spiritually discern their difficulties in life and look above, beyond and away from the here and now. He challenged his audience to move beyond their present problems and to faithfully consider what God was working out on their behalf at the present time and, more importantly, how it would help them in their quest for eternal life. Any message that commands people to quit fighting for the things of this world and, in addition, calls them to patiently endure mistreatment while trusting God to work everything out in the end, is a message from God. Any message that directs people to quit focusing on all the negatives which **can** happen in their life and, instead, start focusing on all the positives that **are** happening in their life, is a message from another realm. Any message that challenges listeners to find perspective instead of finding themselves must have come from someone who had seen the other side and knew that heaven would be the great equalizer. It was a message from someone who was privy to thousands of years of overwhelming proof that God, indeed, could and would cause all things to work together for the good for any believer who would simply choose to stay the course and continue doing what was right (**Romans 8:28**).

Jesus' opening remarks were about possessing the right attitudes. Be humble. Be softhearted. Be gentle. Be godly. Be merciful. Be pure. Be peaceful. Be patient. Be positive. Be faithful. Be happy. These opening lines launched an all-out attack on the spiritual forces of evil. Jesus came with an amazing message of peace that would shake the foundations of the world when applied in any century or setting. Whether it was Gandhi trying to gain independence for the people of India or Martin Luther King Jr. trying to teach a nation the evils of racism, if someone taught it "The Jesus Way," they were moving in the right direction. If they lived out "The Jesus Way," they had arrived!

"You are the salt of the earth. But if the salt loses its saltiness, how can it be made salty again? It is no longer good for anything, except to be thrown out and trampled by men. You are the light of the world. A city cannot be hidden. Neither do people light a lamp and put it under a bowl. Instead they put it on its stand, and it gives light to everyone in the house. In the same way, let your light shine before men, that they may see your good deeds and praise your Father in heaven" (**Matthew 5:13-16**).

Jesus never intended for his message to stand still. His plan was to teach it to some, let those who accepted it put it into practice, then expect those doers of the word to live it out in the presence of others to convince everybody that his teachings were not only right, but workable. Jesus never preached a sermon just to preach a sermon. He expected it to be heard, then followed. He refused to allow his listeners to feel good about merely attending and complimenting him on the wonderful way he communicated God to the people. His message was always, "Hear it, believe it, do it, show it and teach it."

It's a real tendency for religious people (church-goers like you and me) to have higher expectations of others than they do of themselves when it comes to obeying truth. And it is quite easy for them (us) to feel really good and pat themselves on the back just because they came to church and sat through a sermon, even though being obedient to the message they heard isn't a top priority (**James 1:22-25**). Unfortunately, many ministers, due to their fear of stepping on toes and stopping their members from dropping their weekly donation in the offering plate, are inclined to say little or nothing about this sinful practice, thus allowing their listeners to maintain a hypocritical mindset. Not Jesus. His message was from God and hearing it without obeying it did not sit well with him! It wasn't enough to Jesus that people knew his messages were salt. He fully expected his followers to tip themselves upside down and start shaking. It wasn't enough to Jesus that people knew his messages were light. He challenged everyone in his audience to turn on their spiritual flashlights and start walking.

Today, his expectations are still the same. If in the Scriptures you hear Jesus present a truth concerning your marriage, you first need to take it to heart and live it out in your partner's presence, pouring your saltiness on your spouse. If your children are married, they'll need to be sprinkled by your obedient example as well. If the couple across the street opens their door for friendship, it shouldn't be long before they see your "just like you started dating yesterday" joy and then see the need for adding some zip to their mediocre marriage. Soon you'll be invited to pour out your salty life on them.

If Jesus reveals a truth involving the proper attitude to carry into the workplace, you'll be expected to grab your spiritual flashlight every morning before heading off to another busy day in the dark crevasses of capitalism. If your boss is harsh and hardheaded, you'll need to do all you're asked to do with a smile on your face, all the while shining your flashlight in his. If fellow workers are bad-mouthing the new shift manager and look to you for agreement, you can bypass the bashing with sounds of silence, stop the slander with a stern warning to the critics or just quietly walk away and pray for wisdom and strength to be the brightest light possible. With every clocking-in on time, light is present. With every "Not a problem sir," the light shines brighter. With every contented prayer of thanksgiving for a monthly paycheck, the light becomes blinding. Every "Good morning," every "Have a great rest of the day" and every "Can I get you some coffee?" brings extra light into the hallways and nearby offices.

If Jesus proclaims the plan of God concerning the correct way to live on your campus, in your neighborhood or in regard to your dating partner, he expects you to take it from the pew to the public arena. On your way out, you'll be presented with a full saltshaker and fresh batteries for your flashlight. If you come back to hear more of his message and somehow feel like you really don't need a refill of salt or a recharge of your battery, more than likely you didn't invest much in practical application and you're probably better suited for the preaching of a philosopher or Pharisee, but not for the Son of God.

"For I tell you that unless your righteousness surpasses that of the Pharisees and the teachers of the law, you will certainly not enter the kingdom of heaven" (**Matthew 5:20**).

"But I tell you that anyone who is angry with his brother will be subject to judgment" (**Matthew 5:22**).

"But I tell you that anyone who looks at a woman lustfully has already committed adultery with her in his heart" (**Matthew 5:28**).

"But I tell you that anyone who divorces his wife, except for marital unfaithfulness, causes her to become an adulteress, and anyone who marries the divorced woman commits adultery" (**Matthew 5:32**).

"But I tell you, do not swear at all..." (**Matthew 5:34**).

"But I tell you, do not resist an evil person. If someone strikes you on the right cheek, turn to him the other also. And if someone wants to sue you and take your tunic, let him have your cloak as well" (**Matthew 5:39-40**).

"But I tell you, love your enemies and pray for those who persecute you, that you may be sons of your Father in heaven" (**Matthew 5:44**).

Throughout the years, a number of teachers had taught many of those sitting in Jesus' audience some seemingly spiritual lessons. Yet, most of his listeners that day had only heard about a lower form of righteousness. In the few decades prior to the arrival of Jesus, the spiritual bar had been set so low that almost anybody could rise above it. It was simple. Don't strike the first blow. Don't get in bed with the wrong woman. Don't forget the certificate when you cancel your wedding vows. Don't feel bad about paybacks because revenge is only fair. And best of all, if people are your friends, they get lots of love and if they are not, you let them have it. Then along came Jesus to schedule everyone for a spiritual MRI and expose the inner heart. It hadn't occurred to people that anger kills, too. It hadn't entered enough parents' minds that their children completely cowered and changed their view of God when they didn't control their temper while disciplining them. And very few men were open to the idea that their once vibrant and radiant wives had become victims of murder, slowly but surely killed by their bullets of harshness and insensitivity, shot to death by the one man they were supposed to count on the most for understanding and protection.

Most people had never considered lust to be a law-breaker. After all, it wasn't mentioned in the Ten Commandments, except for a brief reference to coveting your neighbor's wife! So the thought of undressing someone in the mind for a momentary rush of sensuality had never been thought of as degrading. Nobody really bothered taking the time to consider that what was underneath a woman's clothing was intended for one man behind closed doors. Did any of them bother to think that the women they stared down felt put down? Did any of them consider how unchecked lust eventually leads to unchecked morals? Did any of them bother to theorize that, if they could learn to control their lust, immoral acts such as prostitution and adultery might become things of the past? Did any of the married men and women realize that giving their heart in lust to another individual during the day often meant withholding love and passion from their spouse later that night?

So because Jesus cared about people, he spoke out against lust. He knew the immense value of every human being and refused to allow any of that value to be diminished. He couldn't stomach the thought of a woman feeling more like an object of sex than a special creation of God. He knew every human body he had created was to be admired and touched in a sexual context only by the one individual in marriage who had vowed to forsake all others.

Divorce, in the minds of most religious people in the first century, was thought to be a perfectly acceptable alternative to an unhappy marriage (**Matthew 5:31**). The popular philosophy of the day was simple and expedient: *"Just as long as everything is legal, everything will be lovely. Moses made the law so that must make it right!"*

Jesus refused to accept these sub-par standards and raised the bar on marriage by reintroducing the garden variety, explaining how God had designed it from the beginning (**Matthew 5:32**). God had always intended for marriage to last a lifetime, but in that day any excuse to move on to the next mate was deemed legitimate. If you didn't like the way your wife performed in bed, you could get yourself a good lawyer and before long get back to the dating scene. If she didn't show you the respect you thought you so richly deserved, your fellow man would gladly respect your decision to dismiss her from her wifely duties. If her cooking was questionable and dinners were medium and not "well-done" as you had ordered, you could cancel any future dinner reservations at home and go in search of the culinary kind. If your spouse became debilitated and couldn't do the work of a wife, you could quickly work up a plan to put her out of your plans and into an institution. No wonder Jesus was disgusted with the current trend. And, like a lot of other trends and patterns, he changed them. What did Jesus see clearly that others refused to even glance at? What did he know about man so deeply that indicated he had become so shallow?

Jesus knew man was fickle. He was certain that as soon as a man found a suitable replacement for his first wife, a flaw would be uncovered in wife number two. What would he do with his second spouse when his new pet peeve about her started driving him crazy? Would he drive her away, too?

Jesus knew man was selfish. Did the husband who was fed up with his wife's character and convinced that divorce was his best option ever consider offering help to his wife in her area of weakness? Did he ever stop long enough to think that maybe something he had done, or was currently doing, was contributing to her latest episode of disrespect? Did he understand that, while his wife was definitely not Barbie, he was a far cry from Ken?

Jesus knew man was faithless. Did prayer ever become a part of that husband's plan to salvage the dying marriage? Couldn't God glue together whatever was growing apart? Couldn't God lead them to meet a happily married couple down the street that could offer them some trade secrets?

Jesus knew man was way too focused on the here and now. Did that husband, who so desperately wanted out of the marriage, ever consider the hours of loneliness he would face after the divorce became final? Was he willing to arouse any compassion in regard to the severe downward slide of self-esteem his ex would experience after the split, and that her regular thoughts of being better off dead could lead to an early departure from the life God had planned for her? Did he attempt to understand the pain and guilt that his children would carry with them after the divorce, or the pain that would persist through their growing-up years and right on into their own marriages?

Jesus knew man didn't fear God and he anticipated some bold attempts by everyone to justify their sin.

"God won't have a problem with it. After all, he divorced Israel didn't he? Of all people, he certainly will sympathize with my situation."

"Even if it is wrong, God is a God of grace. We all have our individual weaknesses, you know. Mine just happens to be I'm pretty picky about who I have to live with."

Jesus knew man's heart was inclined to become hardened. He stated this as the reason for the flexibility factor in getting a divorce, offered to man under the leadership of Moses and the guidance of the Law. Jesus was there to announce that those days were finished and that it was time to go back to the beginning and back to the basics—no adultery, no divorce! Jesus spoke in his era what no one else had the courage to communicate and, in doing so, re-established marriage as the relationship God spends the most time viewing in his moment-by-moment observations of the human race.

Then it was on to the subject of getting even and biting back. Jesus turned some heads when he sounded off on turning the other cheek and handing over your coat to the one who had already ripped off your robe (**Matthew 5:38-42**).

Jesus really roused the enemy when he laid out the expectation of loving your enemy. He was never interested in what anyone could do naturally but what they were willing to accomplish with God in all that didn't come naturally (**Matthew 5:43**). He really riled up his religious audience when he dared to put the pious Jew in the same category as the pagan tax collector (**Matthew 5:46**). And he had the fortitude to challenge his audience to add their greatest foe to their daily prayer list (**Matthew 5:44**).

> *"So when you give to the needy…"* (**Matthew 6:2-4**).
> *"And when you pray…"* (**Matthew 6:5-15**).
> *"When you fast…"* (**Matthew 6:16-18**).

Jesus saw the need in this sermon to remove any and all confusion coming from the popular idea that being religious was equal to being right. For Jesus, that idea was clearly wrong. Where others found contentment in simply performing their religious acts, Jesus found disgust. While others focused primarily on cleaning and polishing their outer selves, Jesus looked to do his scrubbing on the inside. Jesus cared more about heart and motive than any man who ever lived. God had long been tired of checkmark followers and Jesus came to check them off his list of true disciples.

> *"Pray for thirty minutes. Check!"*
> *"Turn in my weekly tithe. Check!"*
> *"Fast one day this week. Check!"*
> *"Attend synagogue service. Check!"*
> *"Receive one compliment today. Check!"*
> *"Feel really good about myself. Check!"*

Jesus seemed completely uninterested in recruiting anybody who was content with the current religious standards and, instead, sought a different kind of follower, one who might be heard saying some of the following to the Father:

> *"God, I really need you and I have some things I must confess. Thanks for taking the time to listen."*

> *"God, I know this isn't much money. Please help me to get into a better position so I can give more each week."*

> *"God, help me to look healthier than ever while I fast and please keep people from asking me why I'm not eating."*

"God, I can't wait to be with the people who love you. While I'm worshiping you, help me to focus first and foremost on you and then on anybody who might need some extra love and encouragement while I'm there."

"God, I pray you will keep my heart pure today and help me not to go fishing for compliments or wait for a pat on the back."

"God, I know even after I serve you today I won't deserve to have your grace. My worth is not found in what I feel about me, but in what I know you feel about me."

Who else but Jesus would have recruited strange and sinful people to be the foundation and core of a religious movement that would need to rock the world? Who else would pick the prostitute who was too ashamed to pray before selecting the religious man with the most eloquence in prayer to be the one most likely to move the heart of God to action? Who else would pick a pagan with no prior fasting experience instead of choosing a Pharisee who put down the fork twice a week to be a part of his all-important inner circle? Who else would select a tax collector who often stole people's money before choosing a temple attendant who always tithed his own to be the one to join him and preach against the evils of materialism?

Only Jesus had the guts to make all of these weird-to-the-world choices, as well as all of his other seemingly ignorant roster moves. But Jesus didn't care what his fellow Israelites thought about his choices. He knew who he was looking for and he was completely unimpressed with spirituality that was only visible on the surface. While others may have stood in awe of religious appearance, Jesus rapidly removed man's thick layers of piety, pride and public approval and went straight to the heart. What he found there determined his applause.

"Do not store up for yourselves treasures on earth, where moth and rust destroy, and where thieves break in and steal. But store up for yourselves treasure in heaven, where moth and rust do not destroy, and where thieves do not break in and steal. For where your treasure is, there your heart will be also." (**Matthew 6:19-21**).

In the first century, seeking after and acquiring material wealth was often considered noble, even spiritual, according to religious people. Many believed the more a man owned, the more he had been blessed by God. If you had a chariot, you were God's friend. If you owned two, you must have been a relative. If you owned a home, no doubt you were going to heaven. If you also had a vacation getaway, the red carpet would be rolled out upon arrival. Jesus saw it differently.

Jesus refused to equate money with blessings or cash with the Creator. He called people to contentment. He called his disciples to be easily satisfied, waiting for heaven to reveal their eternal reward rather than roaming the world in a frantic search for earthly treasure.

He had no problem with downsizing. He knew the square footage of heaven and wasn't impressed with the mansions of earth.

He had no problem with the simple life. He had seen the heavenly banquet spread and was bored with the delicacies of earth.

He had no problem with giving his money or letting people take his money. He had walked the golden street and sailed the crystal sea and yawned at the notion of saving for a chariot fit for a Caesar or a yacht for enjoyment on the Sea of Galilee.

The teachings of Jesus contained no information about making lots of money, developing land or constructing bigger and better buildings. He wasn't personally interested in getting rich and he never promised it to any of his potential followers. Gaining wealth, going to war against Rome or getting back full possession of the Promise Land were never heard in any of his speeches. His desires were not focused on acquiring more property, but more people. He expected people to live as though heaven was already theirs and the things of the earth never were. He called people to trust and not to take up arms. He never said no to a beggar. He never owned a home. He never hosted a fund-raiser. He never sought political office. He never held a rally against the evils of the Roman occupation of his homeland.

If followed wholeheartedly by those of us living today, his teaching on true treasure would end all suicide bombings, terrorist attacks and wars. If adhered to, his teaching would eliminate all hunger, homelessness and poverty. Obedience to his teachings would keep the Smith family focused on keeping up with each other and not on the Joneses.

If his teachings were taken seriously, the lawyer would be inspired to become best friends with the janitor. Young people would consider social work and teaching as two of the most desired full-time positions, and every last one of us would think that becoming rich was only a fleeting temptation. Every father would love to come home for dinner each night of the week, more excited to attend their children's special events than staying at work through the evening, scratching and clawing in an all-out attempt to get a promotion.

"Therefore, I tell you, do not worry about your life, what you will eat or drink; or about your body, what you will wear…" (**Matthew 6:25-26**).

"Who of you by worrying can add a single hour to his life?" (**Matthew 6: 27**).

So do not worry, saying, "What shall we eat?" or "What shall we wear?"
For the pagans run after all these things, and your heavenly Father knows that you need
them. But seek first his kingdom and his righteousness, and all these things will be given
to you as well. Therefore do not worry about tomorrow, for tomorrow will worry about
itself. Each day has enough trouble of its own" (**Matthew 6:31-34**).

The teachings of Jesus were centered on calm. They were all about
slowing people down and teaching them to think. Jesus encouraged people
to look around at the creation and contemplate (**Matthew 6:26**). He directed them to go find a flower and figure it out (**Matthew 6:28**), to notice a
nest and, in doing so, not panic (**Matthew 6:26**). His were teachings to turn
people away from the hustle and bustle of life and turn them heavenward.
His teachings emphasized God's personal and daily involvement in every
individual's life. They were teachings designed to stop the under-employed
and the unemployed from stealing because, somehow, God was going to
work out their future employment (**Matthew 6:33**). His teachings offered
sound emotional counsel and were powerful enough to cure psychological
dysfunctions. Jesus was presenting God truthfully, as a real father who never
forgets any member of his spiritual family. This same God would also give
power to all of his children, enabling them to forgive and overcome any
hurt they might be experiencing due to the lack of love they received in
their physical family (**Matthew 7:7-11**). His teachings were deep, spiritual
truths designed to lead people into their closets to pray instead of into their
closets to consider the need for another apparel acquisition (**Matthew 6:
6**). If followed, his teachings would help to fill up the empty pew spaces
at midweek services with men who chose the need for fellowship over the
need for fixing up the basement or watching the big game. The teachings
of Jesus would motivate a woman to turn down a huge promotion in a new
city where she would be a stranger and, instead, decide to keep earning her
modest income in a city where best friends and believers had helped her to
stay focused and God-centered for the past ten years.

"Do not judge, or you too will be judged. For in the same way you judge others,
you will be judged, and with the measure you use, it will be measured to you. Why do
you look at the speck of sawdust in your brother's eye and pay no attention to the plank
in your own eye? How can you say to your brother, "Let me take the speck out of your
eye," when all the time there is a plank in your own eye? You hypocrite, first take the
plank out of your own eye, and then you will see clearly to remove the speck from your
brother's eye" (**Matthew 7:1-5**).

Jesus taught a lot about mirrors and he implored his listeners to look into them often. One of my biggest problems is that, when it comes to considering my own flaws and faults, I look through the wrong end of the binoculars. Try it sometime and you'll discover that what should be real clear is barely detectable. But when it comes to picking others apart and seeing their weaknesses, I become a scientist. I get my microscope out, put people on a slide and look long and hard to detect even the slightest sign of sinful behavior. If that's unsuccessful, I'll locate the telescope and bring into focus those far away objects in others that clearly show why I'm not at fault. I love my scopes and, unfortunately, they work magnificently every time. They offer clear insights to help me feel better about myself. They reveal the tiniest of impure motives in others to momentarily take me off the hook. I don't think I'm alone, however. Every last one of us owns at least one of these powerful scopes of justification and rationalization. Jesus tells us to put them away. Or, better yet, keep them out but only use them on yourself. Put yourself under the microscope and look for strange little creatures of bitterness, selfishness and envy. Turn the telescope around on yourself and see if you have rings of laziness, hatred and deceit around your personal planet.

This is a simple teaching, yet it's rarely heard—be a *lot* harder on yourself than you are on anybody else. Be slow to judge others and quick to judge yourself. Spend hours developing film of your own heart in a spiritual darkroom and blow up every picture. Allow any negative film you have of others to be exposed by the Son and, therefore, useless in your mind. Spend a lot more moments confessing your sins to God and devote huge chunks of time thanking him for the good qualities you see in those around you.

In 1988, during the first few months of our stay in the ministry in Denver, Patty and I had been at each other's throats on a daily basis for an extended period of time. We drove dangerously over marriage bumps that were slowly destroying the undercarriage of our marriage, but we couldn't see the damage. Thankfully, God placed people in our lives to encourage us to look below the surface. Preston and Sandie Shepherd led us to the truth that would set us free to be the partners we needed to be for each other.

Our problem was simple and one that has existed since Adam and Eve were brought before God for questioning way back in the beginning.

"She did it. It was her fault, God" (**Genesis 3:8-12**).

"I didn't do it. It was the serpent's fault, God" (**Genesis 3:13**).

What we heard from our ancestors was filling our minds as well, leading us to some very prideful observations: *"If you could only see what I see, and hear what I hear, then you would know what I know, God."*

And that was exactly where we had lived for a few months. The Shepherds told us to get a new address! They reminded us of the teaching we had casually put on the back burner and told us to quickly move it to the front and turn on the stove. Then they introduced us to a month-long plan to help us realize we actually had married the right person.

Every morning, before we did anything else, we would get out of bed, get down on our knees, hold hands and pray. Now, when you're fully convinced your spouse is the problem, this is not an easy exercise. But our prayers would sound different than they had recently. Prayers, for a change, that God might be willing to hear. I would begin and confess specific things I knew were a part of my sinful nature and any sin I had specifically committed against Patty the day before. Then I would spend the next five minutes thanking God for all the great qualities I saw in Patty and all the godly things she had done for me and for others the day before. Patty would pray next and do the same thing in regard to her sins and my strengths. We would repeat this scenario every night—the very last thing we did before going to bed. If one of us had a late-night appointment and came home to find the other already asleep, we would wake the other one up and get down on our knees to pray. It was our focus the first thing in the morning and the last thing at night. We did this for one solid month, not missing a single time of prayer. Sure, at times it was hard—physically hard if either of us was the one who had to be woken up to pray. Sometimes it was emotionally hard because we didn't feel the warm-fuzzies for each other. And sometimes it was spiritually draining because we were fighting the devil on the most difficult front of all—our pride! But we did it. And, boy, did it ever change our lives! I found the woman I married! Of course, she hadn't gone anywhere, but I had sent her away in my mind and in my spirit with my critical attitudes toward her. Ironically, once I stopped using my telescope on Patty, I could see she was a shining star once again. Patty put hers away as well and I'm thankful to say there hasn't been an episode like that in our marriage for the past 16 years. Anytime we sense this to be a problem for other married couples, with roommates or close friends, we share our story about the time the Shepherds led us back to the Good Shepherd and his infatuation with the mirror.

That first sermon had a lot to offer. It touched on issues many had rarely considered, and if they had, they lacked the courage to bring them to the forefront. In wrapping up his initial message, Jesus filled his hearers with more clear and colorful words. He used pigs and pearls to preach on caution (**Matthew 7:6**). He heralded the three-step plan of ask, seek and knock to teach people about boldness and persistence. (**Matthew 7:7-8**). He contrasted bread with stone then fish with snakes to communicate the heart of God in regard to giving (**Matthew 7:9-11**). He gave us the Golden Rule wrapping up the entire Old Testament in just one sentence (**Matthew 7:12**). He showed us two open gates leading to our ultimate eternal destiny and warned us about the width of both (**Matthew 7:13-14**). He told us to look beyond the wooly outside of some so-called sheep and look at the facts like Little Red Riding Hood (**Matthew 7:15-20**). He made it clear that "Lord, Lord" must line up exactly with "life, life" or on judgment day we would be in for the shock of our lives (**Matthew 7:21-23**). He made his last point in his first preaching platform with a blueprint for building your house of life in anticipation of bad weather (**Matthew 7:24-27**). And when he finished, the crowds who were privileged to be there and hear the greatest sermon ever delivered went home amazed at the words Jesus spoke and the way that he spoke them (**Matthew 7:28-29**).

There were many more sermons in his three-year stint on the preaching circuit. To those bogged down in the legalism of their current tradition, Jesus spoke of a rest for the soul and a release from the burdens of life (**Matthew 11:28-30**). To those hurling outlandish accusations about Jesus keeping company with the devil, he coined a phrase that has been copied for centuries by teaching, *"A house divided against itself cannot stand"* (**Matthew 12:25-28**). He taught of the impossibility of adults making it to heaven without mimicking children's humility (**Matthew 18:1-3**). He revealed the top two teachings of all-time with a simple call to love your God and love your neighbor (**Matthew 22:34-40**). He cooked up a sizzling rebuke for all hypocrites with illustrations of gnats, camels, dead men's bones, whitewashed tombs and snakes, yet seasoned it with a closing remark and reminder of how much he had loved and longed to save each one of them (**Matthew 23:1-39**). He taught about making heaven your center of joy and not your earthly results (**Luke 10:17-20**). He revealed the true definition of good in the story of the Good Samaritan (**Luke 10:25-37**). He cleared up the burden of guilt in regard to birth defects (**John 9:1-3**), opened our eyes to the truth of spiritual blindness (**John 9:39-41**), warned of the dangers of emotionalism and altar calls (**Luke 14:25-35**), prepared us for persecution (**John 15:18-27**) and excited us with the re`sume` of the coming Holy Spirit (**John 16:5-16**). He constantly taught about the reality of God's love while never diminishing the reality of hell (**Mark 9:42-49**).

He never deleted a controversial point from any sermon when warned a critic or two might be present (**Matthew 23:1-39**). He never pouted or questioned his strategy when all but a few deserted him (**John 6:60-67**), and he never boasted about his church-growth success when thousands decided to stay. He never swerved erratically to avoid an interrogation (**Matthew 21:23-27**), yet was always aware of any trap by the enemy that deserved a silent reply (**Matthew 22:15-22**). He didn't apologize for who he was or what he expected from his followers (**Luke 14:25-34**). He never received an honorarium for a message or preached because he liked the popularity (**John 2:23-25**). He was, to put it simply, all about God and getting God's message out to as many as possible (**Mark 16:15-16**).

Yes, the baby grew up and had something to say. He had a lot to say! And every time he did, the crowds were amazed.

Even his enemies knew they had met their match. More accurately, they knew they had lost their match. So they did the only thing they could possibly do to shut Jesus up and shut down his ministry: They killed him. But two thousand years later we still hear him preach. The faithful few who hung on to every word Jesus spoke knew that his teachings were truly of God, unparalleled with any teaching anyone had ever heard before, containing truths that would never be matched in the future. So the disciples made sure that those born in future generations (you and me) would be able to hear the words he spoke and the way he spoke and come away with the same conclusion as those who were there to hear the Sermon on the Mount: *"No one ever spoke the way this man does."*

❦ Chapter Eighteen ❦

What Kind of Man is This?

Then he got into the boat and his disciples followed him. Without warning, a furious storm came up on the lake, so that the waves swept over the boat. But Jesus was sleeping. The disciples went and woke him, saying, "Lord save us! We're going to drown!"

He replied, "You of little faith, why are you so afraid?" Then he got up and rebuked the winds and the waves, and it was completely calm.

The men were amazed and asked, "What kind of man is this? Even the winds and the waves obey him."

— Matthew 8:23-27

It truly was a set-up. With his series of miraculous billboards, God was slowing down the fast and furious freeway traffic called life. Each enormous sign was being used to entice the "I know exactly where I'm going and I need to get there fast" drivers to slow down, move over to the far right lane, take the next exit and check out what seemed to good to be true in the man called Jesus. And it worked. The miracles Jesus performed were prodding many previously uninterested observers to at least pull in for a quick look at his activities. The startling displays of the unexplainable seemed to convince many of them to stick around just long enough to hear what he had to say.

Before encountering the signs of God in the miracles of Jesus, most Israelites were saying they didn't need to waste any time listening to another crazy man who was rounding up a few followers to make a run at the Romans. Most of the Jews were content living in their compromised peace with Rome, being allowed, for the most part, to continue in their worship of Jehovah and the observance of most Jewish laws. They wanted nothing to do with any takeover attempt that might take away their present harmony with Caesar. But the sentiments of many began changing when the weather began changing with no meteorological explanation and caskets began opening and corpses began dancing when Jesus showed up at funerals.

"So Jesus, you say you have some important matters we need to hear?"

"Okay, we'll stay and listen to your new proposal."

"Anybody who can do what you've been doing must have some trick up their sleeve that Rome has never seen before."

So thousands upon thousands stayed to listen to Jesus at least once. That had been the plan of God from the beginning: Drop a miracle on them, then drop the bomb about who Jesus was and what he expected. Whether the miracle was in front of the twelve or in front of the hungry masses huddled on the mountainside, the display was always an attention-getter. His miracles, some said, were clear proof that divine power was nearby. Some were commenting to each other that his miracles were causing them to recall stories of the great prophets of old. His miracles, they all hoped, were the ultimate witness that God was present and ready to make a move on behalf of his people.

The miracles of Jesus sparked the interest of a typical Israelite (**1 Corinthians 1:22**) the way rumors of miraculous events arouse our curiosity today. You know exactly what I mean if you've ever been in the checkout line at your local grocery store and ventured a quick glance at the headlines in the newspapers you would never buy. I was there today.

Noah's Ark Found on Mars.

I must admit that I wanted to buy a copy and read up on this amazing and miraculous discovery. It did get me thinking some wild and crazy thoughts for a brief moment. But you know as well as I do that the ark isn't in outer space! Why, the next thing we'll hear is that Noah's dogs are living on Pluto. That's not really possible, is it?

What if someone came to my house, told me of a miracle-cure for my baldness, touched my head three times and turned desert to rain forest? You bet I'd invite him back to hear what he had to say about more important matters in life! Anybody who can do what Rogaine and regularly begging God haven't accomplished for the past twenty years deserves some of my undivided attention.

In like manner, they flocked to Jesus. What did they see that caused them to later listen to his messages so carefully? What was it with these miracles of Jesus that left so many with undeniable evidence that every word from the mouth of this miracle-maker could be fully trusted? Let's take an up-close look at the miracle on the lake described in the beginning of the chapter, along with a few other eye-openers, and ask ourselves the same question the disciples did after witnessing the miracle: *"What kind of man is this?"*

It had been a typical day for Jesus and his twelve apostles, spending much of the morning and afternoon with the masses and teaching them the word of God. Even Jesus was becoming physically worn down with the rigorous schedule and signaled for a time out. So off to the boat they went, a favorite getaway from the demanding crowds. The weather had been fine that day, all the way through the late afternoon and into the early evening. No storms were in the forecast or on the horizon and, still well before sunset, it appeared to be the perfect opportunity to retreat, refresh and regroup for more Jesus-mania ahead. It wasn't long before Jesus nodded off to sleep in the boat, resting comfortably on a soft cushion (**Mark 4:38**) and grabbing some needed rest before shore and an awaiting throng of admirers, many of them hoping for a chance to be healed.

And then it happened. The fisherman among the disciples had warned the others of the occasional storm that would batter the lake, but this did nothing to prepare them for the terrifying experience about to take place. It was relaxation time for the twelve and the early-evening temperature was perfect. They could anticipate a calm evening, dropping anchor somewhere in the middle of the lake and taking in the spectacular sunset that would be displaying its splendor in a few hours. It would be one of the best nights for them in quite some time and they were especially grateful for their Master's sensitivity to their ever-increasing workload. But their perfect world would soon end with the arrival of the perfect storm. And the perfect one who lay asleep in the boat would soon wake up and turn their chaos and fears of imminent death into the best boat trip of their entire lives and one they would never be able to forget.

Light rain began to fall, but lasted only seconds before large droplets of hail were pummeling the boat and the disciples on board. The gale-force winds made it impossible to steady the boat, so the twelve simply tried to steady themselves and keep from falling overboard. Massive amounts of water from the towering waves began to fill the boat and bucketing and bailing efforts were useless. At this rate, it wouldn't be long before the boat would sink and, if that happened, they would all most likely drown. Swimming to safety was not an option as the storm had steadily moved the boat away from the shore, and the seas were too rough to overcome for even the best swimmer. Boats able to withstand the elements were nowhere in sight and certainly no rescue attempt could be expected during the fierce downpour. What could the disciples do now? No human effort was going to help turn the tide as the wind and rain were increasing in strength, and the sky was growing ominous, brightened only by the frequent and nearby bolts of lightning. Only God could intervene now! Jonah's trip overboard came to mind but none of the disciples were convinced a big enough fish lived in those waters (**Jonah 1:1-17**). Prayers had been frantically sent upward since the storm set in but the heavens kept answering with more rain. So they woke up Jesus. Just exactly what they expected him to do isn't certain, but they were surely out of other options. Would he fix the sail? Would he help to bail? Would his prayers be honored for a safe return to shore?

> *Lord, save us! We're going to drown* (**Matthew 8:25**).
> *Teacher, don't you care if we drown?* (**Mark 4:38**).

Jesus was in the middle of a nap and they were in the middle of the biggest crisis of their lives! Perhaps that's what Jesus was hoping for all along. Was this storm the only way the disciples could come to appreciate who they had been hanging out with for the past few months? So Jesus woke up, and with a loud rebuke rocked the storm to sleep. High-flying kites soaring in similar winds would have suddenly plummeted to the ground. Daring body surfers and boogie boarders taking full advantage of similar storm-created waves would have called it a day. What had felt like a hurricane was now a hush. As quick as the storm had come, it had disappeared even faster. The storm-stoppage was so sudden, even the rainbow remained backstage.

With only a few words, Jesus told the wind to get a grip and ordered the rain to take a hike home. Then it was the disciple's turn to be humbled by the Master.

> *Why are you so afraid? Do you still have no faith?* (**Mark 4:40**).

And on the way home they asked the same question of each other again and again—*"What kind of man is this?"*

Here are some other ways the question could have been asked.

*"Has a **man** ever done this before?"*

*"Could a **man** do what we saw done here today?"*

*"Since when does a **man** have complete control over nature?"*

*"Is Jesus just a **man**?"*

"Is Jesus the Son of God?"

"Is this God in our presence?"

The disciples were rapidly moving in that direction with each glance toward the bright blue skies they enjoyed while rowing back to shore. Jesus had done it again. Would he ever miss? Every paralyzed man he told to walk, walked perfectly without follow-up therapy. Every demon he told to depart, left immediately saluting him as the Son of God. Every leper he touched was cured on the spot. And now it's the weather!

But for the twelve apostles, this miracle was different because it was all about them. **They** were saved. **They** didn't drown. **They** were the recipients of a rescue mission. And they had never been so personally grateful for the power they had witnessed from their leader and friend only moments after waking him up from his early evening nap.

What conclusions would you have made about Jesus if you had been on that boat? How would your life have changed? Would you have decided to finally believe his claims even though they still seemed a bit bizarre? Would you have acted differently during the next storm you encountered? Would you have watched Jesus a bit more carefully knowing you were watching deity? Would you have ever doubted a future promise made by him? Would you have listened to his teaching more cautiously knowing that God was giving the lesson? Would you have been prouder to tell your friends and family about him?

This miracle was similar to all the other miracles of Jesus. It would not only give us goose pimples but, more importantly, give us proof. It would not only bring about bewilderment but, more importantly, belief. It would not only cause us to quiver but, more importantly, question: What kind of man is this? Let's take a closer look at the miracle and do our best to capture the same amazement as the disciples did that day.

First, the storm came totally without warning. The disciples had no idea it was coming. The fishermen on the boat would have been quick to tell Jesus about the dangers of sailing on such an evening when the bad weather would likely become an issue. But there were no signs of foul weather and they loved the idea of being out on the lake and away from the crowds for at least a little while.

Allow me to play the devil's advocate for a moment and consider some possible normal explanations for that evening's events. Was the stormy scenario a masterminded plan of Jesus? Was he simply looking for the perfect opportunity to fool his disciples into believing his audacious claims of being the Messiah and nothing could be better than this boat ride to belief? Could he possibly have staged a weather-altering miracle such as the one we read about here in Mark? Could a mere man pull off something like that? If so, Jesus would have to have been aware that a storm was coming, displaying more knowledge than all the other weather experts in the area who had encouraged boating and other outdoor recreation for the entire day? If so, he would have to have known in advance all about the duration and intensity of the storm? He would have to have known that there would be a brief but intense storm, known exactly when it was going to begin, wait just long enough for the disciples to panic, wake up just prior to when he knew the storm would probably cease, then command the weather to suddenly change as if he were in control? Did Jesus have this meteorologist-like knowledge or some other inside information about all the past and present weather patterns on the lake? If so, did he conclude his chances were excellent that this latest storm would act according to the percentages? And if Jesus had cleverly planned out this episode, what if he had failed? What if the storm never came? What if it came at the wrong time according to his scientific calculations? What if it came, he shouted for it to stop, but nothing changed? What if it came, he shouted for it to stop, it did, but then five minutes later a worse storm came upon the sea that caught him off guard? His perfect opportunity to pull one over on the disciples would have failed had any of these scenarios come to pass, and any further attempts by Jesus to gather a following of disciples would have been futile.

But Jesus wasn't a mere man, a master deceiver or the greatest meteorologist of his time. He knew the storm would come. He knew when it would come. He knew he would be sleeping when it came. He knew he would get woke up by his frantic friends who were looking to be bailed out. And he knew he possessed the power to stop it at any time he so desired. This was not a clever set up made by a foolish man looking to impress some of his naïve followers so they would take it up a notch for him. This was a clever set up by the Son of God. He was looking to convince his impressionable followers that he was more than just another good man on a religious crusade. He wasn't just attempting, like so many other past and present zealots, to change his country's current situation under Gentile rule. He was convincing them that he, and he alone, must be listened to. He was leaving proof that his words and his ways could be fully trusted and the storm silencing was another opportunity to solidify that in the minds of his disciples. This was not just another storm they would weather. This was not just an inopportune time to have a storm become a little more in-tense than what you were expecting. This was a never-seen-before coming and going of a never-seen-before storm. Some of the disciples on board were very much "in-the-know" about storm patterns. Their experience as fishermen had taught them to have a great respect for the dangers of bad weather, and nowhere in the annals of lake fatalities, boats being capsized and near-death experiences on the water was there an account of a storm that had come so completely out of nowhere or a storm that had said fare-well so fast.

Secondly, it was a furious squall. Thirteen miles long and eight miles wide, this was no small lake. Surrounded on three sides by mountains and cliffs, the lake is situated in a bowl up to 3,500 feet in depth from the bottom of the lake to the top of the Golan Heights. With the air temperature dropping rapidly in the afternoon, it is not uncommon for an avalanche of cool air to flow rapidly downhill, resulting in violent windstorms on the lake. This storm wasn't planning to just calmly subside unless the one who controlled the weather said, "Enough is enough."

Third, the storm ended abruptly. The rains didn't lighten up, they left altogether. The wind didn't diminish, it ceased completely. The dark skies didn't turn to blue over the next few minutes, but in an instant. The waves did not go from ten feet to three, the water went flat. Something supernatural stopped the storm in a most spectacular way.

Fourth, the storm stopped the moment Jesus said it would. Was this a mere coincidence? Was this just a lucky first attempt at weather changing? Or, was the voice of Jesus the same voice the rain had been accustomed to hearing for centuries? Did the wind obey his voice of authority just like it had been doing since the beginning? Was the invisible one who controlled the world's weather by hovering over the surface of the deep also riding with them in the boat?

All of these questions gave the apostles their answer: **God is with us!** This and every other miracle Jesus performed left convincing proof of his deity and little room for other possibilities. Anticipating the many doubters he would have among these twelve men (and the rest of mankind), the miracles of Jesus would make it next to impossible for them (and us) to cling to humanistic explanations.

The water-to-wine miracle was getting confirmation from everyone who had enjoyed the wedding reception that Jesus had also attended (**John 2:1-11**). An invalid of thirty-eight years was cured by the touch of Jesus and those who knew him knew it was for real (**John 5:1-15**). A man blind from birth was given sight by Jesus and medical explanations could not be given to nullify the miracle—not by the man himself, his doctors or his parents (**John 9:1-33**). Lazarus had been dead for four days, smelled like it and was wrapped in grave clothes when he emerged from his tomb (**John 11: 38-44**). What medical examiner was going to come forward and announce that he had only been in a deep coma? The woman who had suffered for twelve years from regular bleeding episodes and then was instantly healed by Jesus could have brought forward a few of the doctors she had sought help from throughout her illness to verify the cure (**Mark 5:25-34**). Could all of these witnesses to a miracle of Jesus have been duped? Could all of these recipients of his miracles have been on drugs at the time? If so, surely one of them would have been able to discount the sketchy evidence and announce him as a hoax.

My personal favorite is a miracle we never actually see occur in the Scriptures but, nevertheless, we can be confident took place. During a discussion on temple taxes and the need for Jesus to pay the piper, Peter was given direction on how to locate enough money to cover the tax bill for he and Jesus.

But so that we may not offend them, go to the lake and throw out your line. Take the first fish you catch; open its mouth and you will find a four-drachma coin. Take it and give it to them for my tax and yours (**Matthew 17:24-27**).

If you believe this miracle actually took place, what can you say but **WOW**! How did Jesus know that one fish, out of perhaps hundreds of thousands of fish in the lake at the time, would have swallowed a four-drachma coin? And even if he knew which fish it was, how would he know Peter was going to drop his line in the water at just the right spot, at just the right time and catch just the right fish?

Was this an early version of the Don Knotts-dolphin on **_The Incredible Mr. Limpett_** (ask someone from the 60s if this title is leaving your brain incredibly limp) and was Jesus on the line with the fish making arrangements? Maybe Jesus caused the four-drachma coin to land in the mouth of the fish at the exact moment Peter snagged it? Maybe Jesus summoned the fish by name and led it beneath Peter's boat to surrender its life and, more importantly, what was in its mouth. Was Peter alone in the boat while Jesus, from a distance, was creating a coin from nothing the moment he knew Peter would land his first catch of the day? How did Peter know where to go and when to drop his line? How did Jesus know where Peter would go and when he would drop his line? None of these questions matter if you calculate the sum of all the miracles in the ministry of Jesus and discover the answer—Jesus could do whatever he wanted, whenever he wanted, wherever he wanted, however he wanted and for whomever he wanted.

These miracles, and all the others performed by Jesus, were never attempted in the hope they could somehow be accomplished. Jesus never gave it his best shot and was never encouraged with, "Nice try" or "Better luck next time." His miracles were always perfect and always whole.

Most of the rain didn't go away, but all of it. Most of the wind didn't stop blowing, but all of it. Most of the waves weren't tamed, but all of them.

Most of the disease wasn't dealt with, but all of it. Most of the dead person didn't come back to life, but all of him.

The conclusion is simple. ***Most*** would indicate a man who had access to some power and one who might possibly be connected with God. ***All*** speaks of a man with unlimited power who is God. The miracles of Jesus were ***all*** all of the time.

If you also consider the purity of motive behind each of his miracles, Jesus becomes even more astonishing. His miracles were never performed to show off. They were never done as "I told you I could do it" statements. You never heard Jesus say, "Well, if you don't think anything of that, what about this?" None of his miracles led to any individual's harm, only to help and healing. One miracle was even performed for an enemy as Jesus restored the severed ear of a soldier who had come to arrest him (**Luke 22:49-51**).

> *Sadly, even with all of these unbelievable displays of power, the miracles were still not enough for some people to drop their disputes and doctrinal disagreements and follow Jesus.*

Those who witnessed the miraculous wonders of Jesus occupied a free, front-row seat at a perfect performance by the Master of the universe. Even his critics wrote of the amazing, never-seen-before abilities of the prophet who proclaimed to be the Son of God. Sadly, even with all of these unbelievable displays of power, the miracles were still not enough for some people to drop their disputes and doctrinal disagreements and follow Jesus. Why did some people still not believe in the miracle-maker even after seeing these signs? Why did so many who saw the miracles choose to ignore or dismiss them? Here are some possible reasons.

Their long-believed-in doctrinal positions on many spiritual matters were being put to question by Jesus, so they would question his origin and claim he had access to the powers of the devil (**John 8:42-59**).

Their military strategy differed from that of Jesus, so they looked for a strategy to do away with him quietly so the miracles would cease (**Matthew 21:45-46, 26:3-5**).

They didn't like the way Jesus jumped on their case, so the case of the calmed storm was still up for debate (**John 8:31-59**).

God never forces people to surrender to him. And he will never make you believe in his Son or follow him, either. But he will give you every reason to make an educated decision to do both.

The teachings of Jesus had never been heard before and his display of miracles had never been seen before. And just like those who witnessed Jesus in person, you can also say that God has touched your eyes and your ears. Now let him touch your heart.

❧ Chapter Nineteen ❧

Jesus Wept
❧ ❧

*When Jesus saw her weeping, and the Jews who had come along with
her also weeping, he was deeply moved in spirit and troubled. "Where have you
laid him?" he asked.*

"Come and see, Lord," they replied.

Jesus wept.

Then the Jews said, "See how he loved him."

—John 11:33-36

It had been a long four days for the two sisters. They appeared
overwhelmed by the constant reminders of the sad reality neither wanted
to face. Relatives and friends had come from many nearby towns to pay last
respects to their deceased brother, Lazarus, a highly thought-of man in the
village of Bethany. Some had brought food for the family. Others shared
tears or listened compassionately to the grieving sisters as they expressed
their pain. Many visitors related a memory of some special interaction they
had had with Lazarus, one that would hopefully help to make the pain of
his loss a bit more bearable for Mary and Martha.

Jesus, one of Lazarus' closest friends, still had not arrived and Mary
and Martha were deeply troubled by his unexplained delay. They had sent
for him a few days earlier when the first signs of failing health appeared in
their brother. Certainly, they had thought, if Jesus could get there soon, he
could fix whatever the doctors said was too late to fix. They had seen him
do it so many times in the past with complete strangers, but their brother
Lazarus was a dear friend. Surely, his love and their faith in his ability to
remove the dreaded disease would lead to a cure. But Jesus did not come.
Had Mary or Martha done something to irritate him? Had Lazarus angered him recently with something he had said or done? Had they completely misread the man they believed to be the greatest example of love
they had ever encountered?

Those four days seemed like four years to Mary and Martha. The visitors certainly meant well, but it was all so very draining. Even people they didn't know that well were stopping by saying, *"I'm so sorry"* and *"If there's anything we can do, please let us know."* It was kind, but it just wasn't enough. They wanted their brother back. He was their strength and had been for many years. How would they survive without his love and care? And if they couldn't have Lazarus back, at the very least they really needed to see Jesus. Maybe he could help them come to terms with the death of their beloved brother. Jesus had been there during earlier times of crisis in their lives and he had brought peace on every occasion. But now, in their most difficult hour, Jesus was nowhere to be found. Even the guests were contributing to the sisters' growing doubts and dismay.

"Did Jesus show up yet?" many asked.

"Didn't you send for him a long time ago to see if he could heal him?"

"So, do you know why Jesus isn't here?"

Mary and Martha were trying desperately to hang on to the many memories of love they had experienced with Jesus since he had entered their lives, but questioning comments and confusing moments were being used by Satan to loosen their grip. Each time they remembered the sight of their brother's lifeless body, they felt deeply hurt and disappointed by Jesus' unexpected absence. No longer was saving their brother's life a possibility, they just wanted an explanation. So they waited. And they waited. Then the word finally came. Jesus was on his way. Martha wasted no time and hurried off to meet him before he arrived in Bethany (**John 11:20**).

Lord, if you had been here... (**John 11:21**).

Martha's cautious attempt to place blame for her brother's death on his tardiness didn't bother Jesus. Without flinching, Jesus spoke of Lazarus rising again and, at the same time, dealt with Martha's misunderstanding of his immediate plan for her brother. Once again, Martha wasted no time and hurried back home to let Mary know of the Teacher's arrival and his desire to see her. Upon hearing Martha's report, Mary rushed off to find Jesus. She was desperate to open her heart and reveal her most anxious thoughts to the one she called Lord. In days past, her desire to open her mind and listen to his teachings had been appreciated by Jesus (**Luke 10: 38-42**), but now she was feeling the need to speak her mind.

Lord, if you had been here... (**John 11:32**).

Mary was weeping as she spoke. Many others who had followed Mary were weeping as well. Martha had spent more time crying than not for the past four days. Sadness hovered over the town as one of Bethany's brightest and best had been taken. Many of its residents were shocked and grief-stricken and couldn't imagine life without Lazarus. They, too, had wondered about the delay of the one who had the power to prevent this awful outcome. They, too, were wrestling with doubt and disappointment.

Could not he who opened the eyes of the blind man have kept this man from dying? (**John 11:37**).

The answer was "Yes" in most of their minds. But the bigger question was "Why?" Why didn't Jesus come when he could have done something about the illness? Jesus was aware of the unspoken criticism toward him. And he could see the tears and feel the pain of those affected by the tragedy. So Jesus did what God had been doing in regard to his creation for thousands of years when they didn't get it—he wept (**John 11:35**).

He could have rebuked them for their unjustified bitterness toward him. He could have simply performed the resurrection miracle from a distance and been on his merry way. He could have walked away and done nothing, justified by his knowledge of Lazarus' positive eternal condition. He could have told them to toughen up and learn the lesson that pain and suffering from the death of a loved one are part of the necessary challenges of earthly life, used to encourage the family and friends left behind to focus more on heaven. Or, he could have taught a long lesson on trusting God in trying times.

But Jesus did here, near the end of his public ministry, what was consistent with what he had been doing since the beginning—he loved. Jesus knew all along what he was about to do, but for Jesus it had never been just about doing. It was always a whole lot more about loving and showing sensitivity. He was most interested in feeling what other people felt and offering them compassion. He always lowered himself to man's level and listened to his pains and fears, rather than expecting him to rise up to his lofty and unreachable position. After all, that was the plan all along—God reached down, came down and sat down beside us to see if he could offer a helping hand.

One of the reasons I believe Jesus wept that day was simply because he knew that the people he loved were very sad. He knew it had been a rough four days for all of them and he wanted them to know that, even though he hadn't been physically present, he understood what they had been called to endure. God has always cared about our pain, and Jesus came to make that truth known in flesh and blood, this time with tears.

It was love that brought Jesus there to Bethany that afternoon, and it was love that led him to the tomb to wake up Lazarus. It had to be something extraordinary to move Jesus to call Lazarus away from the Paradise party he had been enjoying for the past four days. Jesus had changed the man's earthly life and his eternal destiny but, for some reason, he felt the need to bring him back to a world full of trouble and an appointment ahead for another dying day. What could explain this strange decision? What was moving in the heart of Jesus and troubling him so? We'll never know for sure, but since love was the driving force in all that Jesus did, consider some of the following options.

Did Jesus have concerns about Mary's future faithfulness to him if Lazarus were to be left alone? Did Jesus see a bitter root of doubt and resentment growing inside of Mary? Would Satan gladly use it to cause her to turn away from him altogether? Was raising Lazarus the only way to raise Mary's spirits and keep Satan from tempting her to return to the old life that had brought her much emptiness and pain?

Maybe Jesus did it all for Martha? He knew, more than anyone, about Martha's tendency to worry and fret about almost everything. Perhaps Jesus could see a nervous breakdown on her horizon without brother Lazarus in her life to help stabilize her anxious ways. Perhaps Jesus anticipated Martha saying a sarcastic, "Jesus, Jesus, you weren't worried enough about this one thing." Perhaps those words, if spoken, would have hardened Martha's heart and driven a permanent wedge in her relationship with him (**Luke 10:38-42**).

Could the miracle have been performed for the townspeople of Bethany? Maybe those in Bethany weren't quite spiritual enough to accept this date of death for Lazarus and bitterness and blaming God would have ended their quest of pursuing Jesus. Did Jesus raise Lazarus just to give them more time to grow spiritually so they'd be ready to accept the next difficult-to-understand death in their town?

Perhaps there was just one person among the mourners who would have wandered away from being a disciple of Jesus if not for the resurrection miracle. Did Jesus do it all for that single sheep?

Maybe Lazarus had a reclusive neighbor who he had nearly convinced to become a disciple of Jesus. Maybe he needed one more lesson before surrendering to the lordship of Jesus and Lazarus was the only one he had ever trusted enough to come into his home and get into his heart.

Perhaps Jesus raised Lazarus because he wanted to give his critics one more incredible chance to change their stance before voicing support for the Jewish ruling council's plan to eliminate him. Not that he was looking to save himself from physical death because, in Jesus' mind, that was a foregone conclusion. Instead, he would do it to grant all of the religious leaders who wanted him out of the picture a greater opportunity to avoid making a decision that would harden their heart for good.

Maybe Jesus loved Mary and Martha so much that he simply wanted them to enjoy worldly treasure for a few more years, and no treasure was greater in their minds than family.

Did Jesus need a few more powerful moments of fellowship with Lazarus to gain strength for the cross that was imminent in his future? Could he not bear the idea of spending his last days on earth without the benefit of a dear friend?

Whatever it was, it had to be huge! He would need to have a good explanation ready once Lazarus caught a quiet moment to interrogate him about his sudden departure from Paradise. Love would be his ultimate answer and there would be no reason for Lazarus to doubt it. Love was all he had ever seen from Jesus, so why would anything have changed in the four days he had been away? Love was all that anybody had seen if they had been willing to take the time to watch Jesus and keep their hearts open to the possibility that he really was the Christ.

Who else would touch a leper when they could just as easily have cured him from afar? Was it love that put Jesus' hand on rotting flesh to give a leper what he needed more than smooth skin? Or, was it a lack of understanding on the part of Jesus about the stay-as-far-away-from-a-leper-as-possible custom of the day and the huge risk of acquiring the dreaded disease upon contact with one?

Did love lead Jesus on a frantic search for a woman he had just healed? Was his successful mission in locating her more about making sure she knew that what she had just done in boldly coming forward to touch him was awesome and not awful like some may have told her (**Mark 5:25-34**)? Or, was it to challenge her on the need to remember a woman's proper place of subjection in a man's world?

Why did Jesus say "Yes" to feeding five thousand hungry men and their families when it would mean longer hours, harder work and less sleep for he and his disciples (**Matthew 14:13-21**)?

Why did he say "No" to ten thousand angels on rescue watch in the Garden of Gethsemane? After all, their arrival on the scene would have meant that his arrest, the scourging and a painful death on a cross could be permanently shelved (**Matthew 26:51-54**).

Who else besides Jesus had ever bothered asking the demoniac who lived in the graveyard, "What is your name?" (**Mark 5:9**)? Did love lead Jesus to ask him this question, the most basic of all questions? How long had it been since someone had asked the crazy man that question? Did his name really matter to anyone anymore? Did the demoniac finally feel loved for the first time in a very long time and did this I'm-interested-in-you question contribute to his most amazing transformation in the tombs?

What would cause a busy and popular motivational speaker to delay a speech for awaiting adults just to have some additional hang-time and hug-time with a few pre-school children (**Mark 10:13-16**)?

What was behind the challenge Jesus gave to a rich young ruler to sell everything and follow him (**Mark 10:21**)? Was it a selfish desire by Jesus to beef up his troops with the sharp and successful type? Or, was it a loving look into this young man's future along with a desperate call for him to change it, knowing where the love of money would ultimately lead him?

Who else would take time to notice an old lady drop two cents into a billion dollar bucket and, in doing so, make her feel like a million bucks (**Luke 21:1-4**)?

Who else was willing to trash tradition by curing a cripple on the Sabbath, knowing he could have stuck around and performed it the following day (**Mark 3:1-6**)?

What was it that led Jesus to invite himself over for afternoon tea at a despised tax collector's house? Did feeling loved by Jesus have anything to do with Zacchaeus climbing out of a tree and then climbing out of his sinful life (**Luke 19:1-10**)?

Surely it was love that led Jesus to discuss the marital status of the woman at the well (**John 4:16-18**). Love took his mind off the deep and refreshing waters he was thirsting for and love led his heart to hurt over the shallow relationships she had been involved in for years? It was this same love in action that led him to refuse submitting to the traditional silent treatment most women in the first century were given by men. Even the twelve chosen to learn about love in an up-close manner were amazed to see Jesus engaging in this out-in-the-open conversation with a Samaritan woman (**John 4:27**).

It was love that kept an adulterous woman alive while Jesus killed the pride of her firing squad (**John 8:2-11**).

It was love that led Jesus to make a date on his calendar with the man born blind and it was love that scheduled a follow-up appointment to see how his life had been going since his first day of sight (**John 9:1-41**).

It was love that humbly dropped the Teacher to his knees to serve, and it was love that guided his hands to wash the dirty feet of his students (**John 13:1-17**).

It was love that led him to say, "Father, forgive them" to the insensitive and insolent mockers who gambled for his remaining personal items while he died on a cross (**Luke 23:32-34**).

It was love that came into view when Jesus came in to view Jerusalem (**Luke 19:41-44**). He wept for Jerusalem because he had wanted so desperately for the people there to enjoy the peace he had been offering. But, with sadness he realized, instead, they would soon feel the pain he would be allowing.

Regardless of someone's status in life, their reputation with others or their relationship with Jesus, when people were in his presence they could count on being loved. Whether they were wealthy or woefully poor, a fellow Jew or a foreigner, distinguished or demon-possessed, pure or a prostitute, very religious or very rarely thinking about God, a dear friend or a determined foe, a member of the family or a member of the mob that called out for his death, an important official or an insignificant slave, a baby in his arms or a bystander in his face, all were loved by Jesus.

> *Regardless of someone's status in life, their reputation with others or their relationship with Jesus, when people were in his presence they could count on being loved.*

If you happen to be familiar with the words that God gave Paul to pen in his first letter to the church in Corinth (**1 Corinthians 13:1-8a**), you wouldn't be surprised if instead it read like this:

Jesus was always patient, Jesus was always kind. Jesus never envied, never boasted and was never proud. He was never rude, he was never self-seeking, he was never easily angered and he never kept a record of wrongs. Jesus never delighted in evil but always rejoiced with the truth. Jesus always protected, always trusted, always hoped and always persevered. Jesus never failed.

He lived like this in regard to every person he crossed paths with in the first century. And this is how he continues to operate with every last one of us today.

In running terms, his teachings got Jesus out of the blocks. His miracles put him in full stride. It was love that broke the tape. And when Jesus looked back, nobody else was even in the race.

❦ Chapter Twenty ❦

God Was One of Us
❧ ❧

Since the children have flesh and blood, he too shared in their humanity so that by his death he might destroy him who holds the power of death—that is, the devil—and free those who all their lives were held in slavery by their fear of death. For surely it is not angels he helps, but Abraham's descendants. For this reason he had to be made like his brothers in every way, in order that he might become a merciful and faithful high priest, in service to God, and that he might make atonement for the sins of the people. Because he himself suffered when he was tempted, he is able to help those who are being tempted.
— Hebrews 2:14-18

"You just don't understand what I'm feeling."

"I really need to talk with someone who's already been through what I'm experiencing right now."

"I haven't been able to find anyone I can relate to yet."

"Nobody really understands me and that's why nobody wants to get close to me."

Most of us have probably uttered similar statements of frustration at one time or another in our lives. Sometimes, our words were spoken in truth. At other times, self-pity or sadness brought them out of our heart and into the public arena. Yet, regardless of what our motives were in sharing these feelings with others, it still seems apparent that all of us do better emotionally and spiritually when we feel connected with and understood by another human being.

Look at the evidence in your life. Don't you desire to spend time with the people who can relate to you on a number of levels? For many of us, if we find we have only one thing in common with another individual, that *one thing* is enough to encourage us to pursue some type of relationship with them. If we have more than one thing in common, we're likely to invest time and energy into that relationship. If we relate on a number of levels, or have many similar interests, we often become best friends. And, in some cases, we get married. Many of these similarities might even be considered somewhat shallow, worldly or unspiritual. Nevertheless, most of us will attempt to start building a friendship based upon these common interests. Things such as where we were born, where we've lived, where we went to school, what we studied in school, where we've been employed, whether we enjoy playing or watching the same sports, whether we listen to the same kind of music, if our taste in movies is similar or if we enjoy participating in the same hobbies—these are some strong beginning points in developing relationships.

For example, if you are originally from the state of Washington or currently reside there, enjoy playing and watching sports, graduated from or have any connection to Western Washington University, consider "roughing it" to be staying at a Super 8 motel with cable television, happen to be an avid Nebraska Cornhusker fan (football that is—is there any other sport in Nebraska?), believe bowling is a **sport** and not a **game** (every man who lettered in collegiate bowling will fight to uphold that truth), love listening to **Yes, Elton John, Credence Clearwater Revival** or **Crosby, Stills, Nash and Young** with the headphones on and the volume up, love reruns of **Leave it to Beaver** and **Everybody Loves Raymond** (ouch, that covers a lot of ground), can't carry on a conversation about computers, the stock market or the latest home improvement technique, or believe that vegetables are good but steak is better—I can promise you right now, we are going to be tight! Just match me on a few of these items and we can probably talk for hours and waste time together with the best of them. Even one similarity will lead me to believe that you're not half bad, and I'll be likely to cut you some slack if you ever need it. You see, I'm pretty excited we have something in common and, even if the rest of the world thinks bowling is for sissies and camping and backpacking are the closest earthly events to a heavenly experience, as long as you and I know otherwise, you've got a friend in me.

Now, obviously, there are more important areas of similarity we will discover in others which can help us in developing a feeling of closeness with them, things such as having gone through the same challenge growing up, or having endured a similar tragedy at some point in our lives. If you've had a similar experience with someone such as having a family member die when you were young, you will likely feel comfortable around that individual on many fronts. You'll especially feel at ease with them when sharing about the emotional pain you went through at the time of the death, or as you discuss the pain you currently feel that, though less than it was at first, never seems to totally disappear.

If you suffered through a challenging childhood because of any form of abuse, or if your parents got divorced and it ripped your heart in two, who better to understand your current crisis than someone who's been through a similar difficulty.

If you had problems completing your high school education, and basic book learning for you seems to be like climbing over a 20-foot wall without a rope or ladder, more than likely you'll probably not be real motivated to begin a friendship with the guy who earned a PhD from an Ivy League school. On the contrary, it probably won't be nearly as awkward trying to build a friendship and getting close to someone who's thankful they were able to earn their high school GED and has no plans to purchase a single textbook at a university bookstore.

If you've been divorced, aren't you more interested in sharing your challenges with someone who knows all about the emptiness that follows when a divorce becomes final? To begin rebuilding your life, wouldn't you seek help and comfort from someone who knows how incredibly scary it is to do something like going out on your first date after officially becoming single again?

If you're having a hard time conceiving a child, isn't it more comforting to spend time with a friend who can completely understand the lump in your throat and the tear in your eye every time a pregnancy announcement is read at church? Wouldn't her heart become quickly engaged with yours if you shared about everything you felt when you noticed a pregnant woman walking through the grocery store?

If your financial picture gets completely out of focus, what type of individual are you going to talk it over with? Would it be a financial planner who's been one step from bankruptcy earlier in his life but has since fully recovered, or would you prefer the son of a millionaire who studied economics in college and has never felt the personal need to balance his checkbook?

If you began entertaining thoughts of giving up your walk with God and the world looked to be the happening place, wouldn't you try to locate the guy who had abandoned his faith once but is now back on track? Wouldn't you try to set up a lunch appointment with him and get his perspective? It's not that the guy who has never considered "a return to Egypt" couldn't help, but can he relate to you like this other guy? Would he or the prodigal son be better equipped to bring you some much-needed perspective on how incredibly easy but unbelievably foolish it is to buy into the lie about how awesome it really is on the outside?

If you're in your fifties or older and feel like physically you just can't keep pace with the church curriculum, will a talk with the wild-eyed, 25-year-old ministry rookie turn you around? Perhaps. Or, would you feel more comfortable being open about your concerns with the 60-year-old woman with terminal cancer who rarely misses a service?

Currently, I find the most comfort in dealing with my health situation when I talk with those who are in a health crisis as well. Two women who have been fighting cancer in the past six months have been some of my biggest encouragers. A simple ten-minute phone conversation with a man who battled serious health problems that were undiagnosed or misdiagnosed for more than a year was the best talk I've had with someone in the past five months. Why? He knew what I was going through. He was well acquainted with the accusing demons that are visiting me. He was quite familiar with the emotional battles of fear, frustration and feeling sorry for yourself that I fight alongside my physical challenges.

I'm not saying that it would be right, in any of these cases, to talk with someone who will minimize the sin that may be interfering with or causing your feelings, or someone who will lessen your responsibility to do what is right in the eyes of God. But sometimes you just need someone who has a little deeper understanding, due to a similar life experience, to be in your corner. Then these individuals who possess the inside scoop can help you turn a spiritual corner in your journey on the narrow road. Talking with someone who can relate to your situation can help to calm your fears and ease your tensions. These conversations can often produce a spiritual security in your life that might be missing if you talked, instead, with someone who's never walked in your shoes, even if that person loves you. We all tend to feel freer to drop our guard and surrender our shield with those we relate to, usually because we're much less likely to feel judged by that individual. Then, with an open heart and motivated by the patience and grace of God, we can discuss solutions to our problems and look to make any necessary changes to help us move ahead. God knew this was true about all of us, so he became one of us.

One of the most frustrating things I encounter being a 45-year-old minister is my inability to connect with certain groups of people. As hard as I try, I'm just not cool, hip or fresh to certain people. Wearing the right clothes, knowing the latest slang or listening to tunes of today is helpful in connecting with teens, but I'm still from the olden days (I was there to see the dinosaurs disappear as my kids remind me), have graying and rapidly thinning hair and, most damaging to my coolness rating, I'm currently a parent of two teenagers. And, though it's true that "I used to be a teen you know," that was, after all, a long, long time ago and, "Things are much different now, Dad." I've learned with teens, the elderly, single parents, those who are going through challenges I've never faced, and in many other situations when been-there-done-that doesn't fit, to simply surrender to the truth and respond with the next best thing, "I can't relate, but I do care." Thank God, Jesus can do both!

Unfortunately, most of us don't view God in this way. We often think the exact opposite and believe God can't relate at all because he hasn't been in our shoes. Oh, but he has. He knows all about our shoes. His became worn out and in need of repair just like ours. His also walked through pain and suffering. His had to dance around temptation just like ours. His were sometimes tight and uncomfortable. He, too, had been one step from wanting to take them off and throw them away, or at least loosen the strings.

God knows how tough life can be. He's not unsympathetic about the challenges we face every day. He's not quick to call us quitters or wimps when we decide for a brief moment to side with Satan and slip on shoes from his store. He knows how tough the devil can be. He knows all about how comfortable any pair of shoes from Satan's store would feel if you were to wear them. He came close to purchasing Satanic shoes on a few occasions himself, but somehow kept the perfect pair he had from the beginning.

Nothing has happened in your life that Jesus can't somehow, and in some way, understand. Anything you are currently dealing with, Jesus has, in a similar way, been there. Sure, he may not have had the exact experience, but he can relate to the overwhelming emotion or the strong temptation that accompanies the situation. No, he didn't deal with old age, but he always knew that death was near. No, he was never confined to a wheelchair, but he surely was limited by and bound to the flesh. No, he wasn't married either, but he can totally relate to the pain of marital crisis or divorce because he daily dealt with his emotions that stemmed from people wanting to quit on him and he knows the devastating feeling of a once-special relationship coming to an abrupt end. No, he never experienced the extreme disappointment of finding out about a miscarriage or a stillbirth, but he did know the sadness of seeing someone he loved come so close to becoming a part of his family, only to watch that individual change his mind just short of the new birth.

Please don't minimize this piece of great news: ***God was one of us!*** The next time you hear the 2000 hit single, ***What if God Was One of Us?***, just drop the "what if" while singing along because God really does know the feeling of being a stranger on a bus. What could be weirder and less securing than being the eternally perfect God from heaven and coming to live for thirty-three years with earthlings? What could be more challenging than Jesus having to be one hundred percent human while hanging on to the fullness of his deity?

Though none of us will ever relate completely to this monumental challenge, there are times in our lives when we, too, experience the not-so-pleasant realities of being away from home and what we are normally accustomed to. A few months after my high school graduation in 1977, I had the opportunity to live in Brazil. But not long after my arrival, I began suffering terribly from that emotionally nauseating feeling called the home-sick blues.

Gerson, a foreign exchange student from Brazil, lived in our home for eight months in 1976 and he invited me to come and stay with him and his family in their hometown of Fortaleza for an entire year. I gladly accepted his offer, then more than gladly returned home after only two months. It would have been two weeks if I hadn't been so prideful and afraid to tell my parents (who paid dearly for the getaway) what a miserable time I was having. The 80-plus degree weather was fantastic. The beautiful, white sandy beaches and aqua-green waters of the southern Atlantic Ocean were incredible. The family I lived with was fairly wealthy and had access to most of the modern conveniences I enjoyed back home. I didn't have any real responsibilities during my time in Brazil, other than to kick back and have some fun. I actually came to Brazil believing I might never go back to Washington, except for an occasional visit. Allow me, then, to tell you all about what happened.

What happened to English?

"Don't you people know English is the universal language, not Portuguese? I don't understand you. Why is everybody laughing but me? Why does Gerson's three-year old brother look at me as though I'm an idiot when I talk to him?"

Believe it or not, at that point I really was longing for a conversation with a three-year old—in English!

What happened to cow's milk?

"Don't you people drink real milk here? No, you're wrong—goats don't have milk; cows have milk! No, it's not better at room temperature! It's best just this side of frozen."

So it was Coke for me—Coke in the morning, Coke at noon and Coke at night. Not only was it "the real thing," it was the only thing. What for me used to be about a half-gallon of glorious milk every day in amazing America was now close to a gallon-a-day of caffeine in big, bad Brazil.

What happened to baseball?

"Don't you know who Pete Rose and Reggie Jackson are?" (Remember, we're in the 70s and Barry Bonds is still in Little League, Alex Rodriguez is still in diapers and Albert Pujols is still three years from being born!) *"You've got to be kidding, you've never heard of Hank Aaron?"*

Sure, I brought my baseball glove to Brazil, but it wasn't something the goalie was allowed to use! So it was soccer. And more soccer! I played more soccer in one day than I had played my entire life. And, of course, I was terrible. Most of the time I played goalie because that was where the natives figured I would embarrass myself the least. They were right. I thought about suggesting we try playing a game of baseball once, but then I remembered I hadn't packed enough baseball gear for two entire teams!

What happened to *All in the Family* and *Happy Days*?

*"Why are reruns of **My Favorite Martian** and **Lost in Space** on in prime-time? Did I come to South America, or am I on Saturn? Why are the actors' lips mouthing English, but what I'm hearing* (but by no means understanding) *sounds an awful lot like Portuguese? Don't you people believe in sub-titles?"*

During my two-and-a-half-month stay in Brazil, I think my total hours logged of television viewing was equivalent to about a week's worth back in America.

What happened to Mom?

"Where's my nightly chocolate milkshake?" (Oh, never mind the milkshake without the real milk!) *You mean I have to iron my own clothes and wake up on time all by myself?"*

My sister had moved out of our house during my senior year of high school to attend college, so for a full year it was just me and my parents! There was an abundant supply of *me* for my mom to spoil. And she did not disappoint! But when I came to Brazil, I was a borderline-stepson to a mom who worked full-time, had a huge social circle and was raising five children of her own ranging in age from three to twenty. *"I WANT MY MOMMY!"*

These, and many more what-happened moments, made me want America more than Columbus did in 1492, and I was even willing to take the Santa Maria to get back there. I really didn't care that I was going back to Washington and soon would suffer through six straight months of steady drizzle. I really didn't care that the Pacific Ocean near my home was about 20 degrees colder than the Atlantic on the central coast of Brazil and that ocean swimming would become just a fading memory. I really didn't care that I would have to go back to work, back to college or back to both, instead of being able to enjoy a yearlong break from employment and the real world. No, I wanted to go home. Dorothy (of Kansas fame) definitely knew what she was talking about! As soon as I could click my heels three times (or get enough money to purchase a return ticket), I was on Pan Am and headed for Auntie Em.

But I can't blame Brazil. Brazil wasn't the problem. The problem was simply this—I wasn't from Brazil. I'm sure Gerson had similar nightmares about English, baseball, cold milk and wicked stepmothers while living with my family in America. And I'm one hundred percent sure that the falling snow in December didn't inspire him to put on three layers of clothing and go out walkin' in a winter wonderland. I'm sure his idea of natural white was centered on sandy beaches and not on six inches of snow in the backyard. The point is simple—we all like home. We don't mind a short getaway, but **short** is the key word here. Two weeks, maybe three weeks, is about as long as most of us can stand being away from what we've come to know as normal. Jesus did it for thirty-three years.

Let's take a moment and think about all the what-happened questions Jesus might have asked while he lived on earth and longed for heaven.

What happened to all the angels? The thousands upon thousands of heavenly beings that used to bow before the Eternal Word were now merely strengthening him for his battles in the flesh. For the time being, all-God had become all-man as well and, as a man, he, too, was made to be a little lower than the angels (**Hebrews 2:5-9**).

What happened to the fantastic fellowship? What once was constant and on-command with the Father and Spirit was now being broken by a need for physical rest, demands from hurting humans and necessary training sessions with the twelve. Prayer to his Father often had to be lifted up early in the morning or late at night, and intentional getaways and mountaintop meetings with him had to be scheduled in advance just to help Jesus stay one step ahead of the maddening assault launched by Satan on his earthly ministry. What was once automatic and instantaneous was now, in the flesh, something that needed to come from a desire and commitment. Jesus' relationship with God wasn't a foregone conclusion. As a man, like all other men created in God's image, the Father refused to program into Jesus a desire for fellowship with him. This privilege had to be pursued by Jesus, just like it has to be for you and me, and then lived out on a daily basis (**Hebrews 5:7-8**).

What happened to intelligent conversation with peers? There must have been some amazing conversation amongst the Godhead those first six days of creation (**Genesis 1:1-31**). Jesus was in this mighty mix and his intelligent words brought forth the seas to be gathered into one place, the sun to be perfectly placed 93 million miles from earth, the moon to moni-tor the ocean's tide and the stars to brighten the night skies. Now, on earth, who could he count on to carry on some meaningful chatter? Who would relate to the wisdom he possessed while creating the world, or who would understand the depth of sorrow he felt when destroying it? Could John the Baptist make things more interesting and exciting for Jesus with his depth of knowledge? Could Jesus cry over the diagnosis of a hard heart that no-body else could detect without John the apostle becoming worried about his emotional state or judging him to be weak? Could Peter offer stability in a peer friendship with Jesus? Hardly! When Jesus diagrammed his winning game plan called a cross, Peter felt the urge to teach his coach a much bet-ter strategy (**Matthew 16:21-23**).

What happened to Satan needing permission slips? It had always been agreed upon by the Godhead that any havoc wreaked by the deceiver must first be allowed or decreed by them (**Job 1:6-12**). But now Satan was everywhere and coming out of nowhere, battling Jesus toe-to-toe. Satan stalked Jesus in the desert and did so without a visitor's pass (**Matthew 4: 1-11**). The devil entered into the heart of one of Jesus' best friends and didn't think twice about it (**John 13:21-30**). Without conscience, Satan unashamedly tempted Jesus in the Garden of Gethsemane, just as he did with Adam and Eve in the Garden of Eden (**Luke 22:39-44**). But in the Garden of Eden, Jesus was administering discipline to the devil, and later to the deceived couple for their failure to trust. Now, in the Garden of Gethsemane, Jesus was being hounded by the devil and he had to hang on for dear life while being severely tempted to abandon all trust. In heaven, Jesus laughed at the devil's feeble attempts to destroy God's plan (**Psalm 2: 1-6**). On earth, he pleaded with the Father for strength to stay fastened to the cross as the devil made one last attempt to destroy in an instant the plan that had been absolutely perfect for the past thirty-three years (**Matthew 26:36-46**).

What happened to being beyond temptation? In heaven, it never crossed his mind to take a lustful look at a woman. But on earth, it wasn't that simple. How many women do you suppose flashed Jesus the "I want you" eyes to help their cause in catching the most eligible bachelor in town? How many women were attracted to his confident but quiet leadership style and looked for a quiet moment with him that might be the spark of a serious relationship? How many curves did Satan throw at Jesus by using women who threw themselves at him in an attempt to catch him in a mo-ment of weakness and end the "Son of God" talk once and for all?

In his daily struggle to push away pride, how many times was Jesus tempted to pat himself on the back for another perfect day? How often did he want to consider himself better than others when he knew all along nobody else was even close (**Philippians 2:3-4**)? How many times did it become necessary to dig deep and fight hard to erase any notion of clinging proudly to being equal with God (**Philippians 2:6**)? When did making himself nothing get eerily close to the point of getting old (**Philippians 2: 7**)? Just how hard was it for Jesus to turn away from desiring and reveling in all the compliments that came his way?

In heaven, prejudice was never an issue with Jesus and prideful thoughts were never considered. But on earth, Jesus faced many tough tests in staying righteous, probably a number of them every day. How did Jesus stay humble when he knew looking at women the way he had for all eternity would mean that most of the public would look at him like he was a fool? Was it easy for Jesus to remain prejudice-free and continue talking to the Samaritans when every time he did it angered most of his Jewish brethren? Was it easy for Jesus to silently disregard the prideful glances of Roman leaders who believed their power was attained through their own greatness? Jesus knew full well that he, himself, had predicted their arrival and put them in their present positions (**Romans 13:1**)? How many times do you think Jesus was tempted to put them in their proper place?

As Satan offered Jesus three solutions to satisfy his strongest desires and show off his heavenly attributes at his private inaugural (**Luke 4:1-13**), did he have thoughts of "Why did I decide to come?" and "How am I going to make it to the end if this is how tough it is at the beginning?"

Had it ever been so easy to allow anger and self-righteousness to well up in his heart as when he saw up-close on earth the impulsive nature of man? With huge, never-seen-before crowds chanting for him to declare his candidacy for King of Israel, Jesus must have entertained thoughts of taking the road most traveled, especially as he contemplated how the crowds would dramatically change their tune a few years later in demanding his crucifixion.

What happened to all that energy? In heaven there were no yawns. There was never a need for a power surge or a power nap to get Jesus through the day. There were no aches and pains such as he experienced daily from walking the rugged terrain of the Holy Land. Jesus never thought about the need to call it a night at a decent hour because a big day was ahead. Maintaining a healthy and balanced diet was never a concern for Jesus until the flesh and blood of the man from heaven weakened and demanded it. He who created energy, gave energy and never needed energy now recognized the need for food, fat reduction and fresh air.

Jesus, once eternally free in the heavenly realms, was now quite cramped in his earthly flesh. He felt the frustration we feel when we long for something beyond the body. Like all of us, he knew how missing a meal can mess us up and move us toward grouchy. Like most men, Jesus felt sickness attack his flesh. Then, in an even stronger way, he felt Satan trying to use the illness to move him toward becoming inward and demanding of others. Jesus also must have felt the onslaught of energy when he began his day of meeting people's needs, only to be matched by the onslaught of emotional and physical exhaustion when it came to a close.

Yes, God was one of us! The mere fact that Jesus left heaven and entered foreign soil means he can relate to every one of us in some way. But there's more. Let's close the chapter by considering a number of situations Jesus faced in his life. Let's see if it's true that, when we experience personal struggles and challenges, Jesus knows exactly what we're going through.

He had no beauty or majesty to attract us to him, nothing in his appearance that we should desire him (**Isaiah 53:2**).

Average Looks

While the beauty of billboard models and movie stars causes all of us, at times, to wish we had been swimming in a different gene pool, the truth remains that the vast majority of us are a whole lot closer to average and simple than we are to awesome and stunning. Few, if any, take second glances our way. It's either our forehead is too shiny, our nose is too big, our ears stick out, our chin is too pointed, our hair is too thin, our teeth are too crooked, our cheeks are too rosy or our wrinkles are too obvious. If I missed your facial flaw, write it down in the margin. When you're finished, come join the rest of us ordinary people. But, not to worry—Jesus will be there, too!

What was it with his looks that prompted the Spirit to indicate to Isaiah that, *"There was nothing in his appearance that we should desire him"* (**Isaiah 53:2**)? Sorry to disappoint you, but God didn't tell us. Forget the picture of him in the hallway of your home that you saw growing up, the one with the near-perfect facial features and the long, flowing hair, and focus on average. That's as much as God has chosen to tell us about Jesus' physical looks. But don't be too concerned that you'll never know ***exactly*** what Jesus looked like. Besides, if it were such an important piece of information, why did God leave it out altogether? Doesn't just knowing that Jesus was average looking make it much easier to take your insecurities and inadequacies to him? Could knowing that Jesus knows the hurt that comes from being overlooked because of looks help you move beyond the recent promotion opportunity at your workplace that was given to the more attractive, less qualified candidate? Could understanding that Jesus had to learn contentment with the mirror's revelation every time he readied himself for the day help you to stop worrying about what you can't really change this side of a plastic surgeon? Maybe a brother or two was blessed with better looks than Jesus. Maybe all four were finer in appearance. Could this help you to once and for all eliminate your envy of a sibling's luck with their looks? Could the fact that God in the flesh chose to be average in appearance help you realize that looks aren't everything and, in truth, looks are nothing?

Okay, that's enough about the face. How do you feel about the rest of your body?

"Okay, if I can't be handsome, at least I can be hard-bodied."

"Okay, if I can't have fine features, at least my figure can get their attention."

What was Jesus like below the neck? Did he turn heads while walking on the Galilean shores by flexing his biceps? Did he look like a lifetime member of Gold's Gym or resemble one of the steroid-studs of the WWE (World Wrestling Entertainment)? Could Jesus have entered the Mr. Middle East competition on his way to claiming Mr. Universe? Or, again, was he just average?

Now don't get me wrong here. I don't think Jesus was way out of shape and unconcerned about his physical condition. Being the son of a carpenter and working in and out of the woodshop with his father, all the while walking the hilly terrain of Israel, Jesus had many opportunities to keep his muscles strong and his heart rate healthy. But was Jesus' body causing the women to jump at a chance to meet him, or making the men envious every time they saw him without his shirt on? Or, was he probably a lot more like you and me? Maybe Jesus was someone the muscle men tracked down and tried to talk into an arm wrestling match just so they could feel good about their manhood? Maybe Jesus had to keep a constant vigil on his waistline, and maybe he had to work hard just to shed a few unnecessary pounds. Maybe if he missed a few days of doing push-ups and sit-ups due to all the hurry-ups it turned his mid-section from firm to flabby. Maybe nothing he wore fit just right. Maybe, like us, he got tempted to not really bother with the body since he knew he would get a new one eventually. Maybe his legs were skinny, but his backside wasn't. Maybe his stomach was strong, but his shoulders weren't.

The next time you're feeling down and discouraged about what you don't have in your physical appearance compared to everybody else, spend some time talking to God about it and understand that your average-looking advocate, Jesus, who is at the right hand of God, knows exactly what you're dealing with at the moment. When you're finished, feel encouraged by the truth that someone else understands the challenge of being just another face in the crowd.

The Jews answered him, "Aren't we right in saying that you are a Samaritan and demon possessed" (**John 8:48**)?

Unfair Treatment

It would be naïve to think that this was the first time Jesus got hit with this verbal jab. More than likely, this punch landed often, beginning early in his growing-up years.

Because of Mary's unusual pregnancy, it seemed to be a simple conclusion to some Israelites that Jesus' father was not Joseph after all. They believed that Mary had succumbed to the lustful advances of a Gentile man and that her fiancé, Joseph, felt sorry for her, forgave her and took her to be his wife. When she finally gave birth to Jesus, Joseph humbly decided to occupy the role of the child's father. Soon, the unenviable label of Samaritan (half Jew, half-Gentile) was placed upon Jesus. It certainly couldn't have been a comfortable label for Jesus to wear because most of his time was being spent around full-blooded Jews who despised what they considered to be the lesser Samaritans. It was this belief about Jesus, combined with what everyone was calling his hilarious cover-up in calling himself the Son of God, that made Jesus a prime target for trash talk.

If you've ever been handed a name that you never asked for or deserved, Jesus knows your pain. Whether the unwanted label was given to you as a statement about some physical deficiency, a slam on your family's reputation or the result of a one-time lapse in good judgment, name-calling never does much for our self-esteem as children, and often follows us right on into adulthood. Don't forget that Jesus is following you to! He gets it. He hurts for you and with you and he wants to help you get past any roadblock you're now facing on your journey to self-worth.

Not only did Jesus have to deal with his own insecurities stemming from the nasty remarks hurled at him, how often do you suppose he felt the agony of having to hear his parents be put down because of their so-called slippery past? How many times did Jesus really want to go at it with the boys when accusations about his mom and dad, which he knew were totally off base, were being thrown in his face?

Jesus knows the emotional challenge of trying to grow up and honor your parents while many of their peers are dishonoring them. He feels your pain as you remember watching your parents come home and cry, wondering why people didn't see the good you saw in them. Perhaps Jesus even experienced the pain of seeing his father, Joseph, move from place to place and from job to job because rumors about him began to circulate at work and the boss had to let him go despite his faithfulness to the company.

If you've forgotten the information discussed in Chapter 16, go back and imagine again what childhood might have been like for Jesus. Then imagine that right now he understands you better than you understand yourself because he grew up with many similar challenges.

The unfair treatment continued throughout Jesus' adult life. He was accused of gluttony, drunkenness, carousing with loose women, intentionally deceiving people for personal gain, representing Satan himself, not upholding the Jewish law, rebelling against Rome, not paying taxes, being insane and undoubtedly many other things that aren't recorded in the Gospels. And the epitome of these wrongful attacks on Jesus came as religious leaders wove together a series of lies about him, presented that false evidence in a completely illegal trial, condemned him to death and convinced the Roman powers-to-be to crucify him as if he were a hardened criminal. Even while hanging in pain on his cross, false accusations and slanderous statements were being hurled at him by those who passed by his execution site.

Unfair treatment was a part of Jesus' life from the moment he was conceived by the Holy Spirit to the moment he uttered, *"Father, into your hands I commit my spirit"* (**Luke 23:46**). Even to this day, people continue to treat him unfairly, making false statements about him with little or no knowledge of his actual life, claiming his entire persona is a complete fabrication, using his name in an outburst of anger or a moment of rage, equating him with other spiritual leaders throughout history and, perhaps most unfair of all, claiming to be his follower and praising his name while refusing to deal with the sin in their life, thus blaspheming the most wonderful name ever known to man.

Then Jesus entered a house, and again a crowd gathered, so that he and his disciples were not even able to eat. When his family heard about this, they went to take charge of him, for they said, "He is out of his mind" (**Mark 3:20-21**).

Family Challenges
Even Joseph and Mary had trouble understanding their son at times!

"Where did we go wrong?"

"We never really saw this side of him before."

"We've got to get him away from there and talk some sense into him."

"He's embarrassing us big-time. We've got to do something, and fast!"

How have you felt being forced to walk through life encumbered with the umbrella you had to carry in anticipation of your parents raining on your next parade? How did you feel when you knew you were headed in the right direction but your parents were totally convinced you had taken a wrong turn somewhere? What was it like, or what is it like, when the very people you most want in your corner are the same ones who have recently resigned from being your trainer?

Maybe you're there today and your mom, your dad or both of them think you've lost your mind and lost your right to keep the family name.

Maybe your commitment to the family of God has been criticized as overly and unnecessarily ambitious and it produces friction when you can't be with your physical family for the length of time they have deemed to be appropriate.

Maybe the man of your dreams wasn't the man of their dreams and now dreams of family unity are dying.

Maybe mom and dad wanted you to attend their alma mater and your choice of a different college was, and still is, deemed foolish.

Maybe you feel the unspoken disappointment of your parents concerning the career path you have chosen. Maybe they said doctor or lawyer, but you said social worker. Now you face the "I-told-you-so" looks and comments when you don't have enough money for a down payment on the home you want to purchase.

Whatever pain you felt, or whatever pain you still carry due to the unfortunate misunderstandings and misgivings of your family, big brother Jesus knows your struggles and looks forward to hearing from you and helping you to work through them on a regular basis.

The king was distressed, but because of his oaths and his dinner guests, he ordered that her request be granted and had John (the Baptist) beheaded in prison (**Matthew 14:9-10**).

When Jesus heard what had happened, he withdrew by boat to a solitary place (**Matthew 14:13**).

Death of a Loved One

For Jesus, this must have been the worst of news: John the Baptist was dead. In his heart and mind, John wasn't just another prophet. He was a relative and, more than likely, a best friend for many years. Nobody else had the ability to understand the challenges Jesus faced, but at least John could relate to some. How many times do you suppose they had sat down and talked about life, the loneliness of being God's voice, the frustration and temptation to feel like a failure when so many refused to repent upon the conclusion of one of their messages, the misunderstanding of family and friends who viewed their radical lifestyles, and so much more? Who else could Jesus turn to for a listening ear? Who else could he spend time praying with and, as a result, be drawn nearer to God? And whenever Jesus would pause to remember John and his death, he knew he was next. In only a short time, Jesus would face his executioners, just like John had. Only his death would be a long and torturous bloodbath.

Who was it for you? Who died and left you hurting like never before? When did the gaping hole first appear in your heart? When did you first suffer the pain of earthly separation? When did you first realize how many tears could be produced in one day? When did you first feel the need to just get away from everything and everybody, and a big part of you never wanted to come back?

Was it your Mom who died? The only one you had ever felt loved by unconditionally was suddenly taken from you and the pain still seems unbearable. What will you do now? Where will you turn for your security? Who will you chat with for hours on the phone? What will Christmas be like without her? Who can you confide in now and talk to about your latest special interest? How can Mother's Day ever be Mother's Day again? And how will you be able to help dad and the others who loved her get through this ordeal?

For some of you it was your Dad who died. Whether you got the news at six, sixteen or sixty, it was devastating. Who will you play catch with now? What will it be like without dad at your sporting events or school plays? Who will help with the math homework? Who will walk you down the aisle on the day both of you had been dreaming of for years, and how will you ever manage to make it through something like that? Who will you turn to now for financial advice or some good, old-fashioned wisdom? Who will come over and fix the leaky faucet? What will your birthday party be like without him there to celebrate and sing off-key?

To others, losing a sibling left you lonely and troubled. Who will tell you now which teachers in high school are those to be avoided? Who will teach you how to throw the curve ball, or who will take you to the mall and help you pick out your prom dress? Who will you spend two weeks with now on your summer vacation? Who will gladly watch your kids when you take off with your spouse for a few days? Who will tell the scary stories at the family get-togethers and who will keep you laughing all night until you're in tears? Who will you choose to fill your foursome for the Saturday round of golf you've enjoyed together for the past twenty years?

For many, it was a son or daughter. Weren't you supposed to die first? Will anything ever be normal again? Will you ever be able to laugh at the dinner table again? Will the sight of a school bus in front of your home always make you cry? Will the haunting "What if" questions producing guilt in you ever go away? Are reminders of "You'll be with her someday in heaven" enough to keep you encouraged while you live out your days on earth? How will you help your other children endure this shocking tragedy when you can't even seem to get through it yourself? How will you be able to take care of the grandchildren and help your son-in-law with everything new he'll be facing?

Maybe for you it was your spouse and your questions abound.

"Who will ever understand me like he did?"

"We did absolutely everything together, so how can I endure such loneliness?"

"How can I ever be for the kids what their mom was for them?"

"How can I even manage to sleep at night without her?"

"When is it okay to move on and pursue new relationships? Are thoughts of remarriage this soon after his death wrong?"

Maybe it was Grandma or Grandpa, cousin, nephew or niece, aunt or uncle, roommate or best friend. Whoever it was who is no longer with you, whatever pain you felt when they passed away and whatever pain you currently experience, Jesus feels it all and understands how it contributes to who you are today. Just knowing this fact should enable you to look forward a little bit more to tomorrow and pray with much more confidence today.

He could not do any miracles there, except lay his hands on a few sick people and heal them. And he was amazed at their lack of faith (**Mark 6:5-6**).

Disappointment

Many of us have experienced the discouragement of working hard for something but seeing little or nothing placed in the results column. Perhaps we poured out our heart to someone we studied the Bible with in hopes of bringing them to Jesus, but their hearts stayed hard. Months and months of prayer, follow-up calls, late-night talks, dinners together, careful examination of the Scriptures and much more spiritual warfare was bravely waged, but the white flag stayed in their back pocket. Now you feel like it was all a waste of time or, even worse, it must have been something you did or didn't do that caused them to turn down the greatest of all invitations.

You're tempted to get less excited about the other lost souls you're currently reaching out to, and you may even feel tempted to abandon future efforts to share Christ with your family, your neighbors or co-workers.

Jesus knows exactly how you feel. He was amazed how people could be so stubborn. He was dumbfounded that people could be ignorant and blind so as not to see who he really was. He couldn't believe his hometown cronies could dismiss his Messianic and Savior claims so quickly. While experiencing these forms of disappointment and frustration, maybe Jesus questioned his need to proceed. Maybe some of the following temptations stood at the crossroads to his heart.

"Why bother moving forward?"

"Why travel to the next city and embrace more discouragement?"

"Why not just give up on man right now and make my way back to heaven?"

"If they didn't get it when I dropped a miracle in front of them, will they get it when I disgracefully die on a cross for them?

So the next time you hear "No" to a church invitation, or when that incredibly awesome, future brother in the Lord you're studying with becomes a persecutor and a painful memory instead, or when nothing on your prayer list gets moved to the answered column, bring it before the throne of God because Jesus, your advocate and friend, knows the full intensity of your temptation to quit and the deep discouragement you feel from fruitlessness. Then find strength in knowing that Jesus is with you in your time of need and, like he did, get back on the campaign trail.

Hopefully, you're already excited about your prayer time tomorrow. Better yet, drop your immediate plans and go talk to God right now with more confidence than ever before.

What else can you count on Jesus to understand?

He experienced physical exhaustion (**John 4:6**), needed an afternoon nap and took it on a comfortable cushion (**Mark 4:38**) and collapsed in complete physical despair as he was forced to carry the cross to his crucifixion (**Matthew 27:32, John 19:17**).

He had intense moments of sadness (**John 11:35**) and emotional pain (**Luke 22:39-44**). He was angry and became upset at people's stubbornness and hardness of heart (**Mark 3:1-5**).

He knows your feeling of not being appreciated. Because of Jesus' kindness and ability to cure, ten lepers received a new lease on life, but nine left without saying thanks to him (**Luke 17:11-19**).

He knows what it's like to not be able to find the time to get away from it all. He understands the challenge of trying to schedule a few moments to fellowship with your two best friends called peace and quiet and he knows the frustration of being interrupted when you weren't through visiting (**Mark 6:30-34**).

He knows the joys and challenges of being wealthy, as well as the empty feeling and fear of being poor. He lived in mansions of heaven, but he also slept on pillows of stone while on the earth (**2 Corinthians 8:9**).

He knows all about the temptation of wanting to show off your credentials and prove your worth to those in a lesser position than yourself (**Matthew 4:1-11**).

He experienced the pressures of having to stay calm in a crowd and righteous in a riot (**Mark 2:1-2, 4:1, 14:43-50**). Surely he can help us find peace while trying to find a parking space. Without a doubt, he can understand our anxiety in an unexpected traffic delay.

Jesus also comprehends our moments of being totally overwhelmed (**Matthew 26:36-39**). He hangs in there with us when we have no idea about how we'll make it one more week with no more money. He knows the challenge of needing to get an assignment done in two days that normally take two weeks. Jesus knows the utter despair of getting the news confirming a terminal illness while you're still so young: He carried with him the reality of death by crucifixion for all eternity.

He knows your deep desire for wanting to take the easier path and how simple it would be to justify it (**Matthew 26:52-54**). He knows the temptation of wanting to say "Yes" to a lucrative job offer that could easily lead you to compromise your commitment to God (**John 6:14-15**).

Jesus knows your lowest levels of loneliness and what it feels like watching friends you should be able to count on not being there for you during your greatest hour of despair (**Matthew 26:40-46**).

He knows what it's like having others around you who are trying to set you up to fall or fail (**Matthew 22:15-22**).

He understands what it's like going from most popular to most pathetic in the popularity polls (**Luke 4:22-30, John 6:60-66**).

He felt frustration with the established leadership and system of government in his day, and was unfairly tried and executed as a result of their decisions (**Matthew 23:1-7, 26:57-68, 27:11-31**).

He wasn't above doing the dirty work. He probably would have much rather fried some fish or washed a dish in private than to walk on water in public. He, better than anyone, knows all about the feelings which lie deep inside the lonely night janitor, the one who works the job that nobody else really wants and the one who nobody bothers honoring for his meticulous, behind-the-scenes scrubbing of the toilets. Yet, he can also relate to the challenges of dealing with unwanted fame and the inability to step out for a bite to eat without being bitten alive by adoring fans (**John 6: 14-15, 13:1-12, 21:7-14**).

He knew the struggle to keep his standards high, and he knew the temptation to wrongly lower the bar to allow a top prospect into his family of followers. Jesus is there for us, first to relate, then to caution us when we move in the direction of allowing ourselves to believe that those we love are going to heaven even though they aren't living the life of a disciple (**Matthew 19:16-25**).

He felt completely abandoned by God (**Matthew 27:45-46**).

He felt intense physical pain for extended periods of time (**Matthew 26:67, 27:26-31**).

He felt the sentence of death.

He tasted death.

Jesus felt it all. God was one of us from A to Z! (Words beginning with X and Z may have been useful in Hebrew or Aramaic, but you'll notice in a moment I couldn't find any of them in English which Jesus might have done to make him better relate to you!)

He ate. He admired. He admonished. He ached. He aged. He analyzed. He asked. He answered. He angered. He applauded. He appealed. He admonished. He argued.

He burped. He bathed. He battled. He bled. He believed.

He calmed. He cared. He carried. He celebrated. He cried. He chatted. He chose. He cooked. He cleaned. He climbed. He coaxed. He commanded. He communicated. He committed. He complimented. He congratulated. He confronted. He contributed. He cooperated. He corrected.

He dared. He defended. He disapproved. He dreamed. He despaired. He danced. He died.

He earned. He encouraged. He exerted. He endured. He enjoyed. He escaped. He evaded. He examined. He explained. He emphasized. He entrusted.

He felt. He fell. He fellowshipped. He fasted. He fed. He forgave. He followed. He followed through. He finished.

He grew. He glared. He greeted. He grieved. He gave. He granted. He guarded. He guided.

He hurt. He hoped. He helped. He hungered. He held. He hugged. He hammered. He hid.

He insisted. He imparted. He inspired. He imitated. He informed. He ignored. He influenced. He inquired. He interceded.

He joked. He journeyed. He judged.

He knelt. He kissed.

He lived. He loved. He laughed. He listened. He learned. He lent. He longed. He lectured. He led.

He marveled. He mourned. He meditated. He moved. He managed. He mended. He ministered.

He nodded. He needed. He nursed. He named. He nurtured. He networked.

He obeyed. He ordered. He offered. He objected. He observed. He opposed. He orchestrated. He organized. He overcame.

He prayed. He preached. He persisted. He persuaded. He pitied. He planned. He pointed. He predicted. He proved. He pushed. He played.

He quieted. He quipped. He qualified. He questioned.

He read. He reasoned. He refrained. He refused. He received. He relaxed. He rested. He reclined. He ran. He rushed. He risked.

He sighed. He spat. He scolded. He served. He sang. He slept. He sweated. He sailed. He swam. He surrendered. He sacrificed. He searched. He shared. He shocked. He shopped. He shouted. He smiled. He socialized. He started. He stopped. He stayed. He strained. He stretched. He submitted. He supported. He sympathized.

He tired. He talked. He touched. He taught. He thought. He thirsted. He thanked. He traveled. He tasted. He testified. He trusted.

He unified. He uplifted. He upset. He urged. He understood. He unsettled.

He visited. He volunteered. He verified. He ventured. He vowed.

He walked. He wrote. He worked. He watched. He wondered. He whispered. He wanted. He wearied. He willed. He wept.

He yawned. He yearned. He yielded.

My dear children, I write this to you so that you will not sin. But if anybody does sin, we have One who speaks to the Father in our defense—Jesus Christ, the Righteous One (**1 John 2:1**).

🌿 Chapter Twenty-One 🌿

Not Even Once

For we do not have a high priest who is unable to sympathize with
our weaknesses, but we have one who has been tempted in every way,
just as we are—yet was without sin.
— Hebrews 4:15

God made him who had no sin…
— 2 Corinthians 5:21

Go ahead and give it your best shot. Make it your all-consuming focus for the next twenty-four hours. Let nothing else enter your mind but this one thought: ***"I will not sin for the entire day!"*** How will you plan on accomplishing this lofty goal? Perhaps you should secretly slip away from the numerous pressures of life and head high up into the mountains for the entire day—just you and your God. Or, you could find yourself a powerful partner who has made the same commitment of saying "No" to sin and keep each other as focused as possible throughout the day. Or, you could stay locked in your house all day long, ask other members of the household to do just the opposite and keep yourself from every possible temptation you typically face in a normal day outside the comforts of your home. Maybe you could put on a thick blindfold and forbid your eyes from moving your heart away from the narrow road of absolute purity. Maybe you could tightly tape your mouth shut and eliminate your lips from letting loose just once to keep the commandment of speaking, *"only what is for the building up of others"* (**Ephesians 4:29**). Maybe you could schedule fun-filled appointments with only your best of friends and others you find easy to get along with. Or, why not volunteer to work twenty-four straight hours at the homeless shelter and serve the needy. Surely you wouldn't think of sinning during your time there because you'll be overwhelmed with gratitude for your richly blessed life. Better yet, you could persuade your entire church family to take the challenge and have a 24-hour worship service full of prayer, singing and Scripture reading.

Could you do it? Could you keep your eyes focused, your mouth muzzled, your mind clear and, most of all, your heart pure for even one day? Honestly, your best bet in reaching this gargantuan goal would be to just go to sleep and not bother waking up for the next twenty-four hours. Go ahead and catch up on all the hours of rest you've been robbed of over the past few months, wake up, then pat yourself on the back for your amazing accomplishment of a day without sin. Then try creating the scenario once again the following twenty-four hours and see how deep you get into the day before Satan has suckered you into seeking out some silly short-term pleasure called sin.

Now imagine not sinning for your entire life! For thirty-three years, Jesus turned down the devil and brought honor to God. Not even once did he slip. In my opinion, this is the most amazing accomplishment ever known to man. Jesus, as a result of this one phenomenal achievement, becomes my hero, my example and my Lord. Nobody else has ever, or will ever, do what Jesus did in delivering a knockout blow to each and every sinful opponent he faced. Nobody else has ever, or will ever, come anywhere close to reaching the high-mark of righteousness that Jesus set for how a human should live out their existence on earth. Any attempt to compare any other human to him is deplorable. Any comment of "You remind me of Jesus" should be shunned, leaving us too embarrassed to respond. Any mention of Mohammed or Buddha in the same category as Jesus is as far-fetched as the earth being flat or war being fun. Any plan to speak of Confucius and Christ in the same breath or on the same level should immediately be demolished. And don't bother bringing up Gandhi, Churchill, Martin Luther King Jr. or any other of the world's twentieth century heroes. Just give me Jesus. The Doobie Brothers (a band that was big in the 70s for those of you in the younger generation) were on the right track, but fell way short. Jesus is more than *"just all right with me"*—Jesus is perfect with me!

> *For thirty-three years, Jesus turned down the devil and brought honor to God. Not even once did he slip.*

But what is even more amazing to me about Jesus is the context in which he remained sinless. Jesus wasn't living in total isolation. He didn't hang out for months on end at the Messiah Monastery. He didn't just sneak out for a quick trip to the nearby deli once a week and cross paths with a few wonderful people along the way. He didn't sail his boat on the Sea of Galilee all day, every day, then put up a "Do Not Disturb" sign when he docked for the night. People didn't come to Jesus by appointment only. Usually, people forced their way into his time and space. He spent just as much time dealing with his enemies as he did teaching his friends. He never wore a bag over his head to maintain purity and he never avoided conversations or spending time with women to maintain his lust-free status. People rarely understood Jesus, regularly questioned his motives and were looking for ways to get him to sin just once.

Satan had a target on Jesus since the stables of Bethlehem. Who knows how many vicious attacks were launched to destroy Jesus after he reached the age of accountability and in the many years he lived before he began his three-year public ministry, announcing himself to the world as the one who had never sinned? After his baptism and prior to his first public appearance as the pronounced Messiah, and having just spent forty food-less days in the desert, a starving Jesus was the target of the devil's flaming arrows. Three years later in the Garden of Gethsemane, Satan unloaded his entire arsenal upon Jesus while he was in the midst of his deepest sorrow, anticipating the suffering he was about to endure to become the offering acceptable to God for the sins of the world.

Throughout the lifetime of Jesus, Satan had one thought: *JUST ONCE!* He cleverly had demons positioned at every turn of Jesus. He made personal appearances where the best opportunities were available and launched hell's fury in Jesus' path. And all he needed to do was succeed once. One sin would be enough. One sin would end the eternal plan. One sin would increase hell's population by the billions. One sin would send the heavens and the earth into an eternal frenzy. One sin would cancel all Christmas celebrations. One sin would eliminate all printing orders for church hymnals. One sin would end the need for this book. One sin would bring down Jesus to the level of every other man and woman who has ever lived!

But one sin never happened. Not once in private. Not once in a crowd. Not once during a heated debate with the Pharisees. Not once when thinking quietly to himself. Not once during forty lonely days in the desert with no food and water. Not once when enjoying plentiful food and fellowship. Not once when falsely accused. Not once when properly identified. Not once when given the cold shoulder. Not once when being praised. Not once when looking at a woman. Not once when thinking about a woman. Not once when the world's riches were at his disposal. Not once when the world's wrath was on his doorstep. Not once when he agonized in physical pain. Not once when he enjoyed physical prowess. Not once when he wondered why God had forsaken him. Not once when he was confident that God was close by. Not once when his best friends abandoned him. Not once when his best friends worshiped him. Not once early in the morning. Not once late at night. Not once when nobody was looking. Not once when everybody was staring. Not once while lying in bed. Not once while walking the busy streets of Jerusalem. Not once when he rebuked. Not once when he encouraged. Not once when he was full of energy. Not once when he was physically exhausted. Not once when he was emotionally drained. Not once when he was on an emotional high. Not even once.

Add to all this the fact that Jesus lived with the pressure of knowing he had to remain sinless, even though temptation would visit him constantly, and that you and I, two-thousand years later, were depending upon him to succeed.

Steering clear of sin is no easy task. Even when we set out to do good works, our hearts are constantly being tested and found to be falling short of perfection. In the spring of 2002, many disciples in the St. Louis Church of Christ worked downtown and parked cars in area lots before Cardinals baseball games. It was one of the ways we encouraged church members to raise money if, on their own, they weren't going to be able to meet their financial pledge for our yearly Special Mission's Contribution. Many of us who had already reached or exceeded our pledge still participated, taking what we earned and applying it toward someone in the church who still needed help in reaching their personal goal. I participated a total of five times and was very grateful for each opportunity to do so. But, I also discovered a few troubling things about my heart and I quickly realized how far I still needed to go to be more like Jesus.

On one occasion, I had no real desire to be there, and I found myself becoming critical toward some members in the church who I felt needed to be working but still hadn't participated once. I saw self-righteousness rise to new heights right before my very eyes. I proudly thought, "I'm better than others," then, "I'm obviously more spiritual," and finally, "No wonder I'm the minister," all because I was going above and beyond the expectations I had set for myself in this service to the Lord. *SIN*!

I repented of that nasty attitude and looked forward to my next opportunity to help in the fund-raising. This time I cautiously guarded my heart and refused to consider who was there and how many times they had worked compared to me. Unfortunately, I dropped my shield just long enough to allow Satan the necessary time to carefully aim his bow and shoot his fiery arrows my way, piercing my heart with more pride and arrogance. For the four hours I was parking cars, the thought of "I'm sure glad I don't do this for a living" penetrated the spiritual layers of my heart, seeping into those same invisible chambers that I'd been working to strengthen for the past two decades. I began to look down on those who worked full-time as parking attendants and, once again, began considering myself better than them. ***SIN!***

Thank God I fought off those terrible thoughts. I returned from my sinful journey to once again realize that preacher of the word and parker of the car had equal worth in the eyes of God.

My third opportunity to serve the Lord in this capacity started off terrific. I was determined to stay righteous in the areas I had sinned in earlier, and I felt little or no temptation to return to those ugly thoughts for personal gratification. And just when I was beginning to think the parking lot demons had been cast out and conquered, along came Satan.

On this particular day, I was parking cars in the lot closest to the stadium where many of the wealthiest patrons park, along with family members of Cardinal players, Cardinal coaches and various other stadium personnel. Top of the line SUV's, BMW's and Mercedes proceeded my way, and my job was to check each driver's credentials and usher them into the correct area. And then it hit me: The thought I had never thought about getting.

"I wonder if these people think I work here full-time or if they know I'm a volunteer?"

"I hope people know I'm doing this to help out those less-fortunate than me."
SIN!

Can you believe it? Here were complete strangers who, more than likely, I would never see again, and I was worried about their impression of me. What did it matter? Why was that such a big deal to me? Was I again thinking this job was below me? Did the same sin from trip number two come back to bite me, only this time from the mouth of a different dog? Why should I care about what people think? If I really were living as a follower of Jesus, wouldn't I want to let the wealthy ones know that people parking cars were just as important to God as those performing surgeries, or those performing wonders on the field inside the stadium? But wait a minute! Why did I need to let the wealthy people know anything? Why couldn't I just do my job, smile and be kind to everybody who entered my lot regardless of income? Why couldn't I just spiritually waltz through my four hours of labor with much joy and gratitude, thankful I could stand, work and help God and his kingdom in some small way? ***SIN!***

Believe it or not, I actually looked forward to each of those parking endeavors (tests). I had two more opportunities and, both times, I came downtown with the same goal: Be much more like Jesus this time than the last. But each time I quickly realized that this no-sin thing was tough business, even after I had asked myself some tough questions to aid me in my efforts to be more like Christ. Questions like, what will I need to do to be better prepared this time and what side-door of my heart will Satan try to enter and how can I lock it before he gets there? While this self-interrogation exercise was helpful, it was by no means a fail-safe method in fending off the devil.

And then there's church-league basketball—a two-month opportunity to recreate and have some extra time with the brothers every Sunday night. After four years of sitting out from any type of competitive basketball due to back and neck surgeries, I gave myself clearance to play, pleaded with my wife and my physical overseers (the other brothers on staff with the church who didn't want me dying prematurely) to let me compete and got signed up to play. Two weeks into the season, my back was doing just fine. It was my heart that needed the help. With everything from keeping track of how many points I had scored, to why my teammates were taking those stupid shots, to why the referee missed an obvious foul on one of my shot attempts that made me look ridiculous, to wondering if people saw my sweet Michael Jordan-like move and would they make any comments on it later on, it was much more repentance than round-ball for me. I'm pretty sure that's why week three's court disaster occurred. After scoring 13 and 11 points in the first two games (see, I did know how many points I scored), I was shut out in game three with a big, fat goose egg. I scored zero points on zero for four shooting. After every game, I spent some time analyzing where my heart and spiritual focus had been during the competition, then made it my goal to show growth in any areas of weakness in the following week's game. While I could never guarantee anyone how my court skills would be displayed on a given night, I could tell them that after the game I would be wrestling with that repentance thing one more time.

Then there's the daily battle of driving and the devil riding in the passenger seat. Getting behind the wheel of my vehicle has to be one of the biggest ways my true inner issues come to the surface. Whether it's in regard to the idiot who's following too close, the ignoramus who's driving too fast or the imbecile in the front car at the stoplight who can't seem to find the accelerator when the light turns green (causing me to sit and view red for the next two minutes), my behavior is often irrational. *SIN!* What's the big deal anyway? As if I've never given a hint to a fellow driver with a near kiss to his bumper. As if I've never acted as though I'm in a time trial for the next NASCAR competition when I'm late for an appointment. As if I've never heard a horn or two from behind when my daydreaming and late afternoon space-out moments cause a three-second delay in recognizing green!

Finally, we have to talk about one of my favorite pastimes, watching sports. I've discovered Satan loves watching, too! When ***my team*** is on the tube, back off! Don't you dare walk in front of the television and block my view. I don't care if it's during the huddle, that's ***my team's*** huddle. And don't be rooting for the ***other team***. You have a television in your own home and nobody will bother you there. Don't be saying that was a poor call by the quarterback. I'm the only one who can criticize ***my team***. And Mr. Referee, you're in danger of the fires of hell due to that horrible call and God's going to get his revenge in the end. "It's just a game," I keep telling myself. None of this really matters anyway, does it? Even if my team loses twenty straight, God will use those losses to humble the athletes and maybe they'll become Christians then, right? Say it with me: **IT JUST DOESN'T MATTER!** Then why does it? *SIN!*

So watch yourself! Whether you're traveling to the game, watching the game, parking cars at the game, playing in the game or could care less about the game, Satan's in the game. He entered the contest when you were thrust from your mother's womb, and he or his demons have been following you ever since. Satan also entered the game of one young man more than two thousand years ago. And for thirty-three years, the man we simply call Jesus didn't make a single error or miss a single shot. Not even once.

🌿 Chapter Twenty-Two 🌿

The Dark Side
ℐ ℐ

God made him who had no sin to be sin for us.
— 2 Corinthians 5:21

The Lord has laid on him the iniquity of us all.
— Isaiah 53:6

Though he had totally rebelled against every demonic pleading to lust or lose his virginity, on this day sexual deviation enveloped his flesh.

Though loving God had never been considered by him to be second place or below on his list of things to do, on this day idolatry captivated his mind and cleared his schedule of any thought of God.

Though thankfulness was as natural to him as waking up, on this day ingratitude and "I deserve this anyway" were his natural responses to the blessings of God.

Though he had welcomed every opportunity afforded him to elevate others above himself, always leaving the front rows open for anybody else but him, on this day he fought to gain an inch to move closer to the top and demanded backstage passes.

Though the desire for attention and acceptance had been kept tucked away in his humble heart for thirty-three years, on this day he gloried in the masses that witnessed his wonderful words and deeds and basked in the security coming from their admiration and applause.

Though he had carefully walked the narrow road of righteousness and courageously avoided every sinful ditch and devilish detour, on this day he looked for ease and chose every eight-lane highway with low-volume traffic.

Though he had always been content with leftovers, hand-me-downs and open-air nightly accommodations, on this day he expected prime rib from a personal chef, tailored Ralph Lauren and the presidential suite on the Riviera beachfront.

Though he had lived a life of simplicity and often taught about the dangers of greed, on this day he was all about building bigger barns and selfishly enjoying the comfortable life of eat, drink and be merry.

Though he had always made it a point to steer clear of any form of debauchery, on this day he was the party animal with no thought of tonight's foolishness or tomorrow's pain, the impulse buyer with no concern of credit card chaos and the pornography addict longing for release but showing little regard for emptiness and enslavement.

Though he had always cast every temptation of hatred into the eternal abyss, on this day he pulled the pin from the grenade called bitterness, blowing it up in the face of anyone from foe to family member, all those who had wronged him or worked to make his life more difficult.

Though he had always kept his anger under control, on this day he cursed his closest kin for their numerous acts of stupidity and made obscene gestures to any who stared at him or stood in his way of progress.

Though he had paid every tax and left every store with a receipt, on this day he failed to record $10,000 of additional income to the IRS and left the store without paying for something he really needed, feeling justified because the multi-billion dollar chain wouldn't miss it for a minute.

On this day, he judged a young man solely by the color of his skin and stereotyped him out of a fair future.

On this day, he completely lost his cool and viciously slammed the back of his hand onto the tear-stained cheek of a helpless three-year old.

On this day, he cut corners and sought out shortcuts.

On this day, he tipped rather than tithed.

On this day, he brought his mom to tears with a dishonorable tone.

On this day, he stood his father down and labeled him a loser.

On this day, he made prayer secondary.

On this day, he chose sentimentality over standing firm.

On this day, he made a foolish vow.

On this day, he broke a sacred vow.

On this day, he lied about his education on a job application.

On this day, he made fun of the overweight woman.

On this day, he whined and complained.

On this day, he demanded.

On this day, he schemed.

On this day, he deceived.

On this day, he mocked.

On this day, he manipulated.

On this day, he masterminded the perfect crime.

On this day, he murdered.

On this day, he pretended not to see the starving child holding out his hand for help.

On this day, he came to the clinic and allowed a doctor to end the life of an unborn child God was forming.

On this day, he laughed at the radical commitment a friend had recently made to God.

On this day, he came to church to work off the guilt from the immorality he had committed the night before.

On this day, he stood behind the pulpit and preached to gain popularity.

On this day, he selfishly started a war.

On this day, he arrogantly refused to sign a peace treaty.

On this day, he marched six million Jews to their appointed death in the gas chambers.

On this day, he ordered the slaughter of three million people in Cambodia.

On this day, he flew a commercial jetliner into the World Trade Center.

On this day, he toasted champagne as reports of hitting American landmarks were confirmed.

On this day, he walked into a crowded supermarket with explosives strapped to his body, blowing up a young mother and her six-year old daughter.

On this day, he beheaded a man and had it videotaped to show the world that he and his fellow murderers weren't to be taken lightly.

Now before you cry "Heresy, heresy," hear me out! It's clear from the Scriptures that Jesus never actually participated in these sins and atrocities. But as God looked down from heaven upon the cross and doled out the punishment for your sins, my sins and the sins of all mankind, it was as though Jesus had committed them all and God was making him pay dearly. It was on this day that Jesus carried my sin to the cross for its rightful punishment. It was on this day that Jesus carried your sin to the cross for its rightful punishment. But what's even more amazing is this—as he carried our dark side to the foot of the cross, and then allowed himself to be fastened with nails to that cross, he himself refused to participate in darkness down to his final breath. If Jesus were ever going to succumb to sin and delight in the dark side, now would be the ideal time. If he were ever to feel justified in sinning, now would be the moment. But still he remained sinless (**1 Peter 2:21-25**).

They falsely accused him. He didn't answer back.

They unfairly convicted him. He didn't demand a new trial.

They laughed at him. He prayed for them.

They called him names. He called on the Father.

They cursed him. He blessed them.

They beat him with their fists again and again. He entrusted himself to God again and again.

They spat on him. He spared them.

They violently whipped him. He silently suffered.

They placed a crown of thorns on his head. He remained a rose.

They pounded nails through his hands and feet and into the wood. He fought back with the most powerful spiritual weapon at his disposal—mercy, saying, *"Father, forgive them; they do not know what they are doing."*

They looked for more hurtful things to say to ridicule him during his final hours. He looked for more hurting people to save.

They did the worst thing man had ever done. He did the greatest thing man had ever done.

Satan and the evil forces in the spiritual realm were taking their best shot at Jesus, but never did they convince him to change allegiance. He was God's man all the way, but still the dark side had to be overcome and the cross was the only way to win this war against a powerful foe. So the one who had never sinned was now volunteering to accept in his flesh the full wrath of God, the God who had hated every fiber of sin for every second of eternity. It was punishment time.

What was it like for Jesus to die on a cross? How did the guilt of sin taste for six long hours? How did it feel to incur the wrath of God for all the sin man had ever committed and would continue to commit in the future? How was it for Jesus on that day when he received your punishment and became the sacrificial Lamb of God to take away your sin (**John 1:29**)?

Have you made any time in your busy schedule to at least try to understand the intensity of those six hours?

How much time do you take to let him know what that act means to you?

Do you only feel relieved that it wasn't you who received the punishment, or are you overwhelmed with gratitude that Jesus would consider you more important than himself and offer to die instead of you?

> *The cross emphatically states that we will never be acceptable to God because of our good works, our great desires or our grand promises to him that we'll be better from now on.*

Do you try to teach others the significance of those six hours?

Does it bother you that so many seem so casual about those six hours?

Does it ever bring you to tears that billions today don't even have a clue about those six hours?

How much of your life has been lived in imitation of those six hours?

How much of your life in the past few weeks has been motivated by those six hours?

Yet those six hours are the most important hours of your life. It was during those six hours when every last one of your sins was fastened to the flesh of Jesus Christ. The reality and agony of this horrifying moment in time led to an awful awareness that overtook the heart of Jesus, causing him to cry out, *"My God, my God, why have you forsaken me?"* (**Matthew 27: 45-46**).

I believe Jesus knew the answer. I believe *my name* was the answer. I believe *your name* was the answer. Can you believe it? God took your dark side and gave it to Jesus! And in one, never-before-seen meeting of divine love and justice, Jesus donned the dark side, defeated the dark side, demonstrated his hatred for the dark side and emphatically declared that he would go to any length to remove the dark side in all of us.

But he was pierced for our transgressions, he was crushed for our iniquities; the punishment that brought us peace was upon him, and by his wounds we are healed (**Isaiah 53:5**).

The cross of Jesus Christ is, and must always remain, the central focus of Christianity. Its bearer, its horror, its meaning, its eternal implication for every man and woman and its selfless glory must never be diminished. All of these cross truths must remain in our head, in our heart and in our conversations with those we are trying to lead to God. The cross must serve as the constant reminder of our complete inability and unworthiness to approach God in our own way or based upon our own merits. The cross emphatically states that we will never be acceptable to God because of our good works, our great desires or our grand promises to him that we'll be better from now on. Only by the gift of forgiveness, coming through faith in the blood of Jesus, can we be saved from God's wrath in regard to our sin. We do not *attain* salvation by our moral standards or good works. We *obtain* salvation by our acceptance of God's grace. This is God's one and only offer. Our acceptance of the offer begins first and foremost with humility. We must come to a crystal clear understanding and a quick admission of who we are in comparison to Jesus. We must humbly admit what we've done to Jesus and why our only remaining hope for a relationship with God, both now and for all eternity, hinges on our willingness to be washed clean by his blood (**1 John 1:5-10**). While humility is the key in beginning a relationship with God, clearly it is also the key in the middle, in the end and at all points in between.

May the death of Jesus on a cross be the one thing we never forget! May it be the one thing we are proudest to proclaim! And may it be the one thing we cling to more than anything else to help us realize our immense value in the eyes of God.

❧ Chapter Twenty-Three ❦

Arrivals and Departures
✍ ✍

He appeared in a body, was vindicated by the Spirit,
was seen by angels, was preached among the nations,
was believed on in the world, was taken up in glory.
— 1 Timothy 3:16

On his arrival, Jesus cried out and was comforted by the response of his mother and father. He was touched. He was held. He was sung to. He was fed. At his departure, Jesus cried out, "My God, my God, why have you forsaken me?" He was taunted. He was harassed. He was shouted at. He was fed to the ferocious wolves in sheep's clothing.

On his arrival, Jesus was clothed from head to toe to keep warm and comfortable. At his departure, Jesus was stripped of his last item of clothing and left to die cold and in complete shame.

On his arrival, Jesus was completely dependent upon others to protect him from the cruel forces of the outside world. At his departure, Jesus chose to lay down his life and expose himself to the cruel forces of the outside world.

On his arrival, Jesus slept comfortably in the hay of a manger created for his protection. At his departure, Jesus hung in torture on the wood of a crucifix created for his execution.

On his arrival, a star appeared and brightened the night sky, announcing his birth. At his departure, darkness came over the land and hid the afternoon sun, announcing his death.

On his arrival, shepherds were overwhelmed with joy when they laid eyes on the beautiful baby boy Jesus lying in a manger. At his departure, family and friends were overwhelmed with grief when they laid eyes on the bruised, beaten and bloodied body of Jesus hanging on a cross.

On his arrival, Mary watched Jesus sleep and wondered with great faith about what was ahead. At his departure, Mary watched Jesus cry out in unbearable pain and wondered with great doubt about what was ahead.

On his arrival, the child was given the name Jesus, Savior of the people. At his departure, Jesus was given the name deceiver, seducer of the people.

On his arrival, many fell to their knees and worshipped him. At his departure, many stood stiff-necked and waylaid him.

On his arrival, wise men opened their treasures and gave to him. At his departure, foolish men closed their hearts and took from him.

On his arrival, angels were loud and jubilant as they announced his birth. At his departure, angels were silent as they analyzed his death.

On his arrival, many spread the word that the true Messiah was finally here. At his departure, many spread the word that the false Messiah was finally gone.

On his arrival, all who heard about Jesus were amazed. At his departure, all who heard about Jesus were appalled.

On his arrival, Jesus was washed clean of his mother's blood, bathed and handled with care. At his departure, Jesus was covered in his own blood, beaten and handled with cruelty.

On his arrival, those nearby marveled and commented about his precious hands and feet. At his departure, those nearby mocked and commented about the nails pierced through his hands and feet.

On his arrival, he was offered warm milk in the embrace of the mother who would raise him from birth. At his departure, he was offered wine vinegar in the torture of the cross, awaiting his father who would raise him from death.

On his arrival, his mother held him close, sighed and kissed his forehead. At his departure, his mother watched him from a distance and sobbed while blood poured from his forehead.

On his arrival, God became flesh and dwelt among us. At his departure, God became sin and reached out to us.

On his arrival, God said, "Let it begin." At his departure, Jesus said, "It is finished."

On his arrival, Jesus began his earthly battle against the devil. At his departure, Jesus declared his eternal victory over the devil.

On his arrival, God said, "Watch my Son." At his departure, God said, "Imitate my Son."

❦ Chapter Twenty-Four ❦

My Lord
and My God
❧ ❧

*Then he said to Thomas, "Put your finger here; see my hands.
Reach out your hand and put it into my side. Stop doubting and believe."
Thomas said to him, "My Lord and my God!"*
— John 20:27-28

When you're reading the above account of the resurrection found in the Gospel of John, isn't it easy to forget your own sinful tendency, the one that typically demands an over-abundance of physical evidence before believing anything out of the ordinary? Usually, our so-called forgetfulness is a result of pride and self-righteousness, leading us to look down with disdain upon Thomas, as if we would have been quicker to commit were we in his shoes.

"What was the problem with Thomas anyway?" we ask arrogantly.

Hopefully, most of us will humble ourselves before too long, jump off our high-horse, saddle up the Shetland pony and admit that we, too, take Thomas' trip to belief way more often than we should. Granted, at times, it is hard to embrace the believing part without the seeing part. But why should Thomas, or if we had been there, why should we have been surprised that Jesus had actually risen from the dead? For that matter, why should anybody have been surprised? Nothing about Jesus had been normal or ordinary for three decades, so why would anything be different now?

What did it matter that this kind of thing had never been done before? Nobody had ever walked on water or lived their entire life without sinning either, and Jesus had already accomplished both.

What did it matter that this "coming back to life" claim was medically impossible? It was medically impossible to make leprosy disappear, but Jesus didn't seem to have a problem with that.

What did it matter that there were Roman guards stationed at the tomb to prevent Jesus from exiting if he were somehow able to resurrect? They would be of no concern to Jesus. If he could wake up those who had been dead for a few days without any difficulty, couldn't he turn the tables and put to sleep those who had been put in charge of watching his grave?

What did it matter that there was a huge stone covering the entrance to the tomb? Hadn't Jesus gotten himself out of a number of impossible predicaments before this? And didn't John the Baptist say something about God's uncanny ability to take real stones and turn them into real people without much effort (**Luke 3:8**)? Couldn't Jesus have easily made a live-action Mt. Rushmore out of that big boulder?

The resurrection, amazing as it is to us, was merely another day at the office or walk in the park for Jesus. The bodily resurrection of Jesus is simply one more truth about this amazing man that separates him from any possible competition about whom you and I should choose to honor and obey as our final authority (**Matthew 28:16-20**). His birth. His fulfillment of specific prophecies in the Old Testament. His miracles. His teaching. His love. His perfection. His death. And now, his resurrection! Throughout the ages, those who have attempted to stake a claim for being God's one and only mouthpiece have displayed nothing even remotely close to the credentials needed to back it up. But the greatest proof that these are unworthy candidates is that all of them remain in their graves, waiting for the day when they will bow before the one who escaped from his (**Philippians 2: 9-11**).

Buddha, Confucius, Mohammed and many others throughout the centuries have claimed to be God's final messenger. Today, billions still cling to the teachings of these men from earth, but they know little or nothing about the Man from heaven. How foolish! None of these men ever said they would resurrect from the dead. And, most certainly, none of these men actually rose from the dead. And since it was clearly a non-issue to them, none even bothered to determine how they would go about proving that they had risen from the dead. And check it out with any of the current followers in these religious sects—none of them will gladly give up their lives to tell the world that their leader has risen from the dead. Yet Jesus truly conquered death and was totally unaffected by its lasting sting (**1 Corinthians 15:50-57**).

While Jesus was alive, he wasn't apprehensive or insecure about stating any of it as an already done deal. And when finally put to death and given the opportunity to prove he wasn't just all talk, Jesus walked out of the tomb within three days and accomplished this amazing feat. In regard to his resurrection, let's focus on four truths to help us in our understanding of this most unbelievable achievement.

He predicted it

Talk about pressure! Over and over again, Jesus told his twelve disciples and many others that physical death would not signal the end of his life or his ministry (**Luke 9:21-22**). More often than not, his listeners failed to understand the message of the resurrection or, perhaps they blew it off as merely metaphorical or more than they could handle at the time. Nevertheless, Jesus continued to predict it. He wanted people to hear it. He hoped they would write it down and then wait for it to happen. He looked forward to his critics trying to make sure it would never happen. He knew he had come from God and was returning to God (**John 13:3**) and that the tomb was just a temporary stop. Three days would be enough rest for Jesus, then he would go right back to work preaching, loving, forgiving, interceding and being for a lost world what they still needed him to be—both Lord and Christ (**Acts 2:36**).

He performed it

Then he did it. Early that Sunday morning, life and breath were given back to the crucified Son of God. His brain waves began to function. His heart started beating. His eyelids were opened. His muscles flexed. His blood flowed. He woke up, sat up, stood up and removed his temporary grave clothes. Then, as a company of Roman soldiers shook with fear and froze as though dead, an angel who would make Arnold look like a lightweight rolled the tremendous stone away from the tomb's entrance and Jesus walked out, never to die again (**Matthew 28:2-4**).

He proved it

Now it was time to show his face. He knew many people would still wonder if it were true, even after seeing him. For Jesus, then, it was all about leaving convincing proof. He didn't want anyone who saw him beyond the grave to think he was only a mirage or a make-pretend friend. He was Jesus and he was back from the dead. And he needed to convince more than just a few. So for forty days, Jesus proved this resurrection thing was for real. People touched him and talked with him. A privileged few ate with him and were taught by him. Some received a rebuked from him for their lack of faith as he showed them his crucifixion scars.

He appeared a number of times to different numbers of people. Mary Magdalene was the first to witness his resurrection (**Mark 16:9**). He also had an extended conversation with two disciples somewhere on the road to Emmaus (**Luke 24:13-35**). On another occasion, Jesus had a meal on the beach with seven of his disciples (**John 21:1-14**). He met once with all the disciples except Thomas (**John 20:19-25**). He enjoyed regular fellowship with the remaining eleven apostles and met with five-hundred-plus believers on another occasion (**Acts 1:1-9, 1 Corinthians 15:6**).

His visits were well calculated in anticipation of any doubters who lived then and those who remain skeptical today. What if Mary's resurrection claim wasn't taken seriously because most people perceived her to be an emotional basket-case who just needed some time to help her deal with her grief and move beyond the denial stage after losing a best friend? Maybe a similar claim from two trusted men who spent much of one day with the risen Jesus would carry more clout with the unbelievers. If that still weren't enough proof for some, maybe it would help to have a resurrection rally highlighted by personal sharing from seven no-longer-scared disciples, talking of the time they sat around a fire enjoying some fish and bread with a supposed dead man. Perhaps then this resurrection rumor would establish some credibility. If that were still being concluded as insufficient evidence for the skeptics, could a "he's alive" talk with Thomas put some of their unbelief to death? After all, Thomas was well known amongst his peers for his intellectual skepticism. Maybe a touching testimony from his lips would soften their hearts. What if all of that evidence was still judged to be incomplete and unreliable for some? Could five hundred men standing up and telling the exact same story about the day they saw Jesus beyond the tomb help the cause? Certainly, by this time, the "Jesus is alive" allegations would have gained tremendous momentum and been deemed worthy of serious investigation.

He preached it

Letting a little more than five hundred people in on the most important truth of all time was not the plan of Jesus. He wanted everybody to know and called for the truth of his resurrection to be the cornerstone of his apostle's preaching. So he met with them on numerous occasions and methodically explained this all-important truth from the Scriptures (**Luke 24:44-49, Acts 1:1-9**). He rebuked them for their lack of faith that he would be resurrected and charged them emphatically to let the world know what they had been privileged to witness (**Mark 16:14-16**). For forty days he trained them for their mission. For forty days his physical presence eroded any of their lingering doubts. For forty days he listened as the apostles asked their questions and for forty days he pleaded with them to preach about the answers he supplied. For forty days he encouraged them to cling to the joy of his resurrection and theirs to come. He would remind them that, even if their unpopular preaching led to a martyr's fate, their death would solidify for them an unbelievable resurrection. These eleven apostles were the key to the salvation of all men and women from that day forward. And from what we see documented in the book of Acts and confirmed in the epistles (**Colossians 1:23**), and from the billions who have clung tightly to the wonderful resurrection truth since the first century, they were truly successful in their mission to unashamedly convey that Jesus had indeed conquered death. Today, you and I are the beneficiaries of their boldness!

The resurrection of Jesus is an historical fact! Should we be shocked? Should we be surprised? Should we hope that it happened, or have full confidence? Should we doubt it, or fully disclose it? After watching and listening to an amazing presentation of talent in the life of Jesus, doesn't his encore seem to fit? And if the fireworks display has made you ooh and ah, shouldn't the finale leave you breathless?

Like Thomas, we, too, can confidently and proudly proclaim the same truth he came face-to-face with the day he saw the risen Christ: Jesus—our Lord and our God!

❧ Chapter Twenty-Five ❧

More About
the Messiah
❧ ❧

See to it that no one takes you captive through hollow and deceptive philosophy,
which depends on human tradition and the basic
principles of this world rather than on Christ.
—Colossians 2:8

Satan was, by no means, finished with Jesus. He had failed on every front in his efforts to sabotage God's plan, and he was outraged. Every attempt he had made to convince Jesus to sell out to shortcuts or succumb to sin had been thoroughly rejected. And he couldn't deny that the power Jesus possessed had completely overshadowed his. He knew that the many miracles Jesus had performed were still fresh on the minds of those who witnessed them and that recipients of those amazing acts were still around to relay their stories. What once looked like a convincing victory for his side, as Jesus hung in shame on a Roman crucifix, was now just another sore spot and sour reminder of his own futility, as the triumph and true meaning of the cross was making a public spectacle of him and his defeated troops (**Colossians 2:13-15**). Rubbing salt into his already painful wound, the resurrection exposed a fatal flaw in his fear and intimidation tactics regarding physical death (**Hebrews 2:14-16**). But Satan still had life and permission to roam the earth. Filled with fury, there was still much work to be done by the leader of the dark side (**Revelation 12:12**).

Though he was unable to attack Jesus in the flesh upon his ascension to heaven, Satan quickly shifted his emphasis to attacking the followers of Jesus in the flesh, those courageously spreading the message of his perfect life, his purposeful death and his powerful resurrection (**1 Peter 5:8-9, Revelation 12:7-13**). The devil's goal was simple—keep people from receiving the forgiveness of their sins, thwart them from being filled with the Holy Spirit and distract them from finding their way to the perfect place from where he had been eternally exiled.

Now that Jesus was no longer visible to the human eye, Satan counted on humans to become more open to his lies and half-truths and believed that his deceit could be used to quickly derail them on their journey to salvation. Jesus wasn't around anymore to answer the all-important questions about God and how to please him. And he wasn't there to pop a miracle in their presence and therefore re-establish his claim as being sent from God. So Satan set out, once again, to do what he has always done better than anybody else—*LIE* (**John 8:42-44**)!

But, as always, God was one step ahead. First, the Old Testament truths concerning Jesus, found in the sacred writings, were becoming more available to the common man in the first century. Along with that, the message of Jesus was going forth rapidly by word of mouth from those who knew him best. And within a few decades, people were discovering and rediscovering more amazing truths about Jesus in the letters from Romans to Revelation, much-needed information that was being circulated to every church and every disciple in the first century. These letters were crucial to the continued growth of Christianity in the first and early second centuries. God's plan was to use these powerful reminders of Jesus to blow away any clouds and fog that may have settled in the minds of believers, or potential believers, about his Son. Much heresy, false teaching and demonic misdirection were available to every impressionable listener. So God made sure, through Paul, Peter, John and others, that the truth of Jesus would not die out just because he was physically no longer on the planet. His life and his message of truth and grace would live on.

Praise God we still have access to the same message. In this chapter, let's consider some of the affirmations and re-affirmations found in these writings to help keep us on the straight and narrow in regard to our understanding of Jesus. These reminders helped to solidify the faith of our first century brothers and sisters in the midst of many lies, one being a teaching called Gnosticism. Gnosticism centered around a belief that all flesh was inherently evil and, for that reason, either Jesus was divine but never really came in the flesh, he only appeared to be in the flesh, or that Jesus had come in the flesh but, because flesh was completely unspiritual, he couldn't possibly have been divine. That false teaching was equaled only by a highly liberal "God is cool" philosophy, leading people to believe that they could come to their own individual conclusions about Jesus regardless of how crazy, confusing or clearly unsubstantiated they were in the written word. The valuable information contained in these letters, which helped to silence Satan's spokesmen in the first century (**1 Timothy 4:1-5**), will help to solidify your faith in Jesus and will help to obliterate whatever false teaching might be hovering over you at the moment. When initially presented, these eternal truths rattled the cages of doubting disciples and unbelievers both. When accepted, they provided the key to escape. These truths are meant to do the same for us two thousand years later. Jesus is still the same! Nothing has changed about him, and nothing ever will.

Regardless of the lies and half-truths you may hear about Jesus, the whole truth is still obvious and absolute. Is Jesus just another prophet in the company of Moses and Elijah? Is he merely a mighty angel rather than the mighty God? Is he just a great teacher, one of many that God has used over the years to teach people the deeper meaning of love and good will? Was he merely a ghost, an apparition, not really there in the flesh but only appearing to be? Was his death on a cross a sign of weakness and defeat instead of strength and victory? Did Jesus fail in his first mission to set up his kingdom, so one day in the future he'll try it again?

Many of these questions about Jesus are still being left unanswered, or are still eliciting wrong responses. All are being used by Satan to cloud the minds and clog the hearts of millions. Yet all can be answered in the information left in the early epistles, boldly written with the perfect aid and oversight of the Holy Spirit to remind those in the first through the twenty-first centuries that Jesus was indeed all God and all man and that eternal life is found only in him and through him. Here is a small sampling of what you will learn about Jesus in these letters.

Those in the city of Rome would be struck with the following impressions of Jesus while reading or listening to this great Christian treatise from the Apostle Paul:

> *As to his human nature, a descendant of David*
> *He was declared with power to be the Son of God*
> *Jesus Christ our Lord*
> *A sacrifice of atonement*
> *At the right hand of God and is also interceding for us*
> *God over all, forever praised*
> *The end of the Law*
> *The Lord of both the living and the dead*
> *A servant of the Jews on behalf of God's truth*

Our brothers and sisters in Corinth were reminded of these powerful truths, accurately describing the one they daily declared to be Lord:

> *Christ is the power of God and the wisdom of God*

The foundation
Our Passover Lamb
The spiritual Rock
The head of every man
The image of God
We must all appear before the judgment seat of Christ
God made him who had no sin to be sin for us
Though he was rich, yet for your sakes he became poor

The churches in the province of Galatia and the disciples in Ephesus were left with these morsels of truth on the man from heaven:

Who gave himself for our sins to rescue us from the present evil age
Christ redeemed us from the curse of the Law by becoming a curse for us
In him we have redemption through his blood, the forgiveness of sins
For he himself is our peace
Christ Jesus the cornerstone
The Head
Christ loved us and gave himself up for us as a fragrant offering and sacrifice to God
The head of the church
Christ loved the church and gave himself up for her

Many disciples in Philippi and Colossae were being exposed to a teaching best described as "Jesus-minimizing." They were being falsely taught that Jesus was definitely not deity. Paul quickly brought them back to maximum reality with the following truths concerning Jesus:

Christ Jesus, who being in very nature God, did not consider equality with God something to be grasped
He made himself nothing, taking the very nature of a servant
Therefore God exalted him to the highest place and gave him the name that is above every name, that at the name of Jesus every knee should bow
He is the image of the invisible God
The firstborn over all creation
For by him all things were created
He is before all things, and in him all things hold together
He is the beginning and the firstborn from among the dead, so that in everything he might have the supremacy
For God was pleased to have all his fullness dwell in him

The mystery of God in whom are hidden all the treasures of wisdom and knowledge
In Christ all the fullness of the Deity lives in bodily form
The head over every power and authority
The reality, however, is found in Christ
Christ is seated at the right hand of God
Christ is all, and is in all

Paul took some time to write to Timothy, his former missionary partner, reminding him of some key truths about Jesus. As we read these letters, God takes the time to remind us:

Christ Jesus came into the world to save sinners
There is one mediator between God and man, the man Christ Jesus
He appeared in a body, was vindicated by the Spirit, was seen by angels, was preached among the nations, was believed on in the world, was taken up in glory
Christ Jesus, who has destroyed death
Jesus Christ, raised from the dead, descended from David
Christ Jesus, who will judge the living and the dead

Before reading the messages contained in the books of Hebrews and Jude, many disciples of Jesus were ready to jump ship and abandon their faith. The following information kept them on the boat and rowing:

His Son
Heir of all things
Through whom he made the universe
The Son is the radiance of God's glory and the exact representation of his being
Sustaining all things by his powerful word
After he had provided purification for sins, he sat down at the right hand of the Majesty in heaven
So he became as much superior to the angels as the name he has inherited is superior to theirs
Let all God's angels worship him
But we see Jesus, who was made a little lower than the angels, now crowned with glory and honor because he suffered death, so that by the grace of God he might taste death for everyone
A merciful and faithful high priest in service to God
The Apostle and High Priest

Worthy of greater honor than Moses

Christ is faithful as a Son over God's house

Because Jesus lives forever, he has a permanent priesthood

Such a high priest meets our needs—one who is holy, blameless, pure, set apart from sinners, exalted above the heavens

The Author and Perfector of our faith

The Great Shepherd of the sheep

Jesus Christ our only Sovereign and Lord

The only God our Savior be glory, majesty, power and authority, through Jesus Christ our Lord

And John applied the finishing strokes on the canvass of Christ, closing the pages of God's final written message to mankind with more of the same startling revelations about the one who turned him from fiery apostle to beloved disciple:

The Word of Life

The Life

We have one who speaks to the Father in our defense—Jesus Christ the Righteous One

The reason the Son of God appeared was to destroy the devil's work

The First and the Last

The Living One

He holds the keys of death and Hades

The Lion of the Tribe of Judah

The Root of David

Lord of lords and King of kings

The Root and Offspring of David

The Bright Morning Star

Since the first century, the greatness and supremacy of Jesus have withstood numerous attempts by Satan and his evil empire to either be fully forgotten or brought down to a less lofty status. Many leaders of the Roman Empire made efforts to snuff out Christianity by snuffing out individual Christians, and usually made them suffer intensely until their final breaths could be taken. But his glory continued to be revealed by each of those martyr's refusal to call Jesus anything but Lord, even after being offered amnesty for a simple, one-time denial of the man from Galilee. The

Roman emperor Nero accused Jesus' disciples of arson when fire broke out in the great city. They claimed the only fire they were responsible for spreading was the message of salvation, due to the Holy Spirit that burned within them. The emperor Domitian demanded that everybody, including the Christians, recognize him as deity. The disciples stood their ground and claimed that Jesus was the only one they would ever refer to as God.

When it was finally concluded that Jesus' followers could not be stamped out and defeated, and that persecution against them seemed to be promoting their growth instead, Satan offered up a new plan of attack and Christianity became the state religion of Rome in the early fourth century. But true disciples who were well aware of Satan's schemes refused to accept the compromised, watered down version that was being promoted by the majority and clung tightly to the eternal truths of Jesus.

Throughout the centuries, the greatness and supremacy of Jesus have survived the many wars that have been fought falsely in his name, the inability to mass-produce printed documents revealing his credentials, the criticisms of liberal scholars, both religious and pagan, the low numbers of true Christians at different stages of history and the high numbers of false teachers at others. Today's attempts in movies, television mini-series, books and magazine articles to discount the man, the message he brought and the majesty he rightly possesses haven't changed the truths you just read about Jesus in this chapter. Today's fast-growing churches that see him as powerful but not perfect and delightful but not deity don't change a single thing about who he really is and what Peter, Paul and James were firsthand witnesses to. Even if all seven billion people alive today decide to believe that Jesus is just another man, those beliefs won't take him off his heavenly throne and replace him with our best choice. And one thousand years from now Jesus will still be who his friend John and his brother Jude claimed he was.

Oh, that all of mankind might come to know more about the Messiah and give Jesus the appropriate honor, respect and worship that he so richly deserves. And let it begin with me!

❧ Chapter Twenty-Six ❧

Jesus in Blue Jeans

Since the children have flesh and blood,
he too shared in their humanity…
—Hebrews 2:14

Imagine, for a moment, that you received a letter in the mail from Jesus informing you that he will be dropping by your house on a certain day in the near future. The simple message states that he wants to sit down with you in your living room and chat for a while. How would you prepare for an event of that magnitude? What would you do for the next few days to get yourself and your home ready for a visit from the Son of God?

Compared to other worries you might have about your upcoming visit with Jesus, what I'm about to say will seem a bit trivial. But one of the biggest things you'll have to decide is what to wear on that great day? Would you feel the need to go out and purchase some new and improved threads and bypass the selection currently hanging in your closet? Will you dress up, go casual or land somewhere in the middle? But, before you select the most appropriate apparel for that meeting, you should probably ask yourself another question—*"What will Jesus be wearing?"*

"What type of apparel would the King of kings don to meet me face-to-face for the first time?"

"If he's dressed up, but I'm not, oh no! If he's totally casual and I'm in a coat and tie, oh no!"

Relax! Without a doubt, Jesus would come to your house, my house and the White House wearing blue jeans. It makes complete sense to me. After all, doesn't everybody wear blue jeans? Rich people. Poor people. Middle-class people. Young people. Old people. Middle-aged people. Black people. White people. Asian people. Latin-American people. CEOs and cement truck drivers wear blue jeans. Doctors and ditch diggers wear blue jeans. Heads of state and the homeless wear blue jeans. Professional base-ball players and batboys wear blue jeans.

Now, I'm not sure if Gap, Tommy Hilfiger, Wrangler, Levi or another brand would be his personal choice. And I'm not sure if he'd wear the relaxed fit, straight leg, baggy or boot cut (wouldn't they probably be carpenter jeans?), but definitely, in my opinion, Jesus would come dressed in blue jeans. He wants you to feel secure and at ease. He wants to relate to you. He wants to be as approachable as possible. And, although he is who he is, he has never desired to flaunt it or throw it in your face. He's always been just one of the guys, and he never seemed to have a problem in that role. Jesus was a never-seen-anything-like-it-before man who made it his goal to be ordinary, all so you wouldn't be intimidated to learn from him about how your life can be extraordinary. So, a few minutes prior to his arrival, put on your favorite pair of blue jeans, pour a couple glasses of lemonade and plop yourself down on your couch. But don't forget to answer the door when he comes. He's never been the kind to barge in without knocking or without knowing he's welcome (**Revelation 3:19-20**).

Now that your choice of clothing is causing you much less anxiety, you should ask yourself a question that's a whole lot more crucial than the one about your outer covering. What do you suppose Jesus will want to discuss with you? What "inside" information will he be seeking to uncover from you? What questions will he ask you and in which direction will the conversation turn? What topic will Jesus start with? What will interest him the most about you? Will it be your trophy collection? How about your stock portfolio? Sure, he'd be interested in discussing your athletic endeavors, but wouldn't he be more concerned with how you're competing against your sinful nature? Sure, he'd probably check and see where your investments are going, but wouldn't he care a lot more about where you're investing your time and energy? And what will he try to change in your life? Will your furniture or favorite team become a topic for change? Probably not! More than likely, Jesus would sit on anything, cheer for anybody and welcome you to join him in both. Will your job or savings account balance make it into the conversation about change? Maybe. But more than likely he'd be happy you're gainfully employed. And, as far as your finances are concerned, he'd probably focus on making sure you always remembered that whatever amount of money you ***did*** have, it wasn't really yours, and whatever amount you ***didn't*** have, it wasn't really needed to make you happy. What about your hairstyle or your hobbies? How about your choice of vehicles or upcoming vacation plans? Would these things really matter that much to Jesus? From what I've found in the Scriptures, let me propose to you four areas in your life that I believe Jesus would look to change during his one-on-one visit in your home and on your couch.

First, Jesus will try to *change your self-esteem*. More than anything else, he will want you to know that you're deeply loved. He will want you to hear that all-important, three-word phrase coming from his lips, and he'll want you to feel it deeply and believe it is true. He will want you to gain security from that love, and he'll undoubtedly want you to feel special and unique, a one and only "I made you to be you" creation of God.

Unfortunately, most of us don't feel very good about who we are. Things happened early in our lives, or are still occurring, convincing us we're has-beens or never-will-be's. We picked up these strong vibes, whether right or wrong, from our parents, our peers, our failures in life, our looks or lack thereof, our weight (usually too much of it) and our authority figures, those who through the years told us "That's not good enough" or "You'll never amount to much." Oh, we act like we're secure and important, but most of us, deep down, don't really believe it's true.

In the summer of 2002, our family was able to enjoy a vacation on the Gulf of Mexico in Gulf Shores, Alabama. Most of our relaxation took place in and around the water—pool to beach and beach to pool, and then we repeated the process a number of times throughout the day. Every man I encountered in the pool or on the beach seemed to have little or no struggle with enjoying the opportunity to wade, jump, dive, float and swim without the hassle of wearing a shirt. Not me. I was born with what is medically termed *pectus excavatum*, a birth defect that left me with a large cavity in my chest due to a deformed sternum. Yes, I swam without my shirt, but not without high doses of insecurity and simply feeling like an oddball. You would think, at my age, I would have been over that silly stage. But I wasn't then and I'm still not. I did my best to cross my arms across my chest in order to hide my flaw, or I waited until the coast was clear to exit from the water.

For whatever reason, this chest problem seems to sink my spirit, and it has contributed to many moments of low self-esteem in my life. I know what many of you are saying: "Get over it already!" You're absolutely right! But you have your flaw too that shrinks your confidence level. And you know what? I'd probably tell you to do the same thing: "Get over it already!"

Unfortunately, most of us have more than one leprous spot we wish would just go away. A second one I deal with off and on is a four-inch scar on the right side of my face that came as a result of poor judgment and panic while riding a motorcycle in close proximity with some barbed wire.

Sure, most of the time I forget it's even there. But then, out of the blue, someone notices it and asks me (usually without much sensitivity) how I got "that scar!" It's at those times when I feel like the whole world is centered on my face and that my scar is about a foot long, a foot wide and oh-so-obvious to everybody. I usually struggle for the next few days with wishing "that scar" were gone and wanting to call a plastic surgeon and set up an appointment for him to do his job—remove my scar and once and for all eliminate this constant contributor to my self-esteem crisis.

But even with a scar removal, I'll still have to deal with a lot of other issues and insecurities that seem to make regular deposits in my memory bank. These memories can haunt me, hold me captive or have me thinking about quitting. But I'm pretty sure none of those options are what God has in mind for me.

Here are just a few of my issues and insecurities—things like my past sins of immorality, drunkenness and fits of rage, and the relationship consequences that followed; my many sinful choices of the past which have damaged people's lives and contributed to other hearts growing hard toward God; many episodes of impurity and debauchery, selfish behavior and outright stupidity in high school and college that I'd give anything to rewind and re-do; ministry disappointments like not being able to turn a hurting situation around when those who put me there were counting on me to make it happen; thinking I could have and should have done more to keep some close friends from leaving God and his kingdom; wondering if those leading me in the Lord are talking about me and, if so, is it positive?; wondering if the church I lead really does loves me, and would they be deeply saddened if I was called to lead elsewhere?; hoping and praying that I'm making the right decisions as a parent; worrying that my two children won't be proud of their earthly father and, more importantly, worried that they won't be partnered with their heavenly Father till death and beyond. It's these and dozens of other reminders of my self-focused and sinful nature that love to visit me during a typical day, often throwing me into the I'm-a-failure pit where God's sign clearly says "No Trespassing."

It's so easy for me to move in the direction of self-condemnation. When I was eighteen, I scored a hole-in-one while playing golf, but also recorded a score of 102 for the entire round that day. (More than 100 is good on a history course but not on a golf course.) It's impossible for me to think about the hole-in-one just in the context of the one-hole accomplishment. Almost every time it comes up in conversation, I feel compelled to share about the tragedy that occurred on the other seventeen holes. I've also bowled fifteen consecutive strikes before, but all I can think about is that I still haven't recorded a perfect game. I rolled five strikes in a row at the end of one game and then ten strikes in a row to begin the next game, but left a ten pin on my next roll and finished with a 289. When I'm asked about my highest game in bowling, many times it feels discouraging for me to say 289. Almost every time I get the chance to discuss it, I feel compelled to let people know that, even though I've never bowled a 300 before, I have bowled 15 consecutive strikes, three more than the required amount for a perfect game. Now isn't that silly!

What are your hang-ups and deepest insecurities? What are the roots of your self-esteem challenges? Most of us probably feel much like the leper felt when Jesus stopped by and sat on his couch (**Matthew 8:1-4**).

Let's call him Larry. Nobody but Larry and perhaps a few of his diseased friends had sat on that couch before. Larry was forced by all the smooth skin people in town to hang a sign on his couch reading *"Unclean Upholstery"* so normal and important-to-God people would stay as far away from it as possible, so as not to become unclean and unacceptable themselves. So, for the longest time, it was just Larry and his couch. It was lonely on his couch. And the longer Larry sat there all by himself, the more he became convinced he really deserved that fate. Every once in a while Larry tried to tell himself he was okay, but when the next fifty people who saw him sitting on his couch hurriedly darted away, he was convinced, once again, that he was wrong. Why, even the priests and the teachers of the law never sat on Larry's couch! So, of course, Larry concluded, God definitely wasn't interested in him.

Then Larry saw Jesus coming. He had heard some exciting rumors about Jesus and thought maybe Jesus could perform a miracle on his behalf and cure him of his dreaded disease. If so, Larry once and for all could be set free from the lonely-couch syndrome. When Larry saw him approaching, he rose from his couch and fell at the feet of Jesus, begging him for a cure. Then something incredibly strange happened. Jesus motioned to Larry to move back to his couch. But before he had time to think that this most recent hope for a normal life had just been shattered, Larry noticed Jesus heading for his couch, looking as though he, too, was about to take a seat there.

*"What is this? Doesn't Jesus know me? Is he really going to sit on **my** couch? Could this actually be my first spot-free sofa mate?"*

Before Larry could shout out "Unclean!", Jesus plopped down on his couch and, for the first time since leprosy had been confirmed by his doctors, Larry felt hope. Somebody actually cared. Somebody knew he wasn't totally useless. Then that somebody did what Larry had resigned in his mind would never happen again: He touched him. Not only was Jesus on his couch, which would have made Larry's decade, now he was holding his hand, which made his life. Self-esteem was gushing everywhere. The 'Old Faithful' geyser of good-feeling lying dormant inside of Larry was going off for the first time in ages, and she would never shut down. Larry probably could have lived on as a leper, now that someone had finally sat on his couch. He could have found joy for quite some time just knowing that at least one person found him worthy of touch and talking to. The physical cure that followed was incredible, and much appreciated, but the visitor on his couch and the touch of his hand was what Larry really needed. Jesus did for Larry what nobody else was willing to do—he loved him and made sure he knew it.

Jesus loves sitting on your couch, too. It isn't important how many other people have sat on it so far. He's sitting on it right now and telling you the same thing he told Larry: "You're special, you're important, you're valuable and you're loved." But that shouldn't surprise us, should it? It's what Jesus told every person he ever met.

Now that you've found some much needed self-esteem and security, Jesus would certainly try to ***change your thinking***. The reason he'll make such a huge effort to do this for any of us is due to his knowledge that much of our knowledge is incorrect. Most of us have relied way too much on what we think, what we feel or what we've been taught. But much of the information we've collected through the years is off. Some of it is way off! Jesus just wants us to be on—on-track and on target, especially in matters pertaining to God and eternity. During his famous Sermon on the Mount, Jesus sat on the couch with a number of disciples and did everything he could to change their way of thinking. The phrase *"You have heard it said,"* was followed up each time with a simple *"But I tell you"* (**Matthew 5:21-48**). The teaching so many in that era had been exposed to was old-fashioned, incomplete and, in many cases, just flat wrong. Jesus knew that if these disciples-in-the-making continued in their belief of the popular belief, they would miss out on the full life and, ultimately, miss out on eternity. So Jesus made it his mission to correct; to encourage us to erase our boards and tell us to start over; to direct us to delete all of our computer files and start re-programming. Even the specially selected twelve apostles were totally confused on a regular basis, and Jesus spent three years sitting on their couches changing their wayward thinking.

What have you heard? Is it right? Are you open to being wrong? Would you be defensive with Jesus if he pointed out a major misunderstanding in your belief system? What if he tried to tweak your mind just a bit to help you gain a fuller understanding of an important subject? Could he go anywhere in your brain and scramble things without you pulling the plug on him? Would he find your doctrine to be accurate? Would he see your life as full and headed in the right direction? Would he offer you a better way of treating people than what you're doing at the moment? Would he have to help you calm down and get a grip on how God's hand is involved in **everything** that happens in your life? Would you be willing to refill his glass of lemonade and invite him to stay longer so more of your misunderstandings could be discovered? Jesus will stay on your couch only as long as you want him to. That's how he operated while walking this earth and that's how he determines couch-time today.

Now that you're well on our way to a proper understanding of important truths, Jesus would try to **change your eternity.** For Jesus, it was never enough that people knew what was true but, instead, it was always a matter of their acceptance of it and how those truths were going to alter their daily lives. More than anything else, Jesus wanted people he met to be saved. He wanted to be able, one day, to sit down with every human being on their heavenly couch, to lounge with them and welcome them to eternity. That is, after all, why he came. Eternity and helping people experience it with God were what Jesus was all about. Whether it was one-on-one to the woman at the well or the rich young ruler, to a small group of disciples needing an explanation for a confusing parable or to ten thousand first-time hearers on a hillside, the message of Jesus was always the same: *I want you to be with me forever!*

> *For Jesus, it was never enough that people knew what was true but, instead, it was always a matter of their acceptance of it and how those truths were going to alter their daily lives.*

Jesus would try to ascertain from you what might be standing in the way of his hope becoming your reality. Or, he would make you aware of what you're too focused on right now that's keeping you from focusing more on heaven. He would emphatically elaborate on the fact that **this** life is not **the** life and would plead with you to put all your eggs in the heavenly basket so you won't be broken by the things of this world.

Once Jesus turns your focus toward heaven, he will tell you exactly how to get there. He'll unfold the treasure map on your coffee table and mark out significant points of interest. He'll highlight the roads of faith, repentance, discipleship and baptism. Then he'll boldly star the twin cities of loving God and loving your neighbor (**Matthew 22:34-40**). Finally, he will direct you to the great state of humility, outline it and tell you the grave dangers that lie beyond its borders. Then he'll roll up the map, hand it to you and tell you to read it as often as possible.

Before leaving your home, Jesus will address one final area in your life. He'll try to *change your purpose.* It would be considered incomplete, in Jesus' mind, to secure salvation for someone without calling that individual to be an active witness for him and an activist for the poor and less fortunate. And these were the very things that followers of Jesus devoted their energies to in the first century.

In regard to spreading the word about Jesus, the woman at the well got his message and left with the message to convert an entire city (**John 4: 27-39**). The demon-possessed man in the tombs heeded his call and set off on a ten-city tour telling people about Jesus (**Mark 5:1-20**). The Twelve, along with the thousands who were converted in the first thirty years of the church, gladly accepted the responsibility accompanying their salvation and told the entire world about Jesus (**Acts 17:6, 28:21-22, Colossians 1:23**).

In regard to responding to the poor and needy, the first century church accepted it as part of their discipleship. They knew that Jesus preached about it often, and many had seen him live it out in their presence (**Luke 14:12-14**). Even if nobody else cared, the poor could always rely on the Christians and their leaders to feel their pain and open their pocketbooks (**Galatians 2:8-10**). A leper could always look forward to a few minutes of face-to-face fellowship with the followers of Christ. The sick could count on regular visits, the lame wouldn't be left alone and the prisoner wouldn't be forgotten as long as true disciples roamed the earth (**Matthew 25:31-46**).

Simply put, Jesus will expect you to get off your couch and go searching for those who need physical and spiritual assistance. He truly enjoys the time sitting there with you but, if you're saved, he needs you to leave the house, bring someone back who knows nothing about him, take out the map he left for you, spread it out on your coffee table and start teaching them. Or, he needs you to leave the comforts of your home, go locate someone who doesn't have either and offer them your compassion.

Jesus will definitely ask you what you're living for at this stage of your life. He'll be saddened if he has to inform you that your talents and energies are mostly being spent on the non-eternal. He will challenge you to be, first and foremost, making disciples while you're making money. He'll remind you to offer the ladder to heaven to any of your co-workers as you're given opportunities on your job to climb the ladder of success. He will tell you to get more joy from your children memorizing a difficult Scripture than from scoring the game-winning goal, and congratulate them more enthusiastically for a Bible breakthrough than a buzzer-beater. He'll implore you to remember that gaining disciples is your ultimate goal as you're gaining a degree. He will remind you that people are lost and that heaven and hell are real. He'll paint graphic pictures of the hidden pain living inside those you know, and warn you not to be faked out by their smiling exteriors. He will tell you of the amazing joy that will accompany your efforts to fish for him, and the even greater joy to come when you finally catch someone. He'll tell you to make the extra call, take more chances in inviting people to church, even if it means looking foolish, and never assume anybody is going to be in heaven just because they truly believe they are.

Jesus will also ask you to open your eyes to the many hurting people on the planet, not just those who are thousands of miles away in a third world country, but also those who live in your own neck of the woods. He would point you to the closest homeless shelter and halfway house and ask you to try and make a difference with the people living there. He would offer you the address of the nearest nursing home and tell you to go play Bingo with the residents or hold the hand of an Alzheimer's patient. He would remind you of the orphanage in town and ask you to offer love to a ten-year old who has never seen it. He would ask you to drive by the prison more often and think about what the inmates inside really need and how you might be able to meet it. He would admonish you to not turn the channel on your television when starving people are being shown and donations are being requested. He would encourage you to consider adopting or being a foster parent to give a child a chance to feel welcomed and wanted.

So how have you done on the couch? During this chapter and, for that matter, throughout this entire book, you've been on the couch with Jesus. What have you heard? What have you seen? What have you felt? What have you learned?

Jesus in blue jeans—he has shown himself to be incredibly down-to-earth. He's infinitely kind and completely loving. He's unapologetic about his expectations. And he is, without a doubt, persistent, but not pushy. Was he successful in his time with you? Do you know him better now? Do you love him more now than you did before his latest visit? What can you tell others about Jesus now that you've had your time on the couch with him?

I'm certain many more books will be written about Jesus in your lifetime? More than likely, you'll read a few of them before your days are through. And you will undoubtedly hear a number of sermons that will attempt to uncover his true character and reveal his true glory. Never tire of it! Never think you've had enough! Welcome it! Search out more about him than you think you should. Make it your all-consuming passion to get to know the one who would wear blue jeans if he were to meet with you on earth and the one who will be wearing a crown when he meets you in heaven.

❦ Chapter Twenty-Seven ❦

In His Steps
∼ ∽

But if anyone obeys his word, God's love is truly made complete in him. This is how we know we are in him: Whoever claims to live in him must walk as Jesus did.
— I John 2:5-6

It's a four-letter word that many people who claim to be Christians have decided to completely eliminate from their spiritual vocabulary—**must**. We live in a religious world that focuses a whole lot more on admiration than application when it comes to knowing Jesus. It's one thing to admire Jesus. It's a completely different challenge to imitate him. It's one thing to talk about Jesus. It's another thing altogether to walk like him.

"But Jesus was perfect, and I'm certainly never going to be perfect," many would say quite defensively.

Don't you think God was aware of that truth a lot more than you are now when he chose to include this passage in his written word?

*"I'm certainly going to **try**, but you can't expect too much."* That's the general excuse heard coming from those whose spiritual thermostats are set at lukewarm.

Is the word **try** contained in the text? As Yoda remarked to a young Luke Skywalker after he had just given up hope in raising a disabled starship from a swamp in the classic Star Wars epic, *The Empire Strikes Back*—*"Do, or do not; there is no try!"*

We're so caught up in creating our clever excuses for where we are with God today, many of us haven't grown in years in becoming more like Jesus. We're spiritually stuck! And until we develop a conviction that God is serious about this verse being honored and obeyed, our spiritual starships will remain in swamps of religiosity and mediocrity.

It is high time to take the word **must** to heart and get serious about the call to walk in his steps. No book about Jesus should just tell readers more about who he is. If you know who Jesus is and it ends there, it would be better for the two of you to never have been introduced. But since you're already this far in the book, it's too late for that anyway, and that's exactly how God has set it up. After seeing this most amazing life, why wouldn't you want to figure out how to imitate the man? Assuming this is now your heart's desire, I'll leave you with a few basics and some practical solutions on how to live the time you have remaining *in his steps*.

First, you'll need to swallow your pride and ask for help. God has designed us to both need help and provide help for each other, and there are plenty of people available who would love to help you on this exciting journey (**Hebrews 3:12-14, 10:24-25**). Get all the help you possibly can on a one-on-one basis, but also get involved in some type of small group with people of a similar passion. While Jesus was a master at wowing the huge crowds with his words and wisdom, and while he radically changed a number of lives in one-on-one encounters, most of the training and character building he accomplished with the men who would later change the world was done in a group setting. It is my conviction that, in the right atmosphere of "one desperate student telling another desperate student the information he just received from the teacher about what to expect on the final exam," you will find this true in your spiritual life as well.

Secondly, go at it with passion. Make it your number one focus in life (**2 Timothy 2:3-7**). At different times in my life, I've been willing to subject myself to much focus, pain and humiliation in order to get something I really wanted. I worked an entire summer with my college roommate doing nightly cleanup of flesh, blood and guts at a local slaughterhouse. It was the most disgusting job I've ever had! But I needed the extra cash for dates with my new girlfriend, Patty, and no other would-be employers were offering me the kind of money I was making there.

I also worked for a few years as a city league basketball official. My roommate and I needed sufficient funds to support our sport's addiction, a rented 25-inch color television to watch all the big events and season tickets for University of Washington football games. If you don't know anything about city league basketball, the men you often find playing are former high-school subs who think they missed a shot at the NBA because of bad timing. They play their hearts out for the five fans in attendance and can't believe you would actually make a call that goes against them. I was told where to go on a regular basis and believe me it wasn't over to their house for snacks after the game! But I endured the scorn and shame and suffered for the cause of keeping sports at the forefront of my life. If that's how I was willing to go after an idol, then certainly I can do at least that much while pursuing my God (**Colossians 3:23**).

Next, watch other people you admire in regard to their ability to imitate Jesus and observe carefully how they go about it. It's amazing how much we can learn just by watching someone for a while. Spend some time with these people, ask them questions and elicit their help in your efforts (**1 Corinthians 4:14-17**).

Fourth, read the four Gospel accounts over and over again and keep putting Jesus before your eyes. Much of Christianity is simply relearning what we've already learned but somehow forgot to put into practice. Read through them slowly. Think about what you see. Watch Jesus in action in a specific area then make it your goal that day to imitate him in the exact same way (**2 Peter 1:5-15**).

Next, pray about it every day. What prayer could be more important and more special to God than the simple prayer of, "God, please help me to be like Jesus"? Do you think God might be eager to answer that one? Be specific. Be humble. Admit your shortcomings to him and beg him for wisdom and strength to live up to the name Christian (**Colossians 1:9-13**).

Sixth, get regular reviews. Don't get direction on how to be a better imitator and then find out how you're doing weeks later. Invite people to be daily involved in your life. Ask people from time-to-time to tell you what they see in you that must be changed to become more like Jesus. Ask them to also tell you about any positive results they've seen and the ways they've noticed you growing to become more like him. Remember, we're not the best judges of whether or not we're being formed into the image Christ (**Colossians 1:28-29**).

Next, rest in the grace that's available. Don't plan to fail or fall short, but definitely plan to accept his plan called grace when you realize your shortcomings and sins. Enjoy the continual forgiveness and cleansing promised to you as you take the thrilling ride of discipleship, and take pride in the honor of having a role model and rust-remover like Jesus (**Romans 5:6-11**).

Finally, don't quit. You can be a disciple, and a strong one, all the days of your life! Satan will tempt you to think that it's just not for you, but that's a big, fat lie (**Hebrews 10:32-39**).

While playing in a church-league basketball game in Chicago in 1995, I dove after a loose ball that was heading out of bounds and wound up with my middle-back in the middle portion of the double-doors at the entrance to the court. I knew something was wrong the moment I made contact with the enemy of steel, and it was two long years later before I finally found relief.

At times I felt like giving up and resigning to a life of back pain and limited recreational activity. But I was determined to get back to normal as much as possible. Often, after preaching for only a few minutes or standing in one place for a short time, I would need to lie down on my back for a few hours just to lessen the pain.

I began my journey to recovery by seeing a chiropractor from the church in Chicago. No relief. Then I spent a few weeks going to a physical therapist for treatment. Things remained the same. Finally, they ran a number of tests and concluded that I had three herniated disks and other problems in my neck and lower back that were causing the pain. Shortly thereafter, we moved to Los Angeles and I continued to see a physical therapist. Things were growing steadily worse and my pain was increasing. The physical therapist there recommended I try acupuncture and, desperate for a fix, I allowed a total stranger to stick my body with pins. Those forty-five minutes in his office were wonderful and soothing to every part of my body. But later that same day, the pain prevailed. I continued to see him for about two months in hopes the treatment would stick-it to my pain and defeat it. It didn't help at all.

Many people had discouraged me from seeking surgical solutions, and I had heard some horror stories of those who chose that option. But I had tried everything else and nothing was helping. So after weighing the risks and benefits, I decided upon surgery. I needed two major operations, one on my lower back and the other to repair disk problems in my neck. In September of 1996, I underwent the first of two operations. The final one was performed in December of the same year. I must admit, at times, that I thought I had made the most ridiculous decision of my life by undergoing surgery. Those first few weeks after both surgeries were some of the most challenging times of my life— physically, emotionally and spiritually. But it wasn't long before I was enjoying golf, basketball, tennis and many other sports, just like I had before my back problems began. I can now stand without pain, preach an entire sermon and not need my bed until bedtime, lift weights and enjoy a fairly normal lifestyle for a 45 year-old. Though I lost some flexibility from having a few vertebrae fused, and I still experience some pain and stiffness in my neck and back if I sit too long in an awkward way or stand too long on a hard surface (the malls are the worst, but my wife thinks it's all in my head), I'm grateful to God that he brought me to Los Angeles where my injury could be properly treated. I have absolutely nothing against chiropractors, physical therapists or acupuncturist. I'm sure many others have benefited from their expertise. But for me, the operating table was where I needed to be. I walked for two painful and discouraging years and I'm glad I didn't stop searching until a victory was secured.

What walls have you hit that bring you daily pain? Have you given up hope that the injury to your spiritual life will ever be healed? Keep walking in the footsteps of Jesus and God will honor your determination with a plan to bring you relief. The plan may not be what you expect or want, and it will likely include some pain and self-denial along the way, but it will succeed if you will submit to it. For you that plan might involve getting open with a sin that you can't seem to overcome or telling the whole truth about the sin that is slowly but surely damaging your heart. Or, it might involve apologizing to that individual who you don't feel like apologizing to. The plan may be for you to set your alarm an hour earlier than normal so you can spend some quality time with God in prayer and Bible study before leaving for work. Or, it might mean you'll need to put a block on your computer so you can't access the pornography that has recently imprisoned you. Perhaps the plan involves a break-up with the one you're dating because you're pulling each other down. Or, it could involve a re-arranging of your financial priorities so you can start honoring the Lord with your wealth. Whatever plan God puts on your heart, don't dismiss it. Repentance is a tough step, but times of refreshing are waiting on the other side (**Acts 3:17-20**). My back ordeal has led me to a deeper conviction about maintaining my spiritual health—if I can let a stranger stick my body with pins and allow a surgeon to open me up and leave some screws in my back and neck, I can certainly let a friend poke at my Christianity. And I can definitely invite my fellow disciples to remind me, challenge me and admonish me to be more like Jesus. And I can endure a significant amount of pain and suffering if that's what it takes to be my best for God. If I can have that type of passion to return to normal and healthy physical living, I certainly can have as much, or more, of the same passion in my desire to become like Jesus. So can you!

We have absolutely no choice in the matter of who Jesus is and what he has done. It's history, and a remarkable history at that. We do have a choice, however, about how we're going to respond to what we've seen. Walking *in his steps* is the only choice which will provide you with an abundant life now and also ensure you that one day you will hear those most wonderful words of Jesus as you stand on the doorsteps of heaven: *"Well done, good and faithful servant; enter the joy of your master."*

❧ Chapter Twenty-Eight ❦

Trouble in Paradise

*But if anyone obeys his word, God's love is truly made
complete in him. This is how we know we are in him:
Whoever claims to live in him must walk as Jesus did.*
— I John 2:5-6

My wife and I were able to spend a week in Mexico celebrating our
20th wedding anniversary in the summer of 2002. We stayed in a fabulous,
all-inclusive resort on the shores of the Caribbean in Playa del Carmen,
about forty-five minutes outside of Cancun. Without a doubt, it was one of
the most beautiful places I've seen in my life—breathtaking and bound to
make any atheist rethink his position. We had been thinking about this trip
for a number of years and, after considering other options such as Hawaii,
Jamaica and Bermuda, we settled on Mexico and were all set for one of the
most incredible times of our married life—relaxing, enjoying God's beautiful beaches, dining like royalty and just being together without the typical
pressures of life, parenthood and the full-time ministry. Our excitement
grew as each day passed, bringing us closer to our departure date. We had
never been to a tropical paradise and we were determined, in the words
from a song by Sheryl Crow, to "soak up the sun" and tell ourselves and
everyone else to "lighten up."

We had no idea that poison ivy, parasites and pain were about to
mingle with our Mexican getaway. Three days before we left, I discovered a
rash on my face that looked a bit like poison ivy. I had done some yard-work
about a week before our trip and met the dreaded green enemy somewhere
in my own backyard. I went to an urgent-care facility the next day and the
doctor gave me a shot of steroids and some medicated lotion to apply to
my rash, assuring me that the treatment I received should stop the spread
of the poison ivy. He was wrong.

We arrived in Mexico on a Saturday afternoon and my rash was spreading to my arms, chest, stomach and legs. There happened to be an on-site doctor at the resort, so the following day I went to see him hoping for a miracle cure. He promptly gave me another shot of steroids and put me on some stronger cream medication, then told me to be careful about being out in the sun too long because of the adverse reaction I might get from taking the steroids. I was holding out hope that both the rash and the discouragement I was feeling from missing out on a perfect paradise experience would subside. Neither happened.

On Tuesday, the doctor seemed surprised that my rash was still spreading, so he gave me an even stronger dosage of steroids in hopes that they would do their job and enable me to return to the full life. None of the medications I had been taking were making me ill, and Patty and I still managed to have some fun swimming in the ocean, riding bikes, walking along the beach, relaxing, sleeping in and just doing a fantastic job of vacationing those first few days. Tuesday night changed all that.

Whether it was an adverse reaction to the steroids, something unhealthy I ate or drank, a combination of both or something completely different, I got seriously sick that night and began experiencing some very intense abdominal cramps, rendering me useless and bound to the bed. I couldn't move and I really didn't want to. The next morning, the doctor came to my room and began dealing with my latest problem. A few shots of painkiller and some diarrhea-inducing medication and he said I should be well on my way to recovery. Hanging on to his every word, we envisioned that our final four days would be so amazing that they would make up for the first three days that were less than we had expected. It didn't happen.

My cramps intensified, my rash spread and I was more than ready to leave paradise for the comforts of America and a doctor I could fully understand. I gave up hoping my bodily mess would soon get cleaned up and that we would still be able to enjoy the end of our anniversary celebration. I wanted out of Mexico, and I wanted it fast. For the next three days it was nothing but bed and bowel movements for me, securely fastened to the IV the doctor had decided to put me on to keep me properly hydrated. We tried to arrange a flight back to St. Louis a day early on Friday, but to no avail. We did manage, however, to leave a bit earlier on Saturday than we had planned, and we were in the air by noon. That was, by far, the longest, most uncomfortable plane ride of my life. I was sicker than I could ever remember and now I was dealing with turbulence. Landing on American soil was a tremendous relief, but it didn't bring any relief from the pain. My cramps were worse than ever and it took what seemed like an eternity to finally make it through customs. Those who were meeting us at the airport had arranged to bring our car and I think Patty topped out at a speed of 90 mph on the ten-mile trip to the emergency room.

More pain than I hope to ever feel again came over me as I lay there in the ER waiting to be seen by a physician. I was hyperventilating, my temperature was below 96 degrees and my legs, arms and shoulder had become somewhat paralyzed. Finally, a doctor attended to my illness, gave me some much-needed pain medication and ordered a number of tests to be run to see if he could pinpoint the problem. A CAT-scan and extensive blood-work were done, but neither provided an immediate answer. But I would remain in the hospital for the next few days on an IV just trying to return to some type of normalcy. I had always planned on this trip being something I would never forget. I just didn't realize that most of those memories would be awful.

There I was, in the midst of one of God's finest pieces of creation, lying in bed with absolutely no desire to see any of it. During my stay in the hospital in St. Louis, I found one of the keys from our hotel room in Mexico, and the memories triggered just by looking at the key were nauseating me. What happened? Why was I feeling that way and why, nearly two years later in my life, do I have absolutely no desire to return to that beautiful place? The resort was fabulous. The beaches were magnificent. The weather was wonderful. Playa del Carmen was more than we dreamed it would be. But as of today, I don't want to see that place again. And who knows if I'll ever make a return visit there. I'm pretty sure I'd give Hawaii a shot, but beautiful Playa del Carman will probably never be seen by these eyes again except on a postcard.

I couldn't help but think how so many people are looking at Jesus in a similar way. Many paradise-seekers have had a bad experience with life, religion or both, and sadly these experiences have soured them on seeking and spending time with the most amazing, beautiful, wonderful and magnificent man who has ever lived. Many people have pursued a relationship with Jesus in the past, and even seemed to enjoy it for a while. But somewhere along the way, something got on their insides that made them spiritually sick, and now they have no desire to enjoy him any longer. They're content with the short time they had in knowing him, but for now they've had enough and they've decided there's no pressing need to get to know him any better. Many others, in their pursuit of Jesus, were hoping for something that would be, in their opinion, more comforting and more thrilling. Being under the impression that they had done everything on their part to make the relationship work, they believed they had experienced the fullness of Christ and were deeply disappointed with an outcome they considered to be far from full. These, and many others who have experimented with different forms of Christianity, got spiritually sick of Jesus somewhere along the way. Unfortunately, most of them don't have the energy or desire anymore to leave their rooms and check out the beauty beyond the closed curtains.

I'm not aware of where you are today in regard to Jesus. Perhaps this book has helped you to capture the glory of Jesus for the very first time. Maybe you understood his glory at one time and the book has been used to bring Jesus back to his rightful place of first place in your mind and heart. Maybe he's been your Lord and Savior for a while and the book was an opportunity to add to your "Jesus is amazing" collection. Wherever you are in regard to Jesus, I hope you've been encouraged and blessed by the time you've devoted to considering my thoughts about him.

If you believe you've reached the pinnacle of walking with Jesus, keep walking because there are other glorious peaks ahead.

In closing, let me encourage you to be on the lookout for trouble in Paradise. It's Satan goal to get on your insides, make you ill and leave you in your room so you won't be able to marvel at the glory of Jesus. Resist him! Even a small amount of his poison can lead to spiritual death. If he has already caused some damage in your life, don't despair! In the very same way we see him changing lives while living as a man in the first century, Jesus can remove your rash, cure your cramps, get you out of bed, take you for a walk on the beach, lower you into the warm ocean waters for a soothing swim and help you to relax in the refreshing breeze under the setting sun. If you believe you've reached the pinnacle of walking with Jesus, keep walking because there are other glorious peaks ahead. If you're totally satisfied with your spiritual life, stay on your toes! Satan would love nothing more than to sneak up behind you and drop a parasite or two in the living water you have been enjoying all these years.

If this book has helped you resist the urge to be unimpressed with Jesus, praise God for his power over the Great Impostor's plan to deceive you. If this book has helped you replace despair with hope for a full life, praise God for his power over your discouragement and decision to settle for less. If this book has helped you discover another peak in your spiritual journey, praise God for his power over your plateaus. And if this book has helped you notice the enemy in your rear-view mirror, praise God for his power over the devil's plan to keep you out of Paradise.

Jesus Christ is the Revealer. You have come face to face with his manhood and his majesty while reading this book, and you will be reminded of them over and over again as you study the word of God. Keep these two amazing truths before you at all times and model your life after the one who most deserves your attention and your affection.

❧ Epilogue ❧

Jesus—The Revealer

God's final statement is found in Jesus—The Revealer. Here are the mini-statements God has revealed to you in Jesus that collectively tell you the message he has always wanted you to hear and believe: *I hate your sin, but I am deeply in love with you!*

I visited you. God wanted to give you every opportunity to see what he was really like, so he developed for you the perfect picture in Jesus.

I showed you. God wanted to make it abundantly clear to you regarding the right way to live. He did so by sending Jesus so your one chance of living would not have to be left up to gambling and guesswork.

I related to you. God lived in the flesh in Jesus because he wanted you to know that he knows exactly what you go through and that he totally understands just how difficult day-to-day living can be.

I loved you. God showed you his love by the way Jesus treated the people he came in contact with while living here. How Jesus treated individuals and loved them is exactly the same way God feels about you today.

I died for you. God knew you could never reach heaven any other way. Due to your many sins, an enormous chasm had been created that separated you from God and his standards of holiness and perfection. That hellish valley of sin and eternal separation from God could only be bridged by a cross and faith in the man who died upon it.

I rose for you. In the resurrection, God proclaimed that your fear of death and your worry about the great beyond do not need to seize and control you any longer. When Jesus exited the tomb, he made it crystal clear there was more to living than meets the eye.

I ascended for you. God brought Jesus back home to heaven so the Holy Spirit could be available to you, sending him on a mission to offer you a personal and prolonged visit.

I intercede for you. God wants you to know, through Jesus, that he is still available at any moment you desire to be with him or talk to him, and he loves to work on your behalf.

I will come back for you. One day you will see Jesus again and, when you do, he will guide you to where God has always wanted you to be—with him for all eternity enjoying the heavenly banquet.

I am pulling for you. God wants you to know, through Jesus, that nothing would bring him more joy than to have you as an honored member of his household and for you to be able to fully enjoy the privileges that are included with an eternal membership.

In closing, let's consider some comments made in regard to Jesus Christ that have been made by noteworthy people during the past few centuries:

"If Jesus Christ is not a true God, how could he help us? If he is not a true man, how could he help us?"
Dietrich Bonhoeffer
20th century theologian/concentration camp prisoner

"No revolution that has ever taken place in society can be compared to that which has been produced by the words of Jesus Christ."
Mark Hopkins
19th century railroad tycoon

"Many teachers of the world have tried to explain everything—they have changed little or nothing. Jesus explained little and changed everything."
E. Stanley Jones
Author/missionary to India

"Alexander, Caesar, Charlemagne and I founded empires; but upon what did we rest the creations of our genius? Upon force! Jesus Christ alone founded his empire upon love; and at this hour millions of men would die for him."
Napoleon Bonaparte
19th century French ruler

"If Jesus Christ were to come today people would not even crucify him. They would ask him to dinner, hear what he has to say, and make fun of it."
Thomas Carlyle
19th century author/social reformer

"Had the doctrines of Jesus been preached always as pure as they came from his lips, the whole civilized world would now have been Christian."

Thomas Jefferson
Third American president

"Tell me the picture of Jesus you have reached and I will tell you some important traits about your nature."

Oscar Pfister
20ᵗʰ century clinical psychologist

"Gentle Jesus, meek and mild" is a sniveling modern invention, with no warrant in the gospels."

George Bernard Shaw
Irish playwright/1925 Nobel Prize winner

What statement about Jesus are you ready to make at this time? You might not be considered noteworthy in most people's minds, and you probably won't be sent a questionnaire on Jesus to be included in a book soon to be published. But you are noteworthy to God and he is very interested in what you think and believe about Jesus. And today you're being asked to complete the Father's questionnaire about Jesus and where you stand in regard to knowing and following him. The names of those who have already answered the questionnaire correctly are currently found in the only book besides the Bible that has ever really mattered, The Book of Life **(Revelation 20:11-15)**. Praise God if your name already appears. May it remain there and never be blotted out as you keep on confessing the most wonderful truth known to man, *"Jesus is Lord."* And if it doesn't, praise God if this book in some way has motivated you to search the Scriptures to find Jesus. May you begin to feel his loving concern about your name not appearing, be moved in the near future to receive the forgiveness he offers, then rejoice like never before that you've been added to the eternal roster **(Acts 2:36-41)**.

❧ Study Guide ❦

The Revealer

Chapter 1:

1. What are some of the ways we try to get people's attention and how does that relate to how God tries to attract us?

2. Why do you think so many people are distracted in their pursuit of God and what are the main contributors to this distraction?

3. How does that relate to you in God's efforts to reach out to you in the past?

4. What are the things distracting you from God right now that keep you from giving more of your time and energy to a relationship with Him?

5. Write a list of the specific ways you believe God has tried to get your attention in the past? Were they successful? Why or why not?

6. What might God be doing right now in your life to get your attention?

Chapter 2:

1. In your own words, why is God becoming a man so amazing to you?

2. What is something radical you would have to do to imitate what God did in becoming flesh?

3. Think of the people you find it most difficult to be around. What makes it so easy for us to avoid these people?

4. How is God's nature so different than ours in this regard?

5. What can we do to develop more of God's heart in this area?

Chapter 3:

1. Make a list of some of the "other things" you think Jesus did.

2. Why do you think it's important to consider these things?

3. Why do you think God chose to only include the things he did about Jesus?

4. If you had been able to spend a few days just hanging out with Jesus, what general impressions do you think you would have come away with?

Chapter 4:

1. Why do you think so many people have the wrong impression of Jesus?

2. What were some reasons why you developed a wrong impression of him?

3. What would be the biggest reason today why you might not be able to maintain the right impression of Jesus?

4. What do you think Jesus' main message or emphasis would be to the following categories of people? Americans? Religious people? Wealthy people? Young people? Older people?

5. What events in the past few decades do you think have been used by Satan to lead people away from a positive impression of Jesus?

Chapter 5:

1. What are some lies that have been told about you through the years and how did you feel about them at the time?

2. Which impostor mentioned in the chapter would have been the most enticing for you before you became a Christian?

3. Which impostor is the most tempting for you to believe in today? Why? Select one impostor from the 1-7 list and one from the 8-12 list and locate more verses to combat that false teaching about Jesus.

4. If you were Satan, what strategies would you use to hide the real Jesus?

Chapter 6:

1. Think of someone from your hometown or high school and the roadblocks you would have encountered if they had been announced as the Messiah.

2. What things do you think residents of Nazareth used to dismiss Jesus' claims of being the Messiah?

3. What things have other people used to try and discount your faith?

4. How do you think Jesus felt about his hometown's hatred for him?

5. Why do you think the Jews were so offended when Jesus referred to Gentiles in a positive way in his sermon?

6. What would be some parallels of that today if he were to speak to a group of people in your city or country?

Chapter 7:

1. Which of the five Messiah figures in America from 1940-2005 do you think would have been the toughest to believe and follow? Why?
2. Create the perfect Messiah for your sinful nature. What would he look like and what would he teach?
4. Think of other eras in history and a certain type of Messiah that would likely have been rejected by the masses.
5. What are the hardest things about the way of Christ for you?

Chapter 8:

1. What are some of the popular opinions of Jesus today?
2. How would you go about responding to and countering those opinions?
3. Select three of the negative comments about Jesus in the chapter and discuss why these were such a roadblock to faith for the Jews.
4. Which of the claims about Jesus is most absurd in your mind? Why?
5. Which of the claims seems the most legitimate? Why?
6. Which of the correct claims is the most amazing to you? Why?

Chapter 9:

1. What things did Jesus do in the first century that would still be viewed with a lot of skepticism today? Why?
2. How does the devil go about spreading wrong information about Jesus in the world today?
3. Were you ever a part of that? If so, how?

Chapter 10:

1. Select three of Jesus' comments regarding his true nature and find other passages that confirm them.
2. Which truths about Jesus do you think were the most difficult for people to comprehend? Why?
3. Which truths do you believe had the least amount of resistance? Why?
4. Which of his claims have the most resistance in America today? What about in other parts of the world?
5. Which of his claims are most encouraging to you? Most challenging?
6. List five of his claims and what each means to you on a personal level.

Chapter 11:

1. Who are some other Matthew types in our world today? In your neighborhood? At your school? At your workplace?

2. What is your favorite parable in the book of Matthew? Why?

3. Which of the fulfilled prophecies of Jesus is the most spectacular to you?

4. Which one has the most personal meaning?

5. Which of the miracles would have been the most mind-boggling to you if you had witnessed it? Why?

6. What can we learn about God in his selection of Matthew to communicate Jesus to the Jews?

Chapter 12:

1. What cities might parallel Rome today and what would you do to reach the people living there?

2. Who are some individuals that parallel the kind of people living in Rome in the first century?

3. When presenting the gospel to people, why is it so important to meet them where they are and start at their level?

4. What did people do for you to help you get started with following Jesus? What kind of things have you done to help others get their start?

5. What impresses you the most about how Jesus dealt with different types of people? Which episode is the most inspiring to you? Why?

6. What type of people would Jesus spend time with today that would blow observers away in a positive sense? In a mistrusting way?

7. Who are the people that are easiest for you to ignore? What are some practical things you can do to repent of that?

Chapter 13:

1. Who, like Luke, would you say are the "intellectuals" of today?

2. Make a list of the ones you are in a position to share your faith with.

3. Why is it so intimidating to talk with these kinds of people?

4. List some ways that Luke's background helped him to be more effective.

5. How does your background qualify you to be effective in certain areas?

6. What contents in the book of Luke do you think would be most effective to use in studying with intellectuals?

7. What did Jesus do in Luke's gospel that impresses you the most? Why?

8. What did Jesus say in Luke's gospel that impresses you the most? Why?

Chapter 14:

1. How does the book of John help Christians strengthen their beliefs?
2. Why do you think John was such a good choice for a gospel writer?
3. How did John's background as "a son of thunder" help him in his efforts to tell others about Jesus?
4. What changes in your life do you find most effective in sharing with others?
5. What would you say are the two most amazing changes God has helped you to make since becoming a follower of Jesus?
6. What things about John's Gospel are different than the other three?

Chapter 15:

1. Why do you think God chose such humble means to begin his life? What might some of the other options have been?
2. What would you say were some of the biggest challenges Mary had to face as the mother of Jesus? Joseph? Other relatives?
3. What part of the Christmas story is most meaningful to you? What part is the most radical?
4. If Jesus would have come in similar fashion to America in 2005, what might be a possible scenario for his birth?
5. What "normal" things did Joseph and Mary experience the first two years of Jesus' life? What about Jesus?

Chapter 16:

1. List some of the other things you think could have taken place in Jesus' life from age three to thirty.
2. Why do you think not much was written about him during that time?
3. What are some of your biggest questions about Jesus during this time?
4. What do you think were his biggest temptations during that time?
5. Of the things I mentioned as possibilities in the life of Jesus from three to thirty, which were most meaningful to you?

Chapter 17:

1. In your opinion, what is the most inspiring portion of the Sermon on the Mount? Why? What is the most challenging part? Why?
2. Which of his points in the sermon do you think got the most favorable response? Which received the most criticism? Which were the most difficult to grasp?
3. What impresses you the most about Jesus' approach in this sermon?
4. How is this sermon different from sermons you heard growing up?

5. What things did Jesus use in this sermon that could be used by you as well in your presentation of the gospel to an individual? How about when you have an opportunity to preach to a group of people?

6. Why do you think we tend to feel good just by listening to a message?

7. What practical things can we do to better listen to God's word when it is being preached?

8. What practical things can we do to better carry the messages we hear far beyond our time at church?

Chapter 18:

1. What was it that finally got you to pay more attention to Jesus?

2. What are the miracles of Jesus intended to teach? What specific things do the miracles say to you?

3. What amazes you most about the storm on the lake incident?

4. Which of Jesus' miracles is your favorite? Why?

5. How do you think people would respond today if Jesus were here and performing similar miracles?

6. What kind of miracles do you think Jesus would perform today?

Chapter 19:

1. Putting yourself in Mary and Martha's shoes, what kind of things would you have been feeling when Jesus failed to show up?

2. Why do you think Jesus ultimately raised Lazarus from the dead?

3. What about Jesus makes you feel secure and loved by him?

4. What do you think is his most amazing act of love outside of the cross?

5. What kind of things did Jesus do to make sure people felt loved?

6. What kind of things do we need to do to make sure people feel loved?

7. What are your strengths and weaknesses when it comes to making people feel loved?

8. What practical things can you do to better express your love for people?

Chapter 20:

1. In what specific ways do you often feel like no one can really understand you? How can Jesus understand in those times?

2. Examine your closest friendships. Why are you so close to these people?

3. How can you do a better job in being more relatable to others?

4. How have the following hurt you and helped you in the past? (Looks, physical stature, family challenges, misinformation, death of a loved one and disappointments)

5. Discuss how difficult it must have been for Jesus to be fully human.

6. Which human quality of Jesus encourages you the most right now?

7. How can Jesus understand the two or three biggest challenges you are facing at this time?

Chapter 21:

1. What is the easiest temptation for you to give in to?

2. When and where does your sin get exposed the quickest?

3. What things would Jesus have done to avoid similar temptations to yours and ultimately avoid sinning?

4. What do you think was the hardest temptation for Jesus to withstand?

Chapter 22:

1. In your own words, what does Jesus' death mean to you?

2. Write out the sins Jesus took to the cross on your behalf.

3. How can you do a better job of keeping the cross on your mind?

4. How can we better honor the cross on Sunday mornings?

5. What other horrors over the centuries did Jesus bear on the cross?

6. Why do you think the cross is so hard to grasp and appreciate at times?

7. Why do we so often try to attain God's favor by our works and not by the cross? How can we better avoid doing that in the future?

Chapter 23:

1. Put yourself at the cross the day Jesus died. What do you see?

2. How do you think the following people who were there at the cross felt about what they were witnessing? Mary? John? Soldiers? Bystanders?

3. Why do you think it is so much easier to celebrate Christmas than Good Friday?

Chapter 24:

1. Why do you think the disciples had such a hard time understanding the resurrection, both before and after it happened?

2. Why do we tend to doubt the resurrection at times today?

3. What does the resurrection of Jesus mean to you on a personal basis and how can it change your daily life?

4. How is the resurrection designed to change our views on the world?

5. What are you worrying about or hanging onto in your life at the moment that the resurrection can put in better perspective?

6. How can we bring the resurrection more into our daily discussions with our spouse, our children, our co-workers and even strangers?

Chapter 25:

1. Name some false statements religious people make about Jesus today.
2. What practical ways does the devil use to spread false information in the religious world?
3. Why is it so crucial for us to have the truth on Jesus?
4. Why are people attracted to a different Jesus than the one in the Bible?
5. Of all the truths about Jesus found in the epistles, which one is the most glorious to you? Which is the most difficult to understand?

Chapter 26:

1. If Jesus were coming to visit you, what might his agenda be?
2. What would his notes of encouragement be for you?
3. What would his notes of concern be for you?
4. What would his notes of disappointment be for you?
5. Which of the four messages is the biggest challenge for you today? Why?
6. Which of the four messages is your biggest strength? Why?

Chapter 27:

1. What is the hardest thing about the call we are given to be like Jesus?
2. What part of your life is most like Jesus right now? What do you think the other people who know you best would say?
3. What part of your life is least like him? What would others say?
4. How are you doing in your daily discipleship compared to last month?
5. How about compared to last year? How about compared to when you first began?
6. What practical things can you to do grow in your discipleship?

Chapter 28:

1. What glory of Jesus have you possibly been diminishing?
2. Do you feel your zeal for Jesus slipping at all? If so, how?
3. Write out words or phrases that describe to you the glory and awesome nature of Jesus.
4. In one or two paragraphs, write out who Jesus is to you.

Illumination Publishers International

Toney Mulhollan has been in Christian publishing for over 30 years. He has served as the Production Manager for Crossroads Publications, Discipleship Magazine/UpsideDown Magazine, Discipleship Publications International (DPI) and on the production teams of Campus Journal, Biblical Discipleship Quarterly, Bible Illustrator and others. He has served as production manager for several printing companies. Toney serves as the Managing Editor of Illumination Publishers International, and is the writer and publisher of the weekly "Behind the Music" stories and edits other weekly newsletters. Toney is happily married to the love of his life, Denise Leonard Mulhollan, M.D. They reside in Newton Upper Falls, Massachusetts.

For the best in Christian writing and audio instruction, go to the Illumination Publishers website. Shipping is always free in the United States. We're commited to producing in-depth teaching that will inform, inspire and encourage Christians to a deeper and more committed walk with God.

www.ipibooks.com

Illumination Publishers International
1190 Boylston Street
Newton Upper Falls, Massachusetts 02464
toneyipibooks@mac.com
www.ipibooks.com

ipi

Available at www.ipibooks.com

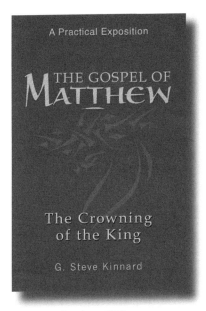

A Practical Exposition

M THE GOSPEL OF
MATTHEW

The Crowning
of the King

G. Steve Kinnard

The Crowning of the King *by G. Steve Kinnard*

Matthew is the first Gospel, in fact the first book, in our New Testament. Because of this, it is often the first book of the New Testament that people read, and it is the first introduction to the life of Jesus for many people. This makes Matthew an important book to study.

G. Steve Kinnard has written a commentary on Matthew that is scholarly in approach, yet practical in scope. Steve began his study of Matthew by translating the Gospel from Greek into English. From that beginning he helps the reader understand the cultural setting of the Gospels and how that helps us correctly understand the text. He attempts to show the historical, geographical, economic and cultural background of Matthew.

Once the task of determining the correct meaning is done, Steve helps apply that meaning to our day and our lives. Steve points out that the Gospel of Matthew is bold, clear, inspiring and readable. No wonder the early church placed this Gospel before the others. Reading this book will help you to know Jesus better than ever, as Matthew has the longest portrayal of Jesus. You will see how Jesus is the fulfillment of Old Testament hopes and prophecy and you'll see clearly that Jesus is the Christ, the Messiah and the King.

Paperback, 304 pages, Retail Price: **$15.00**

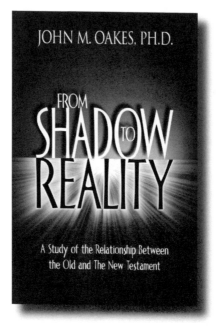